INTRODUCTION

My interest in Dundee church history goes back a long way. In 1985 I p‍‍_____ _____ _____ ‍‍_____‍ congregation of which I am a member, Downfield South Church. The research provided me with quite a lot of information on other congregations in the area, for one congregation does not exist in isolation. In 1990 I supplied Miss Catherine Pullar, Dundee Presbytery Resource Centre Co-ordinator, with some historical notes for a display which she was mounting at the Dundee Christian Festival. When writing to me afterwards, Miss Pullar suggested that a book should be produced with notes on the buildings and a short history of each congregation. Two years later I was asked by Miss Lisbeth M Thoms to carry out some work on behalf of the Council for Scottish Archaeology. This involved gathering material on the Church of Scotland congregations and their sites in Dundee, past and present. All of these activities generated a great deal of data, and whetted my appetite for consolidating it.

In 1989 the Scottish Record Society published The Kirks of Edinburgh 1560 - 1984, edited by the Rev. A Ian Dunlop, a more ambitious and comprehensive enterprise than my work. It seemed to me that a volume on the Presbytery of Dundee, consolidating all the information I could trace on its congregations, might serve a useful purpose as a source for those interested in the origins and history of particular congregations.

This work, therefore, is an attempt to bring together the record of the congregations of the Presbytery of Dundee from the Reformation to date. The information has been gathered from many sources, including congregational and parish histories, booklets issued on special occasions such as anniversaries and bazaars, newspaper articles, congregational magazines, as well as official records of church courts, and the 'Fasti' and other annals. Frequently, names of church personalities appear, many now largely forgotten, and I have added a number of footnotes giving short biographical details which may help to explain their presence, often on the occasion of an important congregational event.

A draft of what I had prepared was offered to the Session Clerk of each congregation, with a request that it be read over and any errors or significant omissions brought to my notice. It was not my intention that this task be left to the Session Clerk, or indeed the Minister. Frequently, there is someone in a congregation with a special interest in its history and a knowledge of its buildings and furnishing. Indeed, as a result of my approach this proved to be the case, and I was put in touch with several such individuals whose knowledge of their churches allowed me to improve on what I had originally written, as well as to avoid mistakes. Having said that, my text was corrected and improved upon by quite a few Session Clerks and Ministers, to whom I am obliged. A number of respondents gave me most interesting current or recent information on their congregation's mission activities. I also received copies of several church histories of which I had been unaware.

I am grateful to all those who have assisted in this way, and appreciate the many favourable and encouraging comments made in the accompanying correspondence. No doubt many errors remain in the text and I accept full responsibility for all of these.

Perhaps the title requires an explanation. 'The Kirks of Dundee Presbytery' seemed more inclusive than the shorter 'The Kirks of Dundee', as quite a number of the charges are, or were, in the landward area. Moreover, only congregations of the Church of Scotland and its constituents are included. To have covered other denominations would have been a very difficult exercise, especially as in many instances their records are not in the public domain and are not readily available. The Presbytery of Dundee was not constituted until 1581, but I have commenced the record in 1558. While the Reformation in Scotland is usually dated to 1560, Paul Methven had preached in Dundee from 1558, in which year elders had been 'set apart'. Having said that, I have attempted to record something of the pre-Reformation history of those churches taken over by the Reformers. The same buildings were used, attended presumably by many of the same worshippers, who in some cases were ministered to by the same clergy.

My objective has been to give for each congregation a brief description of the buildings at the time of writing, and of previous buildings where known, the main furnishings and equipment, the origins of the congregation, its unions and linkings, the succession of ministers, and the principal sources used. In some cases the sources include excellent congregational histories which should be referred to for fuller information.

I am aware that the result is uneven. Much more detail appears for a number of congregations, simply because more was available. It is disappointing that for some churches very little seems to have been preserved in the form of histories or even official records.

I realise that the many secessions from the Church of Scotland cause confusion, as do subsequent unions. I have attempted to explain the principal divisions in a separate essay entitled 'The Secessions'. I trust this article and the lists provided of congregations formed by the main Presbyterian bodies will be helpful.

Apart from those officebearers mentioned earlier, I have been assisted by numerous other people. A number of people who had heard of my project have called or written, supplying me with most valuable information. The staffs of Dundee Public Libraries and of Edinburgh Central Library have been most helpful, as have Mr Iain Flett and Mr Richard Cullen and their staff in the Dundee City Archive and Record Centre. The Reverend Jim Roy, Presbytery Clerk, has given me useful advice and suggestions. Mr Adam Swan of Dundee City Planning Department introduced me to the listed buildings records. I have also received encouragement from my wife, Jean, despite spending a great deal of time in libraries and archives, or in collating data. Jean gave some valuable practical help by reading over the first draft, spotting many errors which I had missed.

I am grateful to the Committee of the Friends of Dundee City Archives for publishing the work. In particular, I am obliged to the Editor, Mr Jerry Wright for his hard work, kind advice and assistance in preparing the text, and also the photographs, for publication. Photographic digitisation is a new technology to me and I appreciate Jerry's enthusiasm and skill with this medium. As a result there are a number of photographs included which he took recently, as well as the historical group. I acknowledge the help with the digitised photographs, taken from the 1916 Dundee Photographic Survey, which I received from the staff of the Central Library Local Studies Department; in particular Mr David Kett and Ms Eileen Moran. One archive photograph I received from another source. Mr Douglas Spence very kindly supplied the splendid view of the congregation leaving St Andrew's Church.

While the volume is basically about Kirks it is also about Dundee, its surrounding area and its people. I trust , therefore, it will make a small contribution to the recording of the history of this part of Scotland. It will serve its purpose if, in the words of Southey:

Yet shall this memorial convey
To strangers and preserve for after-time
Something that else had passed away.

May 2000   Ian McCraw

CONTENTS

Congregations of the Church of Scotland in 1999:

Dundee:

Congregations which have been dissolved or have ceased:

Dundee:

ABBREVIATIONS

A&S	Assistant and Successor
Adm.	Admitted
App.	Appointed, appointment
Asst.	Assistant
C&S	Colleague and Successor
CF	Chaplain to the Forces
CofS	Church of Scotland
Coll.	Collated
DCA	Dundee City Archive & Record Centre
DCC	Dundee City Council
DNC	Dundee Newspaper Cuttings (Held by DPL)
DOB	Dundee Obituary Book (Held by DPL)
DPL	Dundee Public Libraries
DPL Sp.	Dundee Public Libraries, Special Files
Dem.	Demitted
Dep.	Deposed
EC	Established Church
FC	Free Church
GA	General Assembly
Ind.	Inducted
Introd.	Introduced
Lamb	The Lamb Collection, Dundee Public Libraries
Min.	Minister
Mod.	Moderator
NPGS	National Portrait Gallery of Scotland
Ord.	Ordained
OS	Original Secession
PM	Presbytery minutes
Par.	Parish
Pres.	Presented
Presb.	Presbytery
Ret.	Retired
Sec.	Secretary
Term.	Terminable
UAS	United Associate Secession Church
UOS	United Original Secession
UF	United Free Church of Scotland
UP	United Presbyterian Church
YB	Church of Scotland Year Book

BIBLIOGRAPHY

Abbreviations of Books referred to in the Text

DYB	Dundee Year Book
KofE	A Ian Dunlop, *The Kirks of Edinburgh, 1560-1984*, Edinburgh, 1989
Ewing	W Ewing, *Annals of the Free Church of Scotland*, Edinburgh, 1914
FES	H Scott et al (ed.), *Fasti Ecclesiae Scoticanae*, 10 Vols., Edinburgh, 1915-1981
FUF	JA Lamb, (ed.), *Fasti of the United Free Church of Scotland 1900 to 1929*, Edinburgh, 1956
McKelvie	W McKelvie, *Annals and Statistics of the United Presbyterian Church*, Edinburgh, 1873
Norrie	W Norrie, *Dundee Celebrities*, Dundee, 1873
RPC	WJ Couper, *The Reformed Presbyterian Church in Scotland*, Edinburgh, 1925
Scott	D Scott, *The Annals and Statistics of the Original Secession Church*, Edinburgh, 1886
Small	R Small, *History of the United Presbyterian Church from 1733 to 1900*, Edinburgh, 1904, 2 Vols.

Other Works Consulted

FD Bardgett, *Scotland Reformed, The Reformation in Angus and the Mearns*, Edinburgh, 1989

Thomas Brown, *Annals of the Disruption*, Edinburgh, 1893

JHS Burleigh, *A Church History of Scotland*, Oxford, 1960

IB Cowan, *Regional Aspects of the Scottish Reformation*, London, 1978

AL Drummond and J Bulloch, *The Scottish Church 1688-1843*, Edinburgh, 1973

AL Drummond and J Bulloch, *The Church in Victorian Scotland 1843 - 1874*, Edinburgh, 1975

AL Drummond and J Bulloch, *The Church in late Victorian Scotland 1874-1900*, Edinburgh, 1978

AJH Gibson, *Stipend in the Church of Scotland*, Edinburgh, 1961

A Herron, *Kirk by Divine Right*, Edinburgh, 1985

F Lyall, *Of Presbyters and Kings*, Aberdeen, 1980

AH Millar, *The First History of Dundee 1776*, Dundee, 1923

JA Rollo, *The Parish and the Burgh Churches of Dundee*, Dundee, 1897

ES Towill, *People and Places in the Story of the Scottish Church*, Edinburgh, 1976

DCA Collection of inscriptions from War Memorials gathered by Walter Lochhead

Congregational and parish histories used are generally mentioned at the end of the article on the congregation.

ILLUSTRATIONS

Cover Illustration, Doorway of Strathmartine Church

PARISH CHURCHES AT THE REFORMATION

The pre-Reformation parishes in what became the Presbytery of Dundee were for administrative purposes in three Dioceses. This had come about for historical reasons.

The following parishes, later allocated to the Presbytery, were in the Dioceses shown:

St Andrews	**Brechin**	**Dunkeld**
Lundie	Dundee	Abernyte
Liff	Monikie	Auchterhouse
Invergowrie		Tealing
Logie Dundee		
Strathmartine		
Mains		
Murroes		
Monifieth		
Fowlis Easter		
Inchture		
Kinnaird		
Rossie		
Longforgan		
Benvie		

DUNDEE AND THE REFORMATION

The influence of Luther reached Dundee and other Scottish east coast ports through "merchants and mariners, who, frequenting other countries, heard the true doctrine affirmed". These travellers brought Lutheran books, which were legislated against in 1525.

Following the martyrdom of Patrick Hamilton outside St Salvator's College, St Andrews, 1528, those who "drank of St Leonard's Well", a synonym for the adoption of the new religious doctrines, increased in number. However, a Dominican friar who in 1536 preached the reformed faith in St Andrews was forced to flee to England. Previously he had preached also at Dundee where Protestantism had some popular appeal. Dundee friars had been critical of the old order, and in 1528 one of them had preached against the licentious lives of the bishops and the abuse of cursing.[1]

The Wedderburn brothers were the sons of a merchant at the West Kirk Style in the Overgate. James Wedderburn used his poetic and dramatic talents to ridicule the abuses and superstitions of the age. His satirical plays were performed in the town. His brother, John, a priest in Dundee, professed the Reformed faith but, on conviction for heresy, fled to Germany where he heard Luther and Melanchthon. Robert, the youngest brother, went to Paris and was soon in the company of some of the early Reformers. He returned to Scotland, after the death of Cardinal Beaton, and obtained the vicarage of Dundee. He was probably the author of *The Complaynt of Scotland*. John and Robert turned "manie bawde songs and rymes in godly rymes". These were *The Gude and Godlie Ballatis*.[2]

By the mid sixteenth century the parish ministry had been weakened, partly through the system of appropriation, with revenues intended for the maintenance of the church and clergy being diverted to other uses. As a consequence many buildings were in a state of disrepair. The non-residence of priests, simony, and the holding of plural benefices, were other abuses. The wealthy provided for their own chaplains or patronised a local friary.

In 1543 a mob sacked Dundee's two friaries, carrying away chalices and vestments from the Blackfriars' Monastery. There seems to have been particular resentment of friars and their life style. Images were destroyed. Significantly, the burgh churches and altars were not attacked. The iconoclasm in Dundee was symptomatic of the Reformation in Swiss cities and may have been introduced by George Wishart. Wishart preached in Dundee in 1544 and 1545 with general acceptibility. With the arrival in the burgh in 1558 of John Willock, a former Dominican, and Paul Methven "the toun of Dundie beganne to erect the face of the reformed church publiclie, in which the word was preached openlie, and the sacraments trulie ministered". Methven began preaching regularly in July 1558, with open Protestant services being held in Dundee thereafter. In that year elders were appointed to exercise church discipline "to whom the whole Brethren promised obedience". Many of the traditional symbols of the Catholic faith had been removed during the sacking of Dundee by the English.

Notes

1.   Cursing was one of the ecclesiastical censures available to the pre Reformation Church. The full process of cursing or excommunication consisted of a number of steps of increasing severity. The Reformers admitted that, when properly used cursing was " the moist fearfull thing on the face of the earth; for it was the verray separatioun of man frome God". According to Knox a letter of cursing could be bought for fourpence.

2.   The full title of the work, published in 1567, was 'Ane Compendious Book of Godlie Psalms and Spiritual Song collected out of sundrie partes of the Scriptures with sundrie other ballads changed out of prophane sangis for avoyding of sinne and harlotrie with the augmentation of sundrie gude and godle Ballats not contend in the first edition'.

FD Bargett, *Scotland Reformed, The Reformation in Angus and the Mearns*, Edinburgh, 1989
JH Baxter, Dundee and the Reformation (Abertay Historical Society Publication No 7), Dundee, 1960

THE SECESSIONS

The secessions from the Church of Scotland which occurred in the eighteenth century, and the subsequent reunions, are difficult to follow and it may be helpful to explain the main divisions and regroupings.

In 1733 the Reverend Ebenezer Erskine of Stirling and four other ministers formed themselves into the Associate Presbytery, over the issue of Patronage. It was not until 1740 that they were deposed by the Church of Scotland, by which time other groups throughout the country had joined them. However, in 1747 this new denomination split in two over the question of whether or not members should subscribe to the oath required of burgesses in certain towns, by which they acknowledged the true religion authorised by law. The two bodies formed were the Associate Synod (the Burghers) and the General Associate Synod (the Antiburghers).

A further schism occurred at the end of the eighteenth century over the issue of Covenants and the Confession of Faith. Both groups set about revising their testimonies but there were very conservative elements who opposed the changes. When the revised position was approved by the Burghers in 1799 a number withdrew, forming the Auld Licht Burghers, the majority being referred to as the New Licht Burghers. A similar situation developed in the Antiburgher denomination in 1806 with the split resulting in the majority New Licht Antiburghers and the minority Auld Licht Antiburghers.

The Secession of 1733 had now become four separate churches whose official titles were as follows:

Auld Licht Burghers	-	Original Burgher Synod
New Licht Burghers	-	Associate Synod
Auld Licht Antiburghers	-	Constitutional Associate Presbytery
New Licht Antiburghers	-	General Associate Synod

A second secession from the Church of Scotland took place in 1761 when the Reverend Thomas Gillespie and two other ministers met at Colinsburgh and formed the Presbytery of Relief "for the relief of Christians oppressed in their church privileges". The Relief Church was evangelical in doctrine, critical of the association between Church of Scotland and State, and liberal in terms of membership. It showed goodwill to other Christian communities, which is more than can be said for some of the other sects.

Over time some of the differences which divided these sects disappeared, or became less important. The New Licht Burghers and the New Licht Antiburghers united in 1820 as the United Secession Church (properly the United Associate Synod of the Secession Church). It in turn joined with the Relief Church in 1847 to form the United Presbyterian Church. The Auld Licht Burghers rejoined the Church of Scotland in 1839, although most of them left again in 1843 for the Free Church of Scotland. The Auld Licht Antiburghers joined the Free Church of Scotland in 1852, except for a minority which continued as the United Original Secession Church. The Original Seceders maintained a separate existence until rejoining the Church of Scotland in 1952.

The Disruption of 1843, as far as it affected the Presbytery of Dundee, is dealt with in more detail in a separate paper published in *Archives Argus 1997*, the record of the lectures delivered to meetings of the Friends of Dundee City Archives. Nationally, this was the most significant secession from the Established Church with 451 ministers, about a third of the ministry, and a similar proportion of communicants, leaving to form the Free Church of Scotland.

The Reformed Presbyterian Church, constituted in 1743, but which traced its origins back to the Covenanters or Cameronians, claiming to be the true Kirk of the Covenants, joined the Free Church in 1876.

After the Free Church approved in 1892 a Declaratory Article explaining its attitude to the Confessions of Faith, recognising diversity of opinion on such points as do not enter into the substance of the Reformed Faith, a small number, mainly in the Highlands, left to form the Free Presbyterian Church.

In 1900 the Free Church and the United Presbyterian Church joined as the United Free Church of Scotland. Unfortunately a small minority opted out of the union and continued as the Free Church of Scotland, often referred to as 'Wee Frees'. The judgement given by the House of Lords in the court action which the minority raised over the ownership of the property of the Free Church is generally regarded as outrageous. They were awarded the whole heritable property of that Church, which they could not administer or maintain and, following a national outcry, Parliament had to intervene and set up a Commission to allocate the property on an equitable basis. A number of congregations were dispossessed from their churches for lengthy periods until the matter was resolved.

The United Free Church reunited with the Church of Scotland in 1929, although again a small number of the former denomination were unwilling to merge and they remain as the United Free Church of Scotland (Continuing).

CHURCH OF SCOTLAND QUOAD SACRA CHARGES
ERECTED 1843 - 1929

Congregation	Year	Now Represented By
Broughty Ferry (CE 1826)	1863	Broughty Ferry St Aidan's
St Mark's (from 1869)	1871	West
Chapelshade (Relief 1789)	1872	Albany Butterburn
St Andrew's (CE 1772)	1873	St Andrew's
Wallacetown (from 1840)	1874	Trinity
Rosebank (CE 1874)	1875	Albany Butterburn
Broughty Ferry St Stephen's (CE 1871)	1875	Broughty Ferry St Stephen's and West
St Enoch's (FC 1865)	1876	The Steeple
Lochee St Luke's (CE 1874)	1876	Lochee Old & St Luke's
Logie (CE 1874)	1877	Logie & St John's Cross
Lochee (CE 1831)	1880	Lochee Old & St Luke's
Clepington (mission 1872)	1885	Clepington
St Matthew's (CE 1875)	1885	Trinity
Maryfield (from 1886)	1904	Stobswell
Beach (mission 1887)	1907	Broughty Ferry St James'
Fairmuir (mission 1899)	1907	Fairmuir
Downfield (from 1893)	1912	Strathmartine
Balgay (from 1885)	1913	Balgay
Invergowrie (mission 1886)	1916	Invergowrie

Most of the congregations had earlier beginnings and the dates of their origin, frequently as a mission or a chapel of ease (CE), are shown in brackets.

THE SECESSION AND UP CONGREGATIONS FORMED 1738 - 1900

Congregation	Year	Now Represented By
Associate		
School Wynd	1738	Dissolved 1926
Burgher		
Liff	1785	Dissolved 1801
Newbigging	1789	Monikie and Newbigging
Willison	1808	St Cuthbert's; Dissolved 1940
Balfour	1820	Ceased 1845
Antiburgher		
Overgate, later Bell Street	1747	St Cuthbert's; Dissolved 1940
Euclid Crescent (OS)	1802	Dissolved 1968
United Associate Secession		
Lochee	1824	Lochee West
Tay Square	1832	Meadowside St Paul's
Wishart	1837	The Steeple
Broughty Ferry (Union)	1837	Broughty Ferry St Stephen's & West
Relief		
Chapelshade	1789	Adm to CofS 1791: Albany Butterburn
West Port	1792	Ceased 1798
New Inn Entry	1799	Ceased 1819
Seagate	1811	Ceased 1821
Dudhope Road or Dudhope Crescent Road	1821	Dissolved 1909
James'	1837	St James'; Dissolved 1988
United Presbyterian		
Butterburn	1861	Albany Butterburn
Hawkhill	1871	Meadowside St Paul's
Victoria Street	1873	Stobswell
Broughty Ferry Queen Street	1873	Broughty Ferry St Luke's & Queen Street
Ryehill	1876	West
Downfield	1885	Downfield South
Park	1890	Stobswell
Lochee Road	1891	St Columba's; Dissolved 1991
Monifieth	1897	Monifieth Panmure

FREE CHURCH CONGREGATIONS SANCTIONED 1843 - 1900

Congregation	Year	Now Represented By
St Andrew's	1843	Meadowside St Paul's
St David's	1843	St David's North
St John's	1843	West
St Peter's	1843	West
Chapelshade	1843	Meadowside St Paul's
Dudhope	1843	St Columba's; Dissolved 1991
Gaelic later Albert Square	1843	Meadowside St Paul's
Hilltown	1843	Dissolved 1970
Mariners later St Paul's	1843	Meadowside St Paul's
Wallacetown later Baxter Park	1843	Trinity
Willison	1843	St Columba's; Dissolved 1991
Broughty Ferry later West	1843	Broughty Ferry St Stephen's & West
Liff	1843	Lundie & Muirhead of Liff
Lochee	1843	Lochee Old & St Luke's
Longforgan or Invergowrie	1843	Invergowrie
Monifieth or Hillock	1843	Monikie & Newbigging
Monikie	1843	Monikie & Newbigging
Tealing	1843	Murroes & Tealing
Mains and Strathmartine (from 1843)	1844	Strathmartine
Abernyte (from 1843)	1845	Abernyte
Meadowside (from 1802 OS)	1852	St Columba's; Dissolved 1991
Chalmers (from 1851)	1854	Chalmers Ardler
Wellgate (from 1850)	1862	To remnant Free Church 1906
Broughty Ferry East (from 1861)	1863	Broughty Ferry East
St Enoch's (from 1865)	1866	To Est. Church 1874; Steeple
Monifieth South (from 1869)	1871	Monifieth South
McCheyne Memorial (from 1857)	1871	West
Bonnethill (from 1865)	1872	Dissolved 1978
Wilson	1876	Ceased 1879
Ogilvie (from 1868)	1876	Stobswell
Hawkhill or Martyrs (from 1827 RPC)	1876	Balgay
Broughty Ferry St Luke's	1878	Broughty Ferry St Luke's & Queen Street
High Church (from 1875)	1878	High Kirk

* Some congregations had their beginnings in prayer meetings or mission stations which had been organised before Presbytery sanctioned the charge. These earlier years of origin are given in brackets.

All the charges sanctioned between 1843 and 1845 were secessions from the Established Church as a consequence of the Disruption. Later sanctions were new congregations, except where shown as acceding from another denomination.

Where a congregation changed its name the original name is followed by the name on the eve of the Union of 1900.

THE PRESBYTERY OF DUNDEE

This work covers the churches within the jurisdiction of the Presbytery of Dundee as it was in 1999. The bounds of the Presbytery then were very similar to what they were in April 1581, when Dundee was erected into one of the original thirteen presbyteries. The territory embraced the *quoad omnia* parishes of Dundee, Abernyte, Auchterhouse, Benvie, Fowlis Easter, Inchture, Invergowrie, Kinnaird, Liff, Logie Dundee, Longforgan, Lundie, Mains, Monifieth, Monikie, Murroes, Rossie, Strathmartine, and Tealing.

The charges of Barry, Barry East, Panbride and Carnoustie Newton Panbride which united as Carnoustie Panbride, Carnoustie Old and Carnoustie St Stephen's which united as Carnoustie, Newport St Thomas, Tayport Erskine, Tayport Ferryport on Craig, Tayport Queen Street, Wormit East and Wormit West which united as Wormit, were in the jurisdiction of the Presbytery of Dundee following the Union of 1929. They were subsequently transferred to other Presbyteries and are excluded from this volume.

The United Free Church Presbytery of Dundee (1900-29) covered the same area as the Church of Scotland Presbytery.

The Free Church Presbytery of Dundee (1843 - 1900) covered the same area as the Church of Scotland Presbytery.

The United Presbyterian Church Presbytery of Dundee (1847 - 1900) covered the same area as the Church of Scotland Presbytery, with the addition of Alyth, Blairgowrie, Ferryport on Craig, Kirriemuir, and Newport.

The Presbytery situation before the formation of the United Presbyterian Church is complicated. The United Associate Presbytery of Dundee was erected on 12 June 1840 and covered Dundee, Lochee, Broughty Ferry, Ferryport on Craig, Kirriemuir, Alyth, Newtyle and Rattray. In 1840 the Presbytery of Forfar was divided into the Presbyteries of Dundee and Arbroath. Four congregations adhering to the Presbytery of Cupar were transferred to the Presbytery of Dundee. The Relief Presbytery of Dundee was constituted on 8 May 1837, being disjoined from Perth. It included Aberdeen. It joined with that of Perth on 27 May 1845 as the Relief Presbytery of Perth and Dundee. The congregations were apportioned to the Presbyteries of Dundee and Perth at the union of 1847. The Presbytery of Dysart, to which two Dundee Relief congregations belonged at one time, had been formed in 1776. It was suppressed at the union of 1847.

The following Secession congregations are shown with the Presbyteries they adhered to:

Liff Burgher	-	Perth
Newbigging Burgher	-	Perth (1788), later Forfar (post 1820 Union)
School Wynd Burgher	-	Perth & Dunfermline, later Cupar (1820)
Overgate, Bell Street Antiburgher	-	Perth, in 1820 Forfar
Chapelshade Relief	-	Originally Dysart then Perth
West Port, New Inn Entry, Dudhope Road	-	Perth
James'	-	Dysart
Wishart - United Associate Secession	-	Cupar
Lochee - United Associate Secession	-	Forfar
Broughty Ferry -United Associate Secession	-	Forfar

The Quater-Centenary of the founding of Presbyteries in Scotland was marked by a Service of Thanksgiving held in Dundee Parish Church (St Mary's) on 25 January 1981, when the sermon was preached by the Right Reverend Dr William B Johnston, Moderator of the General Assembly.

'The Skailin' o' the Kirk'
St Andrew's Church, Cowgate, circa 1910

ALBANY BUTTERBURN

Albany Butterburn church is situated at 2 Hill Street, at its junction with Strathmartine Road, in the Hilltown area of the city. It is a small, unpretentious, stone building, in keeping with the culture of the Seceders and their descendants.[1]

Albany Butterburn was formed by the union of Albany (formerly Rosebank - Chapelshade) and Butterburn on 26 September 1962.

Butterburn

Butterburn UP became Butterburn UF in 1900 and Butterburn in 1929.

The history of this congregation dates from the beginning of 1861, when the UP Presbytery appointed a committee to examine the Butterburn area, then at the north-east extremity of the town, as a district with no evangelical denomination. The committee secured a hall for Sunday evening worship and a weekly prayer meeting. This may have been in Milton Street. In July Mr David Hay, preacher, began work in the area, and in October the people petitioned to be congregated. On 11 March 1862 Presbytery agreed to form thirty-one persons into a congregation and in August three of their number were ordained to the eldership and a session formed.

After worshipping in Butterburn schoolroom arrangements to build a church were put in hand. A site was obtained in Hill Street and collections for building purposes were organised. The new church, seated for 400, was opened on Sunday, 4 June 1865, by the Reverend David M Croom, Lauriston Place UP Church, Edinburgh. The estimated cost was £850, of which £550 was to be raised by the congregation and Presbytery, with £200 from the Home Board. However, the ultimate cost was somewhat greater for a debt of £500 was not liquidated until 1870.

In 1874 a gallery was erected, increasing the sittings to 600, and a hall was added. The jubilee of the congregation was marked on Sunday, 28 September 1913.

Ministers

1863	David HAY	Ord. To Glasgow, Henderson Memorial UP 1878. (Small I 309)
1879	Robert A WATSON MA	Formerly at Middlesborough. DD (Aberdeen 1891); Dem. 1907. (Died 1921) (Small I 309-10, FHF 382)
1907	John Henderson EDGAR MA	Ord. and Ind. as C&S. To Prestonkirk UF 1920. (FUF 382)
1918	Hugh Cameron HUTCHISON MA	From Dalmarnock UF. Dem.1934 (Died 1954) (FUF 382)
1935	Lionel Cockburn Robb McWILLIAM	Ord. To Kirkconnel St Conal's 1943 (FES IX 506)
1943	Alexander ROBERTSON	Ord. To Aberdeen John Knox Mounthooly 1951. (FES IX 506)
1952	John Thomas Herbertson TAYLOR	From Tullynessie and Forbes. To Alexandria North linked with Bonhill South 1961. (FES IX 506, X 300)

Rosebank

The congregation began as a church extension in 1872, with the first minister being inducted on 14 January 1873.

On 6 November 1872, Presbytery had received a deputation from the 'Subscribers towards the erection of additional churches in Dundee' asking that the Reverend James Nicoll be appointed minister. They presented a petition from 142 members and adherents of the Church in the area, which stated that Mr Nicoll had been working as a missionary among them for over seven months. The mission was in operation on 1 May 1872 when Presbytery approved an application to the Home Mission Committee for a grant of £50 for the missionary 'labouring in the district of Rosebank'. A chapel of ease was constituted on 5 August 1874 by the Established Presbytery and the parish of Rosebank was disjoined from St Mary's, Dundee on 18 January 1875 by the Court of Teinds. A church was built in Constitution Street.

The rectangular building, designed by TS Robertson, architect, Dundee, was described as a 'Gothic church of simple character to accommodate 600 on the ground floor (with provision for 360 in galleries). It is divided into a nave and two aisles by arcades of three bays. The façade to Constitution Street presents a lofty gable surmounted by a floriated Roman cross and is pierced by three lancet windows and a rose on each side. The pulpit is in the middle of the south end'. The building was constructed in rubble with ashlar dressings. The cost was about £1800.

Ministers

1873	James NICOLL	Ord. To Murroes 5 June 1873 (FES V 336)
1873	David Barrie CAMERON BA MA	Ord. Adm. First min. of par. 1875. DD (St Andrews 1906) Died 1919. (FES V 336)
1920	Alexander Forbes BLACK MA BD	From Kiltearn. To Advie 1928. (FES VIII 489)
1928	John MOWAT MA BD	Ord. To Ballater South 1933. (FES VIII 489)
1933	John Henry Horton McNEILL MBE BD	From Gargunnock. Dem. On appt. to Cairo St Andrews 1939. (FES IX 512)

Chapelshade

In 1789 a chapel connected to the Relief Synod was built off Barrack Road, later Constitution Road. The building was seated originally for 800. Those who gave half a guinea and upwards to the cost of the site and building the meetinghouse were considered as having an interest in the church and could vote on matters connected with the property. This seems to have caused difficulties later as the relevant roll of donors was not properly kept.

The first pastor was deposed by the Relief Presbytery because of a dispute on doctrinal questions. He and the congregation were admitted into the Established Church on 7 December 1791. Presumably a minority remained loyal to the Relief Church for, in the following February, a group calling themselves 'the vacant congregation in Dundee' petitioned the Perth Presbytery of that body for 'supply of sermon'. This was the beginning of the short-lived West Port Relief congregation. (q.v.)

On 16 October 1792 an obligation was entered into for the managers of Chapelshade to convey the chapel in trust in connection with the Establishment. This deed was recorded in the Burgh Court Books on 14 January 1793. Later it was to be the subject of dispute.

A paper drawn up in 1843, when it was considered important to determine the efficacy of the ownership of the property, sets out the congregation's beginnings. As it was written within memory of the events, and when records now no longer available were extant, it probably gives a fair explanation of its origins and is worth quoting:

The Church had its origin in an Association entered into among some members of the Established Church of Scotland somewhere about the year 1788, who were of the opinion that it would "promote the interests of religion to build another place of worship in Dundee". It would seem that those parties at first meditated that the church which they proposed to build should be a chapel in connection with the Establishment, but they considered that there would be a difficulty in making an arrangement with the Presbytery of Dundee and on this account agreed in the year 1788 to petition the Relief Presbytery of Dysart to admit them as 'a forming congregation'. They were accordingly admitted into connection with the Relief body but it was not, so far as appears, until the year 1789 or 1790, that they proceeded to erect a place of worship for themselves. In 1790 they obtained a Feu Disposition from Alexander Ritchie, shoemaker, Dundee, of "All and whole that piece of garden ground consisting of about fourteen falls (2) or thereby(on which a church is just now built for said congregation) lying in the East Chapelshade (3) of Dundee" ...

It seems that most of the original members were not strongly attached to the Relief Church. Their first minister, who ironically had come to them from the Relief mother church of Dunfermline Gillespie, was deposed, as previously mentioned. In August 1791 the first moves towards union of the congregation with the Established Church took place. On 13 August the kirk session 'after considering the trouble and inconvenience which the Congregation suffered by their connection with the Relief ... unanimously agreed ... to be admitted as a Chapel of Ease by the Presbytery of Dundee'. A congregational meeting on 2 September approved this decision by a 'great majority'. Out of a congregational roll of 280 over 200 signed a paper of assent.

In 1830 the church was enlarged, 400 sittings and a vestry being added at a cost of £700.

At the Disruption of 1843 the minister and the entire congregation, excepting a few people, joined the Free Church, initially retaining the buildings. They also kept the church plate and furnishings. One report claims that all left 'except three men and an old woman'. This may refer to the attendance on the first Sunday after the Disruption rather than the residual membership. The Established Presbytery took the matter to court and regained possession of the property in February 1847. When the church was reopened by the Established Church on Sunday 2 May 1847 there was an attendance of only 30 in the morning and 15 in the afternoon.

The *quoad sacra* parish of Chapelshade was disjoined from St Mary's, Dundee on 18 March 1872.

The building was described as 'a large plain building with sittings for about 1200 persons'. Improvements, involving the removal of the old desk for the precentor and installation of a new pulpit platform and stairs, had been carried out in 1866.

Ministers

1790 James SMITH	From Dunfermline, Gillespie. Dep. by Relief Church 1791 and joined CofS. Died 1810. (Small 294-5, FES V 324)
1811 William JOHNSTON	From Asst. Rattray. Died 1833. (FES V 324)
1830 William REID	Ord. A&S. Joined Free Church 1843. Min. Chapelside FC 1843-4. (Died 1854) (FES V 324-5)
1849 William Adam SMITH MA	Ord. To Towie 1852. (FES V 325)
1852 John Alexander MACKENZIE	Ord. To Ferryport on Craig 1853 (FES V 325)
1853 George Stewart BURNS MA	Ord. To Newton upon Ayr 1854. (FES V 325)
1854 Peter CAMERON	Ord. To Glenisla 1859. (FES V 325)
1860 William Fergusson WIGHT	Ord. To Auchtergaven 1862. (FES V 325)
1863 Archibald BELL MA	Ord. DD (St Andrews 1894) Dem. 1911 (Died 1913) (FES V 325)
1911 Stephen FORSYTH MA	From Glasgow Springburn, St Serf's. Died 1924. (FES V 325)
1924 Archibald H MITCHELL MA BD	Ord. To Kirriemuir 1929 (FES V 325)
1930 Theodore ANDREW MA	From Walls. To Kinneff 1933. (FES IX 506)
1934 Robert Nicol PATON BD	From Lochgelly, St Andrew's. Min. of united charge 11 Feb 1940. (FES IX 506)

Rosebank-Chapelshade

Rosebank-Chapelshade was formed by the union of **Rosebank** and **Chapelshade** on 11 February 1940. Rosebank church was retained and the Chapelshade church sold in 1943. The hall was repaired and improved. The name of the congregation was changed later to Albany.

Ministers

1940 Robert Nicol PATON BD	Minister of Chapleshade. Died 1957. (FES IX 513, X 304)
1958 Gilbert Mollison MOWAT MA	From Calderbank. Min. of United Charge 26 Sep.1962. (FES X 304)

Albany Butterburn

After the union of 26 September 1962, the Butterburn building was retained and the Albany church sold to another denomination. On 1 June 1986 the congregation was linked to St David's North under the ministry of the Rev. Gideon George Scott MA BD ThM of St David's North.

Minister

1962 Gilbert Mollison MOWAT MA	Min. of Albany. Dem. 1986 (PM, YB)

There are a number of war memorials representing the congregations of which Albany Butterburn is composed. A marble plaque with black lettering at the front of the church is for the First World War. There is a memorial for that war in the vestibule. There are two Rolls of Honour for the 1914 War and a memorial for the Parish of Rosebank Dundee, European War 1914.

Notes

1. Secession and UP churches tended to be plain. They did not require to be as large as parish churches, as they only had to accommodate their own members. A simple building was often more in keeping with the surrounding properties where the members might reside. Moreover, it was functional and did not require the same maintenance costs. Some churches were built in the style of warehouses, in case they required to be disposed of at a later stage. However, some congregations who moved to new (and, frequently, more affluent) districts built more elaborate and expensive churches. Occasionally, where the founders of an entirely new congregation included wealthy people a more ostentatious building would be erected. Ryehill UP church, opened in 1880, is a good example of the latter costing about ten times more than Butterburn.
2. A fall is a land measure equivalent to a perch or 5.03 metres.
3. The name 'Chapelshade' is interesting. The old Scots phrase 'to shed' means to separate and is used in land divisions. The church took its name from the placename which predated the congregation, 'East Chapelside' and 'West Chapelside' appearing on Crawford's map of 1777.

CC Barnett, *The Seven Churches of the Hilltown*, Dundee, nd.
DCA CH2/409, 1218/52
DCA CH3/1218 General Kirk Session Muniment Chest, 9/1 Petition re Chapelshade Church; 9/9 Letter re Chapelshade Chapel dated 8 December 1824; 9/16 Memorial for the Managers of the Chapelshade Church, Dundee, 1843.
DCC Combined Statutory and Descriptive Lists
DPL Lamb 170(6), 171(4)
DYB 1913

BALGAY

Balgay church is situated at 200 Lochee Road, at the junction with Tullideph Road and was opened for worship on 29 December 1902.

The present Balgay congregation was formed on 10 July 1973 by the union of Balgay St Thomas' and Martyrs'. The union, using the Balgay St Thomas' buildings under the ministry of the Rev. John A Macdonald, of Martyrs', had been agreed after the local authority placed a compulsory purchase order on the Annfield Road buildings to make way for redevelopment in the Hawkhill area.

The church interior is cruciform in shape, comprising a centre section of two sets of pews divided by a centre aisle, two side sections, separated from the centre section by stone arches, each with an aisle and pews. Two transepts, with pews separated by a centre aisle, form the short sections of the cruciform. There is a small gallery above the centre section at the opposite end from the chancel apse.

Mr James Binny, builder of the church gifted a baptismal font, and a silver bowl was donated by the children of the Sunday School. The gallery clock was given by Mr James Ogilvie of Planetrees in 1907. A fine communion table and chairs were presented in memory of Mr Edward Robertson, Logie Farm.

A pipe organ was installed as a war memorial in October 1924. The organ which had been used in the church since 1902 was sold to Murroes Church. The pipe organ was in turn replaced by a Hammond electronic organ in the early 1960s. There are two brass plaques as memorials of the First and Second World Wars.

Plans for a new hall had been prepared in 1937 but war held up completion of the work, which cost £7,000, and the building was not dedicated until Easter Sunday, 17 April 1949. After the union of 1973 a hall extension was put in hand, providing additional hall and kitchen facilities, and also forming the Hall of Fellowship between the hall and church buildings. The cost of around £98,000 was funded under the terms of the compulsory purchase order placed on the Martyrs' church buildings.

In 1995 three stained glass windows were inserted in the lights in the apse behind the communion table at an outlay of £15,000, raised by the Ladies' Flower Group of the congregation. The windows, on the theme of praise, depict praise through music, flowers, and praise in the family, were designed by Susan Bradbury. This project had been intended to mark the centenary of the current church building in 2002, but such was the enthusiasm of the fund raising group that the cost of the work was raised years ahead of target. The manse is at 150 City Road.

St Thomas: The Iron Church, Lochee Road
This building was used from 1874 - 1902

Balgay St Thomas

This congregation originated as a Reformed Episcopal church. A number of members of St Mary Magdalene's Episcopal Church, then in Blinshall Street, withdrew in 1868 and formed 'St John's Reformed Episcopal Church'. In 1870 the congregation, asserting its independence, elected the Rev. Joseph Mulkerns as its pastor. They met in various halls until they built an iron church in Logie Den between Dundee and Lochee. The church was opened 22 November 1874.

According to Norrie's Handbook of Dundee:

"St John's Chapel stands upon rising ground south of Logie Toll Bar and on the eastern side of the Coupar Angus turnpike and was erected in 1874. This edifice, which is built to a large extent of iron, is cruciform, the design being a very neat adaptation of Gothic architecture. It seats 500 ... and cost £1,200. The congregation was formed in consequence of the alleged Romish doctrines proclaimed and the ritualistic ceremonies employed in the worship by the then incumbent and subsequently the congregation withdrew altogether from under the Episcopate of Brechin and constituted themselves into what is generally known as a Church of England church."

The Reverends Dr Lane, Mr Taylor, and Mr Jellibrand were successively associated with St John's.

In 1885 the congregation was admitted into the Church of Scotland and renamed St Thomas' Chapel of Ease. A meeting of the congregation on 18 December 1899 agreed to acquire 'the stance at the corner of Lochee Road and Tullideph Road' for a new church. Lord Balfour of Burleigh, the Scottish Secretary, laid the foundation stone on 17 May 1902. The Dundee Church Extension Association had been instrumental in the erection of the church at a cost of £4,900. The architects were Messrs Johnston and Baxter, Dundee. After the new building opened on 29 December 1902 the Iron Kirk was sold and erected at Westgreen [now Liff Hospital] as a chapel. A tenement at 155-157 Lochee Road, known as St Thomas' Place, occupied the old site in Logie Den. The manse was at 13 Lawside Road.

The kirk session of Liff and Benvie had pastoral oversight until the *quoad sacra* parish of Balgay was disjoined from St Mary's and Liff on 7 March 1913.

Ministers

1885 Andrew RUTHERFORD MA BD	Ord. Dem. 1893. *Locum tenens* at Glasgow, St Mungo's. (FES V 324)
1893 John COLVILLE MA BD	Ord. Dem. 1897. After at Lochranza. (FES V 324)
1898 William HALL MA	Ord. Adm. First min. of par. 7 March 1913. Dem. 1924. (Died 1925) (FES V 324, VIII 487)
1924 Cyrus Maxwell MORTIMER MA	Ord. To Roberton 1930. (FES VIII 487)
1930 James Main STEWART MA	Ord. To St Vincent, West Indies 1936. (FES IX 503)
1935 James OSWALD	From Elderslie East. CF 1939-45. Died 1966. (FES IX 503, X 298)
1967 William Alexander DUNDAS MA	From Kilmallie. To Buckhaven 1973. (Died 1979) (FES X 298, YB)

Martyrs'

In 1743 the Cameronians constituted the Reformed Presbyterian Church, claiming to be the true Kirk of the Covenants. They had adherents in Dundee in the late eighteenth century who were granted preachers from time to time. However, it was not until 1827 that application was made for services, and thereafter Dundee was regarded as a regular station. Only one elder resided in the town, and when a kirk session was required in April 1831, elders came from Strathmiglo to constitute it. In the same month a congregation was formally constituted. Attempts to obtain a minister were made in October and November 1831, but the congregation was asked to delay the procedure until they made 'some further exertion for obtaining a place of worship'. They opened a meeting house in rented premises in November 1832.

One of the preachers, Alexander Shand, gave sermons so unedifying that the congregation complained and he abandoned the Church. Further attempts were made to settle a minister and, after seven ministers had been declined, the first pastor was ordained at Chapelshade on 12 October 1836.

A site, later occupied by Albert Square Church, was chosen for a new church in the same year. [see Meadowside St Paul's] The congregation proceeded to build their meeting house, with shops below, against the advice of the Presbytery. The latter's concerns about costs proved correct and a financial crisis developed within three years. £576 remained outstanding on a church that had cost £840 and the resulting difficulties continued to dog the congregation. They were deprived temporarily of their place of worship in 1852 because of the outstanding debt. The congregation was again removed three years later when the bondholder called up the bond but relieved of the debt, since the guarantors of the bond made good the loss.

A new church at Balfour Street, Hawkhill, with 376 sittings, was erected and opened free of debt on 3 February 1856. A long period without a minister resulted in the congregation being reduced to a Home Mission Station. Robert Naismith worked as a missionary for a time but declined a call to the charge. Thereafter John Riddell was appointed and, after a successful year, accepted a call as minister. However, four years later, Mr Riddell and 250 members, most of the congregation, were received into the Free Church by the General Assembly on 1 June 1868. The congregation recovered its numerical strength under the next minister, John Wyllie, who was experienced in mission work in Glasgow.

Under the arrangements for the Reformed Presbyterian Church to join the Free Church, Mr Wyllie, the minister, and the Presbytery Commissioner of what was referred to as 'Hawkhill' Church are recorded as having been received into the Free Church by the Presbytery on 14 June 1876.

Presbytery had approved a request to change the name of the congregation from "Hawkhill" to "Martyrs'" on 14 February 1877, a month before the memorial stone for a new building was laid on 17 March 1877. The church in Annfield Road opened for worship, with 1,000 sittings, on 20 December 1877. Alexander Petrie, Glasgow, was the architect and the building had cost £5,000, with a grant of £1,000 from the Church Extension Fund and a legacy of £832. It had a spire of 100 feet and two halls accommodating 400 and 170. The vacated church in Hawkhill was acquired for the use of Hawkhill UP congregation. [See Meadowside St Paul's] The manse was at 150 City Road.

Dundee Reformed Presbyterian had become Hawkhill Free in 1876, Martyrs' Free in 1877, Martyrs' UF in 1900, and Martyrs' in 1929.

Ministers

1836	Thomas McINDOE	Ord. Dem. 1839. (Died 1865) (RPC 55-6)
1841	Joseph WILSON	Ord. Dem. 1847. (RPC 56)
1852	William STEVENSON	Formerly of Stirling. Dem. 1858. (RPC 56-7)
1863	John RIDDELL BA	Ord. Joined Free Church 1868. To Free Glasgow Wynd 1868. (RPC 57, PM)
1869	John WYLLIE	Ord. Died 1893. (RPC 57, Ewing II 161, PM)
1893	Alexander OSBORNE MA	Ind. Ord. at Sydney, NSW, returned to Scotland 1892. Died 1906. (Ewing II 161, FUF 386, PM)
1906	Alfred Henry CHARLTON	From Kilwinning Mansefield UF. To Marykirk & Muirton UF 1923. (FUF 386)
1923	James LAMONT	From Hamilton Stonefield (CofS). To Wamphray 1934. (FUF 386, FES IX 511)
1935	Douglas BRIGGS MA	From Old Cumnock West. To Dunoon St John's 1939. (FES IX 511)
1939	Ralph Wynne FAIRWAY	Ord. To Glasgow Martyrs' and Robertson Memorial 1945. (FES IX 511)
1946	John Anderson MACDONALD	From Lintrathen and Kingoldrum. Minister of United Charge 10 July 1973 (FES IX 511, X 303)

Balgay

After the union of 1973 the minister of Martyrs' became minister of the united congregation worshipping in the Balgay St Thomas' building.

Ministers

1973	John Anderson MACDONALD	Minister of Martyrs'. Dem. 1985. (FES X 298, YB)
1987	George K ROBSON LTH DPS	From Echt linked with Midmar. (PM)

WJ Couper, *The Reformed Presbyterian Church in Scotland*, Edinburgh, 1925

J Oswald, *The Church and Parish of Balgay St Thomas' Dundee*, Dundee, 1946

A Elliot, *Lochee: As it was and is*, Dundee, 1911

J Lamont, *Historical Sketch 1827 - 1927*, Dundee, 1927

DPL   Lamb 170 (17)

DA   30 December 1902

BARNHILL ST MARGARET'S

The church of Barnhill St Margaret's is in Invermark Terrace, Barnhill. A chapel of ease was constituted by the Established Presbytery on 8 June 1884, the congregation worshipping initially in a galvanised iron church previously used by Craigiebuckler Church, Aberdeen, and then by St Luke's Free Church, Broughty Ferry. This building known as the "Tin Kirk", was purchased for £450 and used for worship until the stone church was built in 1895; thereafter it was used as a hall. In 1968 the original hall was embodied in a new plan, its corrugated walls being harled.

The congregation was formed despite the reservations of Monifieth Parish Church. It achieved full status when the parish of St Margaret was disjoined from Monifieth on 8 March 1907.

The church, designed in Scots Gothic and dedicated to St Margaret of Scotland, was opened on that Saint's day, 16 November 1895.[1] A memorial stone in the porch reads:

"This Kirk was biggit be Godlie men AD 1895 to ye honour of
God and to the memorie of Saint Margaret Queene of Scotland.
Unveiled 18 May 1895 by Mrs Amy Paisley, wife of Rev. Robert
Paisley of Brechin and daughter of Thomas Taylor"

The style of lettering was taken from an old stone in Dunkeld Cathedral.

The nave and transepts were based on sketches by Charles Carmichael, Aberdeen, and modelled on the collegiate church of Biggar of 1543.[2] The original work consisted of the nave and cost £2,500, and was carried out under the direction of Duncan Carmichael, London. In 1932 T Lindsay Gray, architect, Dundee, added the transepts for an outlay of £4,000. The transepts were dedicated and the extended church reopened on 1 January 1933, by the Right Reverend Dr H R Mackintosh, Moderator of the General Assembly. New work was carried out in 1979 when a vestry, session room, choir room, and other offices were added. Two new windows were added to the chancel, which was refurbished. These additions were designed by Lindsay Gray, architect, and cost £36,000. The extension was dedicated on 16 September 1979.

The cruciform building is in pink rockfaced and snecked masonry with buff dressings. It has a green slate roof. The apse and vestry to the east are in brick, harled with polished dressings. The north elevation is five-bayed with a porch which was adapted from St Mary's, Whitekirk, North Berwick.[3] The roof centre boss in the vestibule of 1896 has a lion rampant. There is a sculpted figure of St Margaret in a canopied niche in the crow-stepped gable. The west gable has a large window with curvilinear tracery and a Celtic cross finial. There is a belfry in the apex, the bell being dated 1895. The exterior stone is probably from Brox Quarry and the interior stone from Drumyellow Quarry, Arbirlot.

The original chancel was lined on the east wall with dark panelling from the laird's loft in Newton Church, near Edinburgh, of the family of Wauchopes of Edmonton where the Rev T N Adamson's family had been members. Mr Adamson had it erected as a memorial to his brother, John Archibald Adamson, drowned in the River Congo in 1893. The present light oak panelling replaced the earlier woodwork in 1954 after woodworm had attacked it.

The doorway giving entrance to the nave has two doors, both of oak. The outer door is solid and the inner partly glazed. The latter was the gift and workmanship of James Ellis, an elder, on the occasion of the centenary of the Congregation. This Centenary Door is engraved to show the double strand of sacrifice and victory which runs through the Christian faith. The east panel bears St Andrew's Cross and the Crown of Thorns while, on the west panel, the Cross of St John, or Celtic Cross, symbolises the assurance of the Christian faith.

The interior is in lightly picked and snecked masonry. The braces of the collar-braced roof are supported on corbels sculpted with the arms of European families, some descended from St Margaret. There are seven saints windows in the nave representing the Blessed Virgin Mary, St Bride, St Andrew, St Kentigern, St David, St Margaret, and St Ninian.

A memorial window in the north transept to Norman Pattullo is by Herbert Hendrie, Edinburgh, circa 1937. The central figure of the stained glass is St Andrew. Above the Saint is a jewelled and floriated cross held by two angels, while below is a scene illustrating the call to discipleship of Andrew. At the left is St Columba. Above is the monogram of Jesus and below a representation of the journeys of Columba to Iona. At the right is St Kentigern, bearing a crozier and fish. Below is shown the saint recovering the ring in the mouth of the salmon. The small panels above show angels with instruments of praise.

The south transept memorial to Clement Godfrey is by J T & CE Stewart, Glasgow, and was unveiled on 23 July 1933. This window is divided into nine panels, five of which, in the shape of a cross, depict scenes from the life of St Margaret, her landing in Scotland, her marriage to King Malcolm, her charity, her piety, and her death. At the base on the left is Noah's Ark representing the Old Covenant. On the right are the Chalice and Paten representing the New Covenant.

The stone font was designed by Charles Carmichael and was the gift and work of David Tocher, mason, Dundee. The decoration has the Greek letters IHS, a cross with a crown of thorns, and the monograms of St Margaret and Queen Victoria. The basin is inscribed, "He that believeth and is baptised shall be saved" and "Given for the Glory of God to St Margaret's Church by David Tocher 1887". Evidently it was given in the "Tin Kirk" days, while the Royal Monogram suggests it may also have been marking the Queen's Jubilee.

The carved stone pulpit by Charles Soutar, circa 1912, is in memory of the Reverend Thomas N Adamson. Its panels show the four evangelists and their emblems: Matthew, an angel; Mark, a lion; Luke, an ox; John, an eagle. The inscription reads, "To the Glory of God and in loving memory of Rev Thomas Newbigging Adamson, the first minister of this parish, who died 18 November 1911, after 27 years of devoted service".

One of the church's lecterns was a replica of that which was gifted in 1498 to Holyrood Abbey by Abbot Crichton, when made Bishop of Dunkeld by James IV. The original was stolen in 1544 by the Earl of Hertford's troops and for long was in St Stephen's Church, St Albans, despite Scottish appeals for its return. On St Andrew's night, 1985, it was stolen from St Stephen's and an anonymous caller to newspapers stated that Scottish patriots had buried it in the Highlands. The English church agreed to accept the look-alike lectern from St Margaret's and to give up its claim to the original. Mr Jabez Watson, West Ferry, had given the replica lectern to St Margaret's in 1896.

The present communion table by Lord Roberts Memorial Workshops, Dundee, was gifted by an elder and his wife and dedicated on Sunday, 24 May 1970. Two communion chalices were given by the Rev Mr Adamson. In 1886 Thomas Taylor presented two silver chalices, overgilt by Hart, Peard and Co, London. A solid silver flagon, the replica of one given to St Giles, Edinburgh, in 1618, was given by William M Ritchie and consecrated at Easter, 1914. It may be a copy of a St Giles' flagon given by George Monteigne, then Bishop of Lincoln.

In 1895 an anonymous well-wisher gave a bell cast in the Van den Gheyn bell foundry in Louvain, Belgium. Its inscription reads:

VOCOR EGO
S. MARGARETA
AD TE DOMINE
CLAMABO DEUS
MEUS 1895

"I am called St Margaret. To Thee I shall call, O Lord my God".

On 27 April 1975, a new Allen electronic organ was dedicated. The organ that it superseded was gifted to Richmond Craigmillar Church, Edinburgh. It was ultimately installed in Cults East Church in 1981. The Allen organ was itself replaced with a three manual Wyvern organ on 12 September 1993.

The first minister, T N Adamson, was a high churchman who tried to recover the catholic tradition of worship. As a consequence of some of the practices which he introduced into the worship of St Margaret's he was in conflict with the courts of the Church in what was known as "The Barnhill Case".

Holy Communion was celebrated at 8.30 am. Communicants came forward individually and received the sacrament kneeling at the foot of the chancel steps before the altar which had drapings. The congregation gave responses and sang prose psalms and canticles. There were lighted candles.

Largely as a result of the agitation stirred up by Jacob Primmer[4], Townhill, Dunfermline, Mr Adamson had to give a pledge to the 1903 General Assembly that he would conduct services in accordance with Church custom. Mr Adamson was a member of the Church Service Society which had been founded in 1892, although its prime concern was with doctrine, rather than ritual. He was a follower of the Reverend James Cooper of East St Nicholas, Aberdeen. Previously, Mr Cooper had been a minister of St Stephen's, Broughty Ferry. The founders of the [St Margaret's] Congregation included a group of laymen with High Church sympathies, the leader of whom was Thomas Taylor of Cambustay, a jute merchant. Mr Taylor had been a member of St Stephen's under Mr Cooper. Mr Taylor provided most of the funds for the Iron Church.

A Centenary Service was held on 24 June 1984, when the preacher was the Rev. Professor James A Whyte. As a mark of thanksgiving the congregation donated £2,600 for the work of Darjeeling Hills Bible School of the Church of North India.

A Service of Thanksgiving to celebrate 100 years of worship in the present church was held on Sunday, 19 November 1995. The preacher was the Rev. Douglas Galbraith, son of the Rev. David Galbraith, a former minister of St Margaret's. On this occasion another Thanksgiving Fund which raised £18,960 was disbursed.

The sum of £6,230 was given to Christian Aid and a further £6,230 was shared equally among the Dundee congregations of Camperdown, Douglas and Angus, Mains, Mid Craigie, and Whitfield. The remaining £6,230 was retained for a project within the congregation.

The church is B-listed. McLaren, Sons and Soutar designed the manse, adjacent to the church in Invermark Terrace, in 1912, in the Arts and Crafts style. Mrs Adamson, widow of the first minister, with a £500 endowment, presented it to the congregation. She also gave £1,000 towards the proposed transepts in 1923.

Ministers

1884 Thomas Newbigging ADAMSON	Ord. His alleged ritualistic practices were subject to proceedings in the Church Courts. Died 1911. (FES V 369)
1912 James Fleming Gordon ORR MA BD	From Asst.at St Cuthbert's, Edinburgh. Dem on appt. by Colonial Committee to Nairobi in 1921. (Died 1935) (FES V 369)
1921 George BREMNER MA BD	From Inverarity. Dem. 10 Nov and died 27 Nov. 1946. (FES V 369, IX 503)
1947 James Robert THOMSON MA	From Braemar. To Edinburgh St George's 1915. (FES IX 503)
1952 David Orr GALBRAITH MA BD	From Ardrossan St John's. To Muckairn 1968 (FES IX 503, X 299)
1969 George WATT	From Edinburgh Drylaw. Died 1985. (FES X 209, PM)
1986 Gordon David JAMIESON MA BD	From Elie linked with Kilconquhar & Colinsburgh. (PM, YB)

Notes

1.   Saint Margaret, queen of Malcolm III, King of Scots, was the granddaughter of the English king, Edmund Ironside. She is believed to have been born in Hungary in the mid 1040s. Raised in the Roman tradition, she influenced the process whereby the Celtic church in Scotland was reorganised along Roman lines. She was very pious and founded a splendid church at Dunfermline. Originally a Benedictine priory, it was raised to the status of abbey in 1128. She assisted pilgrims bound for the shrine at St Andrews, the passage at Queensferry being named in her memory. She died on 16 November 1093 and was buried at Dunfermline. She was canonised in 1250.

2.   Biggar is one of a number of collegiate churches still in use as a parish church. In the fifteenth and sixteenth century a number of local lairds of substance established collegiate churches near their castles, instead of founding monasteries or adding to the endowments of existing ones. The collegiate church would be served by a group of secular clergy, who would sing masses for the souls of the founder and his family.

3.   The fifteenth century church of Whitekirk was built near a healing well and a shrine to Our Lady of Haddington. In 1435 it was visited by the future Pope Pius II, to give thanks for his safe deliverance from shipwreck. It is still a place of pilgrimage.

4.   Jacob Primmer was 'pastor' of the chapel of ease at Townhill, Dunfermline. He refused the title of 'minister'. He conducted a long campaign in the Church of Scotland against 'High Church' practices, protesting against the liturgy in St Giles and the reredos in St Cuthbert's. Although he differed widely from his fellow ministers he remained in the Established Church, which tolerated him. Perhaps demonstrating that the Church of Scotland was indeed 'a broad church'.

E S Towill, *People and Places in the Story of the Scottish Church*, Edinburgh, 1976
G Watt, *Story of St Margaret's Church Barnhill 1884 - 1984*, 1984
Pictorial Booklet of Church and Parish, 1984
DCA GD/X100/9, GD/XI13/2/4
DPL Lamb 147(13)
D M Murray, *The Barnhill Case 1901 - 1904*
D D R Owen, *William the Lion 1143 - 1214*, East Linton, 1997

BROUGHTY FERRY EAST

Broughty Ferry East church, situated at 370 Queen Street on the corner of St Vincent Street, is B-listed and was built in 1865 to the design of Andrew Heiton of Perth, who also designed Newtyle church. It is constructed in snecked rubble masonry with polished dressings. The north elevation has five bays and a porch and the south is similar but without a porch. The east elevation has a centred porch with a moulded Gothic arch, surmounted by a gablet terminating in a fleur de lis. Above the doorway is a large window in four lights with tracery in the upper part. There is a rose window in the west elevation. The building has fish-scale roofs with fleur de lis finials, and buttresses. There was provision in the base of the north porch for a tower which has never been added.

The interior has a narthex at the east with a war memorial. The nave has plain plastered walls and a foliate moulded cornice. The roof is pointed and traceried collar braced. There is a gallery to the east and the organ to the west. The building cost about £3,600 and provided seating for 600. A contemporary newspaper account described the church as "the handsomest Presbyterian church of its size that we have yet seen in Scotland. In design it is most elegant; in material it is substantial and harmonious; and in execution most artistic ... Between the windows and at the corners are buttresses of beautiful proportion, which give the church quite the air of some fine college chapel."[1] A vestry and small hall were added in 1870 at an outlay of about £500. The first manse was built at 66 Camphill Road and completed in 1877 for £2,500.

Until 1888 the praise was led by a precentor, but in that year a harmonium was introduced.[2] The harmonium was replaced in 1894 by a pipe organ built by Gray and Davidson, London, at a cost of £650, to the design of the Royal College of Organists. The organ was converted to electric power and modernised in 1939.

The modern lighting installed in the church in 1958, along with a new font and lectern, were a memorial and a generous gift. A new, larger hall was completed in 1960, at a cost of around £13,000. When the church was redecorated in 1961the pews were stripped and waxed and new Flemish glass windows installed. Outside work in 1965 involved repointing of the stonework at an outlay of £3,500 and building alterations in 1968 led to an extension of the hall and addition of a session house and other rooms. The communion table was re-positioned and the elders' stalls replaced with removable chairs when the interior of the church was reordered in 1987. At the same time, the organ console and choir seating were moved to the front of the north transept, a central, raised dais was built in front of the pulpit, and additional storage was provided. Further improvements in the 1990s have included the provision of a church office in 1990, construction of access ramps for the disabled in 1991, and renewal of the roof of the large hall in 1994.

The sanctuary has been enhanced in recent years through a number of gifts: an offering table in 1969, a baptismal flower dish in 1976, a pulpit fall in 1987, and pew bibles in 1992. A table for the vestibule was given in 1974 and pedestals in 1981. A Bluthner grand piano was donated for the hall in 1965 and an amplifier system for the large hall in 1970.

In 1991 the congregation formed an after school care group known as 'Schools Out'. The Princess Royal visited the group, recognised nationally and regarded by the Church of Scotland as a model of its kind, on 23 May 1996.

The congregation plays a full part in the Broughty Ferry Churches Group, with combined Holy Week services, various appeals, and other community events. During six weeks of the summer period united services are held with the nearby congregation of St Aidan's. The manse is at 8 West Queen Street.

On 11 December 1861 the Free Presbytery received a petition proposing an additional church in Broughty Ferry which, it was suggested, should be erected 'somewhere to the eastward of the village'. Presbytery 'highly approved', and a committee was appointed to look into the matter. In the following February, when the initial committee reported favourably, another committee was set up to raise funds and select a suitable site.

It was reported to Presbytery on 9 July 1862, that the station had been opened on the previous Sunday by the Rev. John Lyon, minister of Free West, and that Mr Archibald Henderson, preacher, would officiate for the time being. Public worship was held initially in a hall in Brook Street, formerly an episcopal chapel and kindly granted by a local laird, Mr Erskine of Linlathen. After the hall was burned down, another temporary place of worship was erected on the same site, which is now the location of the YMCA gymnasium at 151 Brook Street. The kirk session was first constituted on 8 October 1862 under the moderatorship of Dr William Wilson of Free St Paul's Dundee.[3]

The condition set by the General Assembly when a ministerial charge was sanctioned on 2 June 1863, 'that a minister shall not be ordained in it till the adherents satisfy the Sustentation Fund Committee and the Presbytery of Dundee that a sum of not less than £100 annually will be contributed to the Fund for his maintenance', was met immediately and Dr Mitchell was elected minister. The Rev. Dr John Cairns of Berwick on Tweed, who preached on the text JOHN XX vv 21-23, opened the church on 21 December 1865. In his address Dr Cairns made reference to the affinity between the United Presbyterian Church, of which he was a member, and the Free Church.[4]

Broughty Ferry East Free became Broughty Ferry East UF in 1900 and Broughty Ferry East in 1929.

Ministers

1863	John Murray MITCHELL LLD	From Missionary at Bombay. To Foreign Mission India 1867. (Ewing II 158, PM)
1868	Alexander Balmain BRUCE DD	From Cardross Free. To Chair of Apologetics and NT Exegesis, FC College Glasgow 1875. (Ewing II 158, PM)
1875	James E SOMERVILLE BD	From Langholm Free. Dem. 1884. (Ewing II 158, PM)
1885	Alexander EWING	From Blyth. Ind. 8 Jan 1885. Died 4 Nov 1885. (Ewing II 158, PM)
1886	James DENNY DD	Ord. To Chair of Systematic and Pastoral Theology FC College Glasgow 1897. (Ewing II 158, PM)
1898	Malcolm Donald MACGILVRAY MA	From Glasgow Union Free. Died 1907. (Ewing II 158, FUF 379)
1907	James MOFFAT DD DLitt	From Dundonald UF. To Chair of Greek, Mansfield College Oxford, 1912. His 1913 translation of the New Testament into modern English became popular reading but the 1924 Old Testament did not. (Died 1944) (FUF 379)
1913	Frank CAIRNS DD	From Pollockshields Albert Road. CF 1914; at Gallipoli 1915. Sen Minister 1938. DD (St Andrews 1938). (Died 1955) (FUF 379, FES IX 504, X 299)
1938	Ironside SIMPSON MC BD	From Grangemouth Dundas. To Glasgow Merrylee 1950. (FES IX 504)
1950	James Fraser McLUSKEY MC BD DD	From Sub-Warden Army Chaplains' Training Centre. To New Kilpatrick 1955. War service earned him sobriquet of 'Parachute Padre'. (Mod. GA 1983) (FES IX 504, X 299, YB)
1956	James Archibald REID BD STM	From Forfar Lowson Memorial. Dem. 1983. (Died 1987) (FES X 299)
1984	Alan H MACKAY BD	From Larbert West.

Notes

1. A newspaper editorial in 1865 on the debate over the proposed new west end Established Church in Dundee and its style of construction declared, 'Let them take an example from the East Free Church congregation of Broughty Ferry and learn that elegance does not necessarily imply extravagance'. This church was opened in 1869 as St Mark's.

2. Nearby Free St Luke's congregation pioneered the introduction of a harmonium in 1880. This resulted in the 'St Luke's Harmonium Case' when the congregation won the right to use instrumental music in worship. The controversy went through the courts of the Free Church to the General Assembly.

3. Dr William Wilson of Free St Paul's was very active in church extension in Dundee Presbytery. He was Moderator of the General Assembly in 1866 and served as its Principal Clerk. In 1877 he became Secretary and Joint Convener of the Free Church Sustentation Fund.

4. Dr Cairns, later Principal Cairns, was probably the most distinguished minister of the United Presbyterian Church of his day, and it is significant that he should have been invited to open the East Church. Moves towards the union of the Free Church of Scotland and the United Presbyterian Church began in the early 1860s with Dr Cairns heavily involved. While a General Assembly overture to Free Church presbyteries in 1870 resulted in the conclusive majority of presbyteries approving union the position taken by the entrenched minority threatened a second Disruption. Both Churches reported the ending of the conversations in 1873.

G Sharpe, *Broughty Ferry East Church 1865 - 1965, A Short History*
J Malcolm, *The Parish of Monifieth*, Edinburgh, 1910
C McKean and D Walker, *Dundee An Illustrated Architectural Guide*, Edinburgh, 1993
Letter of 29 June 1998 from Mr P P Montador
DCC   Combined Statutory and Descriptive List
DPL   Lamb 370(12)
DCA   CH3/9/4
Dundee Advertiser 8, 12 and 22 December 1865

BROUGHTY FERRY ST AIDAN'S

Broughty Ferry St Aidan's, 408 Brook Street, designed by James Black, architect, Dundee, in 1824, has a seating capacity of 800. A prominent church with a square tower and slated spire, it is Gothic and rectangular in plan, in rubble masonry with polished and lined dressings. The third and fourth stages of the tower and spire to the west along with the vestry and south bay were constructed in 1858 by Charles Edward, architect, Dundee. There are four clock faces on the steeple which also houses a bell. The vestry was also used as a classroom. An organ chamber by James Maclaren and George Shaw, architects, Dundee, was added in 1875. The entrance is through a three-bayed porch with a moulded Gothic arch, a two-leafed panelled door and a Celtic cross finial. The church building is B-listed.

The interior is almost square with a semi-octagonal gallery. The lectern to the left is from 1924 and the font to the right from 1921. The organ, installed in 1875 and rebuilt in 1970, and pulpit are at the south centre. The communion table is a war memorial covering both World Wars. Three communion chairs made by the Lord Roberts Memorial Workshop, Dundee, form an additional memorial to the 1939-45 conflict.   Of the five memorial wall plaques, one commemorates James Maxwell Ferguson MD (1817-1909) and the others commemorate previous ministers: Rev James Wilson, Rev William D Fyfe, Rev Andrew MM Giles, and the Rev Keith Campbell.

The stained glass at the organ alcove is by G F Campbell, 1893. The window to the left was gifted by John Watson Wemyss and that to the right was given in memory of James Soote of Reres House. These stained glass windows were designed by Sir Edward Burne-Jones and manufactured by William Morris. As was common, the designs were stock patterns and it may be of interest to note where they were originally used: -

1. St John the Evangelist: The figure designed in 1877 for the church of St Mark, New Ferry, Cheshire. It appears in sixteen other churches in this country, and three abroad.
2. St Peter: First used in 1882 in the church of St Peter, Bramley, Leeds. It appears in six other churches.
3. John and Peter healing the crippled at the Beautiful Gate: Designed by Burne-Jones in 1878 for a window in the church of St John of Beverley, Whatton, Nottinghamshire. There are two others.
4. Calling of Andrew and Peter: Designed for the window of 1878 in Coats Church, Coatbridge. There are five elsewhere.

The land on which the church was built had been feued by Colonel David Hunter of Burnside, and in 1827 his son presented the church with an old bell. Dated 1636 and with a Latin inscription, the bell had been purchased by Col. Hunter in 1772 and reportedly had been hung on a pole at the Eagle Inn and rung on festive occasions. The recasting undertaken in 1827 was possibly not successful since the bell was replaced in 1858.

There are silver communion vessels. The congregation subscribed for an individual communion service. Mrs McPherson sewed the linen cloth for the communion table. Miss Hutcheson gave a reading desk in memory of Alexander Hutcheson. The Junior Choir and Bible Class gave the baptismal font at Christmas 1921, with a basin donated by Miss Hutcheson. The brass lectern for the communion table was bought in April 1937 from a legacy of Miss Euphemia Whyte.

Under the inspiration of the Reverend Keith Campbell, who wished the church embellished by congregation inspired artworks, the St Aidan's Church Enhancement Group was formed in 1990. Expertly guided by Frances Justice DA and Mary Stalker, a dozen ladies worked on small embroidery motifs, which were formed into a pulpit fall and two banners in the vestibule. A larger work of three panels was commenced in 1991, to reflect the ancient and modern flavour of Broughty Ferry: its churches, schools, shops, homes, its castle, lifeboat, and even its pubs. The first panel was hung and dedicated on 19 August 1995.

What is known as 'The Malawi Corner' was developed to celebrate the friendship which has grown since 1991 between the congregation and Chisambe CCAP church, Mimosa, Malawi. Gifts made by the members of Chisambe church are on display and the history of the friendship is recorded in a scrapbook entitled 'Church to Church'. St Aidan's congregation gifted communion vessels to the Malawi church.

The former Eastern Public School, built in 1872 by the Broughty Ferry School Board, was purchased by the congregation in 1913 and converted into halls. The Kippen suite of halls was added in 1979. The manse is at 63 Collingwood Street, Barnhill.

In the graveyard is the tombstone of Dr Thomas Dick of Pitkerro House, scientist and astronomer, who died in 1857. Dr Dick's family were founding members of Newbigging Burgher, later UP, Church.

In the early nineteenth century Broughty Ferry (the name 'Broughty' probably meaning 'the strong point on the Tay') became fashionable for sea bathing and the church was provided to serve summer visitors, as well as the expanding settlements of East and West Ferry. On 13 October 1824 the General Kirk Session of Dundee called for a collection in all churches and chapels of ease towards the cost of erecting Broughty Ferry Chapel. The Established Presbytery opened it for worship on 7 May 1826, it being constituted a chapel of ease by the General Assembly in May 1827. The *quoad sacra* parish of Broughty Ferry was disjoined from the parishes of Dundee and Monifieth on 15 July 1863. The civil area was formed into a burgh in the same year.

Those members, including ladies, who had subscribed a guinea or more, elected the first minister, David Davidson. Although terminally ill, he chose to join the Free Church at the Disruption of 1843.[1] On the Sunday following the secession, his assistant invited members to meet for worship next Sunday in the Victoria Inn. The subsequent ministry of the Rev. Andrew J McIntyre lasted for the exceptionally short period of three months since he accepted a call elsewhere.

The congregation was for long known as Broughty Ferry Parish Church and the Kirkin' of the Burgh Council took place in this church until Broughty Ferry became part of Dundee in 1913. Although one authority suggests that the church had been known as St Aidan's from about the 1860s a kirk session minute as late as 1921 refers to the 'congregation of Broughty Ferry Parish Church'. The name was not changed officially until the Union of 1929.

In 1981 the 'St Aidan's Project' was founded with the object of promoting the training and education, in the widest sense, of physically challenged school leavers. The first students were accommodated in the Kippen Hall, behind the church halls. In 1985 this building became an assessment centre when the main work was transferred to larger premises in Dundee. The project, renamed 'The St Aidan's Initiative' in 1989 and making use of a building in Ambleside Terrace, Kirkton, Dundee, continues to offer an 'Into Employment Service' to young people with learning difficulties. Funding was arranged with Tayside Regional Council and the European Social Fund.

Ministers

1827	David DAVIDSON	Ord. Joined Free Church, 1843, signing the Protest on his deathbed. Died 25 August 1843. (FES V 311)
1843	Andrew James McINTYRE	Ord. 20 Sep 1843. To Strathmiglo 29 Dec 1843. (FES V 311)
1844	John WOOD MA	From Scots Church, Monkwearmouth. LLD (Glasgow). Died 1864. (FES V 311-2)
1856	James LAMONT	From Kelvinhaugh, Glasgow (A&S). To Dalkeith West 1863. (FES V 312)
1864	James WILSON MA	Ord. (A&S) Dem. 1915. (Died 1922) (FES V 312)
1915	William John SYM MA BD	From Balfron. Served as CF in WWI. To Mayfield, Edinburgh 1921. (Died 1946) (FES V 312, KofE 272)
1921	William Dey FYFE MA BD	From Rattray. Served in RGA in 1917. CF in France 1917-18. Died 1924. (FES V 312, VIII 485)
1926	Alexander SMART MA	From Daviot. PhD (Aberdeen 1938). To St Cuthbert's, Saltcoats 1940. (FES VIII 485, IX 504)
1941	Andrew Milne Mitchell GILES MA	From Newmachar. War Service as Chaplain at Kingussie Naval Hospital 1939-41. Dem. 1967. (Died 1981) (FES IX 505, X 299, PM)
1968	Keith CAMPBELL BSc BD NDA	From Edinkillie. Died 1994 (FES X 299, PM)
1995	Caroline JACKSON MA BD	Ord. (PM)

Note

1. According to one unverified report, Mr Davidson was staying in Edinburgh and was able to observe the Disruption procession from his sick room, as the seceders walked from St Andrew's Church in George Street, where the General Assembly was meeting, down Hanover Street to Tanfield Hall at Canonmills, where the Free Church was constituted.

K Campbell, *A Short History of the Church and Congregation*, Dundee, 1976
    (150th anniversary booklet in DCA GD/X100/12)
G D Ritchie, *St Aidan's Church*, 1998
    (Notes for 'Open Doors' day pamphlet)
History of St Aidan's Parish Church
    (Typescript notes prepared for an unattributed and undated manuscript circa 1950)
C McKean & D Walker, *Dundee, An Illustrated Architectural Guide*, Edinburgh, 1984 and 1993
J Malcolm, *The Parish of Monifieth in Ancient and Modern Times*, Edinburgh, 1910
W Norrie, *Handbook of Broughty Ferry*, 1876
St Aidan's Chronicle 1990
DCA CH2/559/1 Broughty Ferry Church Minute Book
DCA CH2/103/18 Presbytery of Dundee minutes 1834-1847
DCA CH2/1218/9
DPL Sp 2.38
DPL Lamb 190(20), 370(10)
DCC Combined Statutory and Descriptive List

BROUGHTY FERRY ST JAMES'

Broughty Ferry St James' church is situated at 5 Fort Street, at the corner with Fisher Street, opposite the Lifeboat Shed, and overlooking the River Tay. It has long been known as the Fishermen's Church.

Designed by Edward & Robertson, architects, Dundee, in 1889, the rectangular church with porches is Romanesque in snecked rubble masonry with polished buff dressings. The vestry and a fishermen's reading room, added in 1896, adjoin the church at the north. The hall by D W Baxter, architect, Dundee, was built in 1907 to the north-west. The church building is C(s)-listed. The manse is at 95 Seafield Road, Broughty Ferry.

The interior has a two-arched aisle, a collar-braced roof, and plaster ceiling. The organ by Scobel and Co, Edinburgh, and formerly in St Rule's, Monifieth, was installed in 1970. There is a fine timber lectern and a pulpit of Romanesque design in memory of the Rev. James Burgess. The choir stalls are a War memorial.

The East Coast Mission, assisted by the Churches in Broughty Ferry, had established a non-denominational mission but withdrew their missionary in 1887. At a meeting on 2 May 1887 it was resolved that the Established Church should take over the work and so the congregation began as a mission, known as Beach. The church, built as a chapel, was opened on 22 February 1890 at a cost of £1,600. £1,000 had been obtained privately, £400 from the Baird Trust, and £200 from the Home Mission Board. The Trustees of the late Mr Cobb of Broughty Ferry endowed the sum of £2,500.

Beach, a chapel of ease from 17 November 1889, was disjoined from Broughty Ferry as a quoad sacra parish on 19 July 1907 when the first minister of the charge was admitted.

Beach became St James' in 1929.

St James' continues to maintain strong nautical links. Members of the congregation are crew members of the lifeboat and the minister is chaplain to the crew and to the local RNLI Association. An annual RNLI carol service and local RNLI annual general meetings are held in the church.

Several times a year an evangelistic literature distribution is undertaken in the parish and a visitation, conducted on a rolling basis, reaches about a quarter of the parish each year. Strong ties are maintained with other Christian agencies, including Scripture Union, Leprosy Mission, Lord's Day Observance Society, Christian Witness to Israel, and Overseas Missionary Fellowship. Five members of the congregation have entered the ministry of the Church of Scotland since 1970 and two have become ministers in other denominations. Six members have been set apart as readers since 1961.

Ministers

1887	Alexander Miller MACLEAN MA	Served from June to Dec 1887. (Afterwards Minister of Paisley Abbey.) (FES V 312)
1887	Andrew ARMIT	App. Missionary. To Nova Scotia 1892. (FES V 312)
1893	John Easton BLACK MA BD	App. Missionary. Dem. 1897. (FES V 312)
1898	John McKECHNIE	App. Missionary. Ord. 1899. To Buckhaven 1905. (FES V 312)
1906	James BURGESS	From Andover, New Brunswick. Adm. First Minister of parish 1907. Died 1924. (FES V 313, VIII 485)
1925	Charles Sydney FINCH MA	Ord. To Glasgow Wilton 1930. (FES IX 504, VIII 485)
1930	Campbell FERENBACH MA	Ord. To Glasgow Ruchill 1938. Author of *Annals of Liberton* 1975. (FES IX 505, KofE 283)
1938	William CAMPBELL MA	From Old Kilpatrick Barclay. Died 1949. (FES IX 505)
1949	John TURNER	From Aberdeen St Nicholas Union Grove. To Riccarton 1954. (FES IX 505)
1955	Malcolm Alexander RITCHIE	Ord. To Strathblane 1969. (FES X 299)
1970	Thomas Parker ROBERTSON	From Dingwall St Clement's. (FES X 299)

C McKean & D Walker, *Dundee, An Illustrated Architectural Guide*, Edinburgh, 1984 and 1993
J Malcolm, *The Parish of Monifieth in Ancient and Modern Times*, Edinburgh, 1910
Letter of 25 March 1998 from C A Webster, Session Clerk
DCC Combined Statutory and Descriptive List

BROUGHTY FERRY ST LUKE'S AND QUEEN STREET

Broughty Ferry St Luke's and Queen Street was formed on 14 June 1953 by the union of Broughty Ferry St Luke's and Broughty Ferry Queen Street. The church is situated at 5 West Queen Street, Broughty Ferry, and is A-listed. A red sandstone cruciform aisled Gothic church with clerestory, it was designed in 1884 by Hippolyte J Blanc, who was also responsible for All Souls Episcopal church, Invergowrie, and Cluny church, Edinburgh. The building, attractively set in its own grounds, is constructed in pink rockfaced and snecked rubble masonry with polished dressings. The roof is green slated with terracotta decorative ridge tiles. The porch at the south-west has a fine moulded Gothic arched entrance on triple nook shafts with foliate capitals and the west elevation has a central moulded Gothic arched entrance.

St Luke's and Queen Street Church, West Ferry

On entering, the narthex is richly detailed throughout and has a fine mosaic floor by Burke and Co, Paris, with medallions bearing the monogram of St Luke. The porch, with a ribbed, timber ceiling, has a door into the vestibule and another leading to the spire that was never built. A timber screen with a stained glass upper portion has doors leading into the three aisles of the nave.

The nave is four bayed with moulded Gothic arches on round Shap granite shafts with octagonal bases and moulded capitals. Two similar, larger, transeptal arches are on Ross of Mull granite piers and a moulded Gothic arch to the chancel has polished Kinsteary granite shafts. The roof is timber-lined and collar-braced and the gallery at the west has timber panelling. The polygonal apse, crowned by a rib-vaulted timber ceiling, houses the communion table and choir stalls. These pews face each other in the centre of the area with the organ situated on the south wall.

Five William Morris stained glass windows, designed by Sir Edward Burne-Jones, were placed in the lancet windows in the apse in 1884 as a memorial to David Ogilvie and his daughter, Catherine. The central window shows the Good Shepherd carrying a lamb upon his shoulders, the drapery being of rich, deep crimson tones. To the right of this figure two windows show, in spirited colour, the figures of Ruth, as a reaper in the harvest field, and Enoch being led through life by the Divine hand. The figures in the windows to the left of the centre represent Mary of Bethany and St John the Divine. Mary is shown in shining white drapery, which enhances the value of the dark red robes worn by the Shepherd and by John.

At the left-hand end of the apse arch is the pulpit which is of grained wood and was meant to be of a temporary character. The original intention was to have an artistically designed stone pulpit in keeping with the rest of the building.

Mr James S Ogilvie and his wife gave the organ, constructed by Gray and Davidson of London in 1884. Inaugurated on 1 February 1895, it has been overhauled and repaired three times: in 1957 for £2,800, in 1983 for £9,900, and in 1991 for £14,400.

A door to the left of the apse leads to various offices. The hall to the rear of the church was built in 1966 and extended in 1970. The manse is at 22 Albert Road, Broughty Ferry.

Broughty Ferry St Luke's

St Luke's Free became St Luke's UF in 1900 and St Luke's in 1929.

This Free Church congregation was organised in 1878 to meet the needs of the growing community. The charge was sanctioned in the same year and the kirk session was first constituted on 9 July 1878. A building, known as the Iron Church, had been erected on a site to the west of the present church and opened on 12 May 1878. Offering accommodation for 375 and used previously by Craigiebuckler Church, Aberdeen, the building had been constructed originally by Francis Morton & Co, Liverpool. It served until construction of the present church began, when the congregation worshipped for a time in the Volunteer Hall and the Iron Church was sold for £450 to St Margaret's Church, Barnhill. The new church cost £8,000; the site, the mosaic floor, and the granite and marble pillars were gifts. It was opened on Thursday, 27 November 1884 by Dr Alexander Whyte, Free St George's, Edinburgh.

St Luke's were pioneers in introducing a harmonium into services. Its first use in 1880 led to the 'St Luke's Harmonium Case' as a result of which the congregation won the right to the use of instrumental music in worship. The controversy began at Presbytery, went to the Synod, and ended at the General Assembly. The harmonium, still in working order, is at the entrance to the south transept.

Ministers

1878	William Wynne PEYTON	From Portsoy Free. Dem. 1892. (Died 1924) (FUF 379-80)
1893	Lewis Andrew MUIRHEAD MA BD DD	From East Wemyss Free. Dem. 1920. (Died 1926) (FUF 380)
1921	William Millar MATHIESON MA BD	From Scone Abbey UF. Died 1935. (FUF 380, FES IX 505)
1936	Thomas Henry KEIR MA	From Perth Bridgend. To Aberdeen Holborn West 1943. (FES IX 505)
1946	Thomas James Trail NICOL MC MA MBE LVO	Formerly CF. Ind. 1946. Dem. on appt. as CF 1949. (Domestic Chaplain to Royal Family in Scotland 1972-79.) DD (Aberdeen 1968) (Died 1998) (FES IX 505, *The Scotsman* 12 August 1998)
1950	Donald Robertson FRASER MA BD	From Newtongrange. Min. of United Charge 14 Jan. 1953.

Broughty Ferry Queen Street

Originally a congregation of the UP Church established after 45 members and 14 adherents in Broughty Ferry had presented a petition to the UP Presbytery of Dundee on 7 January 1873. They claimed that 'a growing dissatisfaction … existed in the congregation' and pointed out that Broughty Ferry was increasing rapidly in size. Presbytery approved the opening of a preaching station on 18 February, and on 22 April reference was made to the 'Second congregation of Broughty Ferry'. They worshipped first in a public hall but a suitable site was acquired and the congregation became Queen Street UP Church.

The Dundee architects James Maclaren and G S Aitken designed the well-proportioned Gothic church, with striped stone gables, a three-stage tower with a tall spire, and a semi-hexagonal chancel to the east. When the distinguished Principal John Cairns opened it on 15 June 1876, the building with sittings for 550 had cost almost £5,000.[1] It remains a B-listed building.

The hall was given to the congregation when the Union Church, to whom it had belonged, united with the West Church in 1925. A number of Union members transferred to Queen Street at the same time.

Queen Street UP became Queen Street UF in 1900 and Queen Street in 1929.

Ministers

1873	Andrew CARTER	Ord. Dem. 1879 (Died 1893) (Small I 344-5)
1879	David Hepburn LAWRENCE MA	Ord. DD (1907) Dem. 1919. (Died 1932 (FUF 379)
1918	James MANSON MA	Ord. C&S. To Alves 1931. (FUF 379, FES IX 504)
1930	Thomas D Stewart BROWN MA	Ord. To Cardross Old 1937. (FES IX 504)
1935	Hugh Baillie MACLEAN MA BD ThM	Ord. War Service as CF. Dem. On appt. as Professor of Old Testament, New Brunswick Theological Seminary 1946. (FES IX 504)
1948	Dugald C ALEXANDER MA BD	Intro. To Thurso St Peter's and St Andrew's 1952. (FES IX 504)

Broughty Ferry St Luke's and Queen Street

After the union in 1953 the St Luke's buildings were retained. The Queen Street property, which had been used as halls, was sold in 1969 and was later converted into a restaurant known as the Gulistan.

Chancel furnishings of a communion table, chairs, lectern and font, surplus following the union, were gifted to Mains of Fintry congregation.

Ministers

1953	Donald Robertson FRASER MA BD	Minister of Broughty Ferry St Luke's. To Forres St Laurence 1959. (FES IX 505, X 299)
1959	Samuel Gilles MACNAB MA BD HCF	From Darvel Irvine & Easton Memorial. Dem. 1994. (FES X 299, PM)
1996	Pauline STEENBERGEN MA BD	Ord. Dem. 1999. (PM)

Note

1. Principal John Cairns personified the life and faith of the United Presbyterian Church. In his own ministry he maintained the ideals of the Seceding ministry; unadorned services with lengthy exegetical sermons unread, backed by regular pastoral visitation. Principal Cairns, then Dr John Cairns of Berwick-on-Tweed, also opened the East Free Church, now Broughty Ferry East, in 1865. At the time he was leading negotiations on behalf of the UP Church for union with the Free Church. These discussions were abandoned in 1873 and union was not achieved until 1900.

C McKean & D Walker, *Dundee, An Illustrated Architectural Guide*, Edinburgh, 1993
J Murray Feathers, *St Luke's UF Church*, 1928
S G Macnab, *100 Years of St Luke's and Queen Street*, 1978
J D F Carnegie, *St Luke's and Queen Street Church*, 1995
       (Notes for use on "Doors Open Day".)
DCC Combined Statutory and Descriptive List
DCA GD/X100/4
DPL Sp 2.61
DPL Lamb 173(10), 370(11,12)

BROUGHTY FERRY ST STEPHEN'S AND WEST

Broughty Ferry St Stephen's and West *was formed by the union of Broughty Ferry St Stephen's and Broughty Ferry West on 8 November 1962.*

The church, built in 1871 and A-listed, stands at the corner of Westfield Road and Dundee Road, Broughty Ferry. Designed by Thomas S Robertson, architect, Dundee, who was a founder member, the building is cruciform in plan, aisled Gothic of multi-coloured snecked masonry. A four-stage tower with a spire stands at its north-east corner. East and west galleries were added in 1875 and the north gallery was enlarged in 1877. The chancel and organ chamber were built in 1880 during the ministry of the Rev James Cooper. The vestry, added at the south-east corner in 1874, has become a counting house since a new vestry was added in 1957.

The nave is galleried with moulded Gothic arches on round columns with finely sculpted foliate capitals. The panelled galleries are supported on cast iron columns. There is a boarded collar braced roof. The timber pulpit and communion table are under the crossing. The pulpit was offset during renovations in 1930. New choir stalls were added in light wood. The present communion table and chairs date from 1969 when the platform was extended. There are organ cases at left and right but the organ was replaced with an electronic instrument in the back gallery in 1969. However, in the early 1990s the electronic organ was brought down from the gallery to the west transept.

The church contains some fine stained glass windows designed by Sir Edward Burne-Jones and executed by William Morris & Company between 1893 and 1915. The splendid three large chancel windows contain Sir Edward's composition of "The Stoning of St Stephen". The majority of the windows were gifted by Mr JJ Watson, Ballinard, a Dundee spirit merchant.

There are war memorials from the constituent congregations on the walls of the sanctuary.

The church hall was built in 1894 but burnt out in 1943 and rebuilt in 1951.

In 1981 the congregation gifted some of its surplus communion silver to the Scots Kirk in Rotterdam. The sacred vessels, including very fine silver given to the Kirk by the City of Rotterdam around 1600, had been stolen. Previously the congregation had gifted communion chairs of the former West Church, surplus on their union, to Colinsburgh church, Fife.

The manse is at 33 Camperdown Street, Broughty Ferry.

Broughty Ferry St Stephen's

The Establishment opened a chapel on 26 November 1871, with the parish of St Stephen's being disjoined from Broughty Ferry and Monifieth on 19 July 1875.

The first minister admitted to the charge, the Rev James Cooper, had High Church leanings and was a member of the small, but influential, Scoto-Catholic party in the Church of Scotland led by the Rev Robert Lee. One of Cooper's followers, the Rev TN Adamson, opened St Margaret's, Barnhill, much of the funding of its temporary church being provided by Thomas Taylor of Cambustay, a layman with similar sympathies, who had been a member of St Stephen's under Cooper.

Ministers

1869	Robert SCOTT MA	Ord to Craig 1873. (FES V 313)
1873	James COOPER MA	Ord Adm. first min of parish 1875. To East Parish, Aberdeen, 1881. Descibed by Jacob Primmer as "more like a monk than a minister". (FES V 313)
1881	James LEASK MA	From Aberdeen Rosemount. DD (Aberdeen 1903) Dem 1918. (Died 1923) A great Greek scholar. (FES V 313)
1919	Douglas William BRUCE MA	From Cadzow. Dem 1925 on appt to Buenos Aires (FES V 313, VIII 186)
1926	James Charles CONN MA BD PhD	From Elgin. Dem 1946, (Died 1969) (FES VIII 486, IX 505, X 299)
1947	Ronald Scott THOMSON MA	From Huntly Strathbogie. To Culter 1962 (Died 1982) (FES IX 505, X 299)

Broughty Ferry West

Broughty Ferry West, which united with St Stephen's in 1962, had been formed by the union of **Broughty Ferry West UF** and **Broughty Ferry Union UF** on 10 May 1925. The West Church was retained as the place of worship for the united congregation. The Union Church was disposed of, the building becoming a grain store that has subsequently been demolished.

Broughty Ferry Free, West Free, West UF

Broughty Ferry Free became Broughty Ferry West Free in 1862 and Broughty Ferry West UF in 1900.

The minister of the *quoad sacra* church of Broughty Ferry (now St Aidan's), David Davidson, came out at the Disruption of 1843 along with many of his congregation. Sadly, Mr Davidson was terminally ill and signed the Protest on his deathbed. According to one unverified account, he was staying in Edinburgh and was able to observe the Disruption procession from his sick room. The seceders walked from St Andrew's Church in George Street, where the General Assembly was meeting, down Hanover Street to Tanfield Hall at Canonmills, where the Free Church was constituted.

His assistant, when taking the last service in the Established Church, invited the congregation to meet for worship on the following Sunday in the Victoria Inn. Until a church was ready services were held in a hall in Victoria Buildings, Gray Street. The foundation stone was laid in September 1843 and the church in Brook Street was opened in March 1844. At the formal opening of the church a snowstorm prevented the guest preachers from arriving and Mr Lyon, the minister, conducted the ceremony. It later became West Free with the opening of the East Free in 1862. A manse was erected in 1849. The church was enlarged in 1856 and again in 1890. The East Free and Monifieth South Free churches were offshoots from this congregation.

Ministers

1843	David DAVIDSON	Min Broughty Ferry Chapel of Ease. Joined FC 1843. Died 25 June 1843. (FES V 311, Ewing II 158)
1844	John LYON	From Banton. Died 1889. (Ewing II 158)
1880	George Emslie TROUP MA	Asst. Broughty Ferry West Free. Ord. Dem. 1918 (Ewing II 158, FUF 380)
1918	James Rae FORGAN MA	From Uddingston Chalmers UF. To Ayr Trinity UF 1921. (FUF 380)
1921	Robert John MACKAY MA LLB	From Petty UF. Min of united charge 1925. (FUF 380, FES IX 505)

Broughty Ferry UAS, Union UP

Broughty Ferry UAS became Broughty Ferry Union UP in 1847 and Broughty Ferry Union UF in 1900.

According to the Old Statistical Account, about the year 1792 the Burghers and the Antiburghers each started a conventicle in the Monifieth area but they were thinly attended. Prior to the formation of a congregation at Broughty Ferry, secession families worshipped in Dundee, five miles from the village. On 2 May 1837, the Rev Matthew Fraser, minister of the Bell Street United Secession church, reported to the Presbytery of Forfar that in April he had opened a place of worship at Broughty Ferry. The building in which this group first met was the property of Thomas Erskine of Linlathen, and was seated for 300. It stood on the site of what was later the YMCA gymnasium. Robert Haldane had erected it as an Independent chapel and the embryo congregation was given the use of it without charge. They styled themselves "The Dissenters of Broughty Ferry and neighbourhood in connection with the United Secession Church". After a trial period they were given some financial assistance and formed into a congregation of the United Secession Church on 16 July 1838.

The first minister called was John Robb who was ordained on 21 May 1839. During the first year of Mr Robb's ministry it was reported to the Home Mission Board that in summer the church was crowded, perhaps reflecting the popularity of the village as a holiday venue, and that even in winter the attendance was "excellent". However, there was dissension in the small congregation and, after two years in charge, Mr Robb demitted to "lessen disunion". An indiscretion alleged against Mr Robb was that he had attended the Established Church.

Following the induction of Duncan Ogilvie as minister steps were taken to erect a new place of worship in Fort Street. This was a period of expansion in Broughty Ferry. The new church, seated for 400, was opened on 22 September 1847. As this was the first church to be opened after the formation of the United Presbyterian Church in that year it was called "Union". With the founding of what became Queen Street UP congregation, and a dispute in 1889 over a proposal to build a church hall, the congregation reduced from 328 in 1889 to 228 in 1894.

Ministers

1839	John ROBB	Ord. Dem. 1841. Ind. To Ramsey, IoM 1845. (Died 1873) (Small I 342)
1843	Laurence GOWANS	Ord. Died 1844. (Small I 343)
1845	Duncan OGILVIE	Ord. To Edinburgh Portsburgh UP 1859. DD (Aberdeen 1869) (Died 1893) (Small I 343, 486, 664)
1860	Hugh Taylor HOWAT	Ord. To Everton, Liverpool 1864. DD (NY 1882) (Died 1888) (Small I 343)
1864	James GRAHAM	Ord. Died 1893. (Small I 344)
1893	Thomas F BEST	Ord. Dem. 1924 To Grange 1924. (FUF 380)

Broughty Ferry West UF

Broughty Ferry West UF became Broughty Ferry West in 1929.

After the union in 1925, the Union Church was sold. The church hall was handed over to Queen Street UF, since a number of members had joined that congregation.

Ministers

1925	Robert John MACKAY MA LLB	Min. of Broughty Ferry West UF (pre union) To Greenock St Columba's 1934. (FUF 380, FES IX 504)
1935	Walter Chalmers Smith ANGUS MA	From Aberdeen High. To Stenton 1949. (FES IX 506)
1950	Thomas Loudon COX MA	From Cambuslang Rosebank. Dem.1962. (Died 1970) (FES IX 300)

Broughty Ferry St Stephen's and West

After the union of 8 November 1962, the St Stephen's buildings were retained and the West buildings disposed of. Broughty Ferry West church at the corner of Church Street and Brook Street was later demolished. Windsor Court flats were erected on the site.

Ministers

1963	Gilbert Stuart CAMERON	From Campbeltown Highland. To Nassau St Andrew's 1974 (Died 1994) (FES X 300)
1974	John Urquhart CAMERON ThD BA BSc PhD BD	Ord. (FES X 300)

C McKean & D Walker, *Dundee, An Illustrated Architectural Guide*, Edinburgh, 1993
JU Cameron, *The History of St Stephen's 1875-1975*, 1975
J Malcolm, *The Parish of Monifieth in Ancient and Modern Times*, Edinburgh, 1910
Conversation with Mr John Grieve, Session Clerk
DCC Combined Statutory and Descriptive List
DCA CH3/91/18
DPL Sp 2.61
DPL Lamb 370(10)
DPL DNC Vol 103

CAMPERDOWN

Camperdown Church is situated at 22 Brownhill Road in the middle of the Camperdown housing estate. This local authority housing development of the 1950s was planned to accommodate workers in the nearby industrial estates where, at their peak, the factories of NCR alone employed 6,500 people. The congregation began in 1959 as a Church Extension charge and was granted full status in 1964. The church was opened for worship on Sunday, 12 February 1961.

The church and hall are built in harled brick. The manse is located at Myrekirk Road.

Ministers

1959	Peter Mitchell GORDON BD	Ind. To Brechin Cathedral 1965. (FES X 300)
1965	John Alfred SHERRARD	From Newtyle. To Galashiels St Columba's 1969 (FES X 300)
1970	George Grant SCOTT	Ord. Dem. 1973 to appt. at Broken Hills, Alberta. (FES X 300)
1973	Robert JOHNSTON MTh	Ord. To Edinburgh St Mary's with St Stephen's 1988. (FES X 300, YB)
1989	Sheila CRAIK BD DPT	Ord. (PM)

DPL   Sp 4.141

CHALMERS-ARDLER

Chalmers-Ardler church in Turnberry Avenue was opened and dedicated on 19 January 1969. The congregation was a Church Extension charge formed by the transportation of the Chalmers congregation on 23 October 1968. Full status was granted in 1972. Constructed in brick and harled, the church has proved to have been poorly constructed and almost £100,000 has been spent on repairs since it was built. The manse is in Turnberry Avenue.

Chalmers Free

Chalmers Free became Chalmers UF in 1900, Chalmers in 1929, and Chalmers-Ardler in 1968.

Chalmers Free was formed following mission work conducted by St Peter's, St David's and St John's Free Churches in the Scouringburn area (later renamed Brook Street). The project was launched at a meeting of representatives of these three congregations held in Free St John's vestry, Small's Wynd, on 27 March 1851. The first service was held in Blinshall Street School on Sunday, 18 May 1851.

After eighteen months preliminary work by Mr William Maxwell, who gathered a congregation, a church was built in Hunter Street and opened on Thursday, 11 November 1852 by Dr Thomas Guthrie [1]. The first minister, the Rev William Tasker, conducted the services on the Sunday following the dedication. The building, which cost £630 and was described as "Perpendicular Gothic", was designed by one of the Maclaren family of architects in Dundee. Mr Maclaren had been somewhat restricted in his design, since the Home Board had stipulated that it had to be after the style of West Port Free, Edinburgh, built in 1847.

The General Assembly sanctioned the charge, which had been known originally as Chalmers Territorial Church, in August 1854. A school, which had been erected in 1852, was used later as church halls. A gallery was added to the church in 1866.

In 1863 Chalmers took over a mission in the Scouringburn previously run for about two years by the Gaelic congregation. Some of the work was suspended shortly afterwards due to the death of the minister, Mr Stirling. However, weekly prayer meetings were kept up. Following Mr Bell's induction he and Mr Riddell, minister of the Reformed Presbyterian Church, Hawkhill, conducted Sunday evening meetings in alternate churches.

In July 1872 the Deacon's Court was informed that "a house being built in Windsor Street by Mr Lickley has been purchased for a manse". Shortly afterwards the Deacon's Court was asked to approve the opening of an entrance to allow access to Windsor Street, but turned down the application because of the cost.[2]

The jubilee of the congregation was celebrated on 2 February 1904. The centenary of the opening of the church was marked in 1952 and that of the obtaining full status for the congregation in 1954. In that year Mr Peter Lawson gifted a beautiful oak baptismal font and a matching oak lectern was subscribed for by the organisations of the congregation. Also in the 1950s, Mr and Mrs Andrew Crichton gifted two oak communion chairs as a memorial to their son killed in the war. Following the union of Tay Square and St Paul's churches the magnificent communion table of the former was gifted to Chalmers which, in turn, gave their old table to a mission church near Slamannan. The Very Reverend Professor George Duncan of St Mary's College, St Andrews, preached when a Martinette electronic organ, donated by Mr and Mrs Archibald Briggs, was dedicated in January 1959.

Following the transportation of the congregation, the former church in Hunter Street was demolished to make way for University extensions.

The congregation continued its evangelical approach after the move from Hunter Street. Missionaries have been sent and supported for spells in Israel, India and England. In 1998 a member was assisted to go into the Arab World Ministries. The congregation has maintained strong links with Romania: smuggling bibles from the early 1970s; sending teams of young people, led by the Minister and Deaconess, to deliver bibles, clothes and medical aid; as well as giving financial and spiritual support. Chalmers-Ardler has sent out seven ministers, two readers and four missionaries to serve the church in other areas.

Around 1990 the Chalmers-Ardler Trust was established to work alongside the congregation, but with its own funding. In its first six years it assisted families in breaking the cycle of unemployment, low skill levels and low income. Those helped through the Children and Family Project have been predominantly women, mostly lone parents and their under school age children. An educational programme, counselling, self help groups, guidance on budget and diet, and activities, outings and parties have enabled the developing objectives to be achieved. In 1998 the Trust extended its activities to include a project for the elderly.

Ministers

1854	William Arnot STIRLING	Ord. Drowned while bathing at Broughty Ferry 1864. (Ewing II 159, Lamb, PM)
1864	Henry W BELL MA	Ord. To Aberdeen Free High 1871. (Ewing II 159, PM)
1871	Robert MILLIGAN	From Wolflee Free. Drowned while bathing at Montrose 1888[3] (Ewing II 159, PM)
1888	Robert Hannay LOGAN MA	Ord. Died 1905. (Ewing II 159, FUF 382)
1905	Frank GORDON MA	From Rathillet UF. To Durris UF 1913. (FUF 382)
1914	David LAWSON	From Belhelvie & Sheils UF. To Lumphanan UF 1919. (FUF 382)
1919	William MAXWELL MA	From Newtyle UF. To Montrose South UF 1926. (FUF 382)
1926	James Anderson BISHOP	From Innerleven UF. Known as "Bishop of Hawkhill". To Scone West 1934. (Died ca 1954) (FUF 382, FES IX 506, Lamb)
1934	Edwin Sprott TOWILL MA BD DipEd FSAScot	Ord. To Edinburgh Newington and St Leonard's 1940. Author of *People and Places in the Story of the Scottish Church.* (FES IX 506, KofE 482)
1940	Alexander Duncan CAMERON MA	Ord. To Slamannan 1946 (FES IX 506)
1946	John Shand PHILLIPS MA	From Moyness and Darnaway. To Fintry 1950. (FES IX 506)
1951	Alexander Stark FARROW	Ord. First minister of transported charge. Died 11 December 1968 - never having had an opportunity to preach in the new church. (FES IX 506, X 300)
1969	James Ernest POWRIE LTh	Ord. Dem. 1995. (FES X 300, PM)
1997	Kenneth D STOTT MA BD	Ind. (PM)

Notes

1. Dr Thomas Guthrie was a leading figure in the founding of the Free Church. As well as arts and divinity, he had studied scientific subjects at Edinburgh, including anatomy under Dr Knox, of Burke and Hare infamy. His medical knowledge was useful in his first charge at Arbirlot during a cholera outbreak. He was a great social reformer, being involved in the Temperance Movement and starting "Ragged Schools" for destitute children. His statue stands in Princes Street, Edinburgh.
2. According to Dundee directories, the manse was at 13 Osborne Place in 1900 and at 27 Windsor Street in 1929. This may have been the same building, the address having been changed.
3. The writer of Mr Milligan's obituary stated: "The wretched state of the poor in his mission district weighed heavily on his heart. Their sorrows were his. He was very tender of heart and wept with those who had cause to weep. Nothing made him happier than to see his people happy."

AS Farrow, *A Short History of Chalmers Parish Church Dundee 1851-1958*, Ramsgate, 1959
Chalmers-Ardler Trust, *Children and Family Project, Sixth Annual Report 1996-1997*
Letter of 10 March 1998 from E Shepherd, Session Clerk, Chalmers-Ardler Church
Piper o'Dundee, 29 August 1888
DCA   CH3/791
DPL   Lamb 170(5)
DPL   DNC Sp 15
DYB   1904

CLEPINGTON

Clepington church is situated on a triangular site at the corner of Main Street and Isla Street. Built to the design of Alexander Johnston, Dundee, at a cost of almost £3,000[1], it was opened on 18 May 1881. The main, or west, gable is broken by three light windows and terminates in a cross. Below these windows, five small windows give light below the gallery. On the southwest corner of this gable a small tower rises 65 feet in height, finished with crow stepped gables on two sides and corbelled parapet courses on the other two. A bell chamber is located in the upper part of the tower. One of the entrances to the church is in the ground floor of the tower. The other entrance is through a porch, with buttresses and an embrasured parapet and cope, on the northwest of the main gable. On both sides of the church are four windows with buttresses between and the two transepts at the east end have two windows each. Two large windows break up the back, or east gable. The pulpit, octagonal in form with a panelled recess at the back, is placed at this end of the church. The vestry is entered through the transept to the right of the pulpit. The older building beyond, now used as a hall, was originally used for services. An additional larger hall was officially opened on 29 April 1933.

An organ fund had been established before the Second World War but the efforts were suspended until after hostilities ended. The project was revived and the new organ was installed in the gallery in 1957. Two marble plaques, below stained glass windows, are memorials of the First and Second World Wars.

Expansion of the Town around 1870 led Presbytery to look for additional church accommodation and Clepington dates from this period. The congregation had its origins in a mission station opened in a two roomed house at 17 North Ellen Street on Sunday, 18 May 1873 by the Established Church. David R Robertson, who was to become the first minister, was at that time set apart as missionary. What was described as "a neat little chapel", built on the present site at a cost of £500[1], was opened on 27 June 1875. This building was incorporated as a hall in the complex when the new church was built in 1881. The parish was disjoined from St Mary's on 12 January 1885.

A Jubilee service was held in 1923. The Centenary was marked by a programme of events in May 1973: a "Family Meal" in the Angus Hotel on the 16th and a service on Sunday 20th when the Rev Professor James A Whyte preached.

In the early years of the congregation the minister appears to have resided at 5 South Ellen Street but, following the financial success of the Celtic Bazaar in 1898, a manse was bought at 23 Albany Terrace. It was sold in 1959 when a house at 17 Adelaide Place was purchased. It was disposed of in turn and for many years the minister resided in his own dwellinghouse. 17a Claypotts Road, Broughty Ferry, was bought as a manse in 1997.

Ministers

1875	David Rae ROBERTSON MA BD	App. Misssionary 1873. Ord 1875. Adm.first minister of parish 1885. DD (St Andrews 1909). Dem.1917. (Died 1921) (FES V 325)
1918	George McWILLIAM MA BD	From Peterhead East. To Auldearn 1926. (FES V 326, VIII 487)
1926	David DICK MA BD	Ord. CF TA 1930. To Torthorwald 1935. (FES IX 506, VIII 487)
1935	Wiliam Alexander MACDONELL MA	Ind. Adm.from Presbyterian Church of Canada 1934. To Finzean 1947. (Died 1951) (FES IX 506)
1948	David REID MA	From Kirkcaldy Victoria Road. To Sorn 1967. (FES X 300)
1967	Raymond Richard HUNT BA BD	From Buckie South. Died 1970. (FES X 300)
1970	John Edward HAWDON BA MTh	Ord.by Methodist Church. Adm.by GA 1970. Dem. 1995. (FES X 300, PM)
1997	Arthur A CHRISTIE BD	Ord. (PM)

Note

1. These figures are taken from the Centenary Booklet; other sources give amounts of £4,000 and £1,000 respectively.

CC Barnett, *The Seven Churches of the Hilltown*, nd
Clepington Parish Church Centenary 1873-1973, Centenary Booklet 1973
DPL   Lamb 170(7)
DCA GD/X100/3

CRAIGIEBANK

Craigiebank church, which stands at the intersection of Craigie Avenue and Greendykes Road, was erected in 1937-8 and is B-listed. The 1931 design, in Scottish Romanesque style, was by Frank Thomson, architect, Dundee. The church forms part of the Craigie Garden Suburb planned by James Thomson, father of Frank, and designed by his other son, Harry, in 1919. The building, which is cruciform in shape, is in harled brick with stone dressings and has a tower, but no spire as originally intended. The interior has stone columns to arcaded aisles. A 3-manual organ by Frederick Rothwell and Sons, Harrow, may have come from a bombed London church. The manse is at 244 Arbroath Road.

After the First World War the Government encouraged the development of local authority housing and, taking advantage of the relatively generous subsidies available under the 1919 Housing Act, Dundee proceeded to build high quality housing at Taybank and Craigiebank. There was provision in the concentric plan of Craigiebank Estate for a church at the centre. The Church Extension Committee reported to the Presbytery on 3 December 1929 that a site had been purchased for a church at Craigiebank. Early in the following year the Home Mission Committee of the General Assembly awarded a grant of £1,200 towards the cost of halls. A church hall with vestry and a small hall and session room were built in 1932. Late in that year Presbytery encouraged Old St Paul's congregation to transfer to the new area, bearing in mind the lack of membership within its parish and the drift of population to the new housing areas. The proposal was rejected and the new Craigiebank congregation began as a Church Extension Charge.

In February 1998 Presbytery agreed that the congregation should be linked with the congregation of Douglas and Angus on 11 March 1998, both churches to continue as places of worship. The manse at 244 Arbroath Road became the manse of the linked charge.

Ministers

1933	John Douglas ADAM DD	Adm. By GA 1927. Dem. 1934 (Died 1949) (FES IX 507)
1935	John Houston YULE MA BD	From Monigaff. To Edinburgh Stockbridge 1945. (FES IX 507)
1946	Alexander Lumsden WALKER MA BD	From New Byth. Died 1963. (FES IX 507, X 301)
1964	John Hubert Innes WATT	From Arrochar. Dem.on appt to Hamilton College of Education 1966 (FES X 301)
1967	James BEWS MA	From Wick Central. Dem. 1981. (FES X 301, YB)
1982	David JH LAING BD DPS	Ind. To Kirkcaldy St Andrew's 1989 (YB)
1989	Charles A LEGGAT	From Coatbridge Townhead. Dem. 1995. (Died 1997) (PM)
1998	Michael VA MAIR MA BD	From Aberdeen Holburn West (PM)

DCC Combined Statutory and Descriptive List
C McKean and D Walker, *Dundee, an Illustrated Introduction*, Edinburgh, 1984
The Steeple Church Dundee 1789-1989, Dundee, 1989

DOUGLAS and ANGUS

Douglas and Angus church is located in Balbeggie Place in the 1950s local authority housing development of Douglas and Angus.

The congregation originated in November 1953 when Mr Alex. Watson, divinity student, began work under the supervision of the minister and kirk session of Dundee St Mary's. The first gatherings were held in houses in the area, with monthly evening services being conducted in Mid Craigie church in 1954. As a result of an anonymous gift, a hall church was erected and opened on 9 September 1954. On the induction of the first minister in 1955 the congregation became a Church Extension charge, achieving full status in 1968. The Right Reverend Dr George F Macleod, Moderator of the General Assembly, laid the foundation stone of the church on 22 February 1958.[1] The building in harled brick cost around £22,500.

Douglas and Angus was linked with Craigiebank congregation on 11 March 1998, with both churches continuing to be used for worship.

The manse was at Balbeggie Street, but following the linking it was sold, the Craigiebank manse at 244 Arbroath Road becoming the manse of the linked charge.

Ministers

1955	Arthur William Alex. MAIN MA BD	Ind. To Kirkintilloch St David's Memorial 1964 (FES X 301)
1964	Alistair SKINNER BD	Ord. To Edinburgh Priestfield 1975 (FES X 301)
1976	David John Henderson McNAUGHTON MA BD CA FSAScot	Ord. To Killin and Ardeonaig 1983 (PM, YB)
1983	James McNAUGHTAN BD DipMin	Ord. To Kilmarnock St Marnock's 1989 (PM, YB)
1990	John R NOTMAN BSc BD	Ord. To Portlethen 1997 (PM)
1998	Michael V A MAIR MA BD	From Aberdeen Holburn West (PM)

Note

1. Dr George Macleod, Lord Macleod of Fuinary, Moderator of the General Assembly in 1957, was one of the most distinguished ministers of the Kirk in the twentieth century. In 1938 he founded the Iona Community

Letter of 25/3/98 from Mrs Grant, Session Clerk
DPL 3/24

DOWNFIELD SOUTH

Downfield South church is situated at the top of Haldane Street facing onto Strathmartine Road. The church was opened for worship on Thursday, 26 September 1889, the Rev. John Smith, Broughton Place, Edinburgh, conducting the service.[1] The architects were C & L Ower, Dundee, and the cost was £1,400. A contemporary description stated that it *is Gothic in style and it forms a striking and attractive feature in the landscape.*

The main entrance is at the centre of the west façade, above which is a tower and spire of 70 feet. Access to the gallery is by a staircase from the vestibule. The front of the building is built of scribbled courses and the sides of scribbled rubble with white freestone dressings. There is a 2 light window with pointed divisions above the doorway, with windows on either side. The pulpit is placed centrally at the east end with a large circular window above. Six Gothic windows light the building on either side. The windows contain small panes of tinted cathedral glass. A door on either side of the pulpit leads into the vestry on one side and to the session room on the other. Originally the building was seated for 406 in the area including the choir, with sittings for 20 more in the small gallery. Alterations to the gallery were carried out in 1896, increasing its seating capacity. The organ was installed in 1911 and substantially renovated in 1968.

The church occupies quite a large site, it having been intended that a manse would be erected. A hall and additional offices in stone were built on to the rear of the church in 1896, creating an L-shaped building. A second larger hall, with a kitchen and other offices, connected to the older buildings, was erected in 1959. This hall was refurbished in 1996 as part of a major upgrading of the church complex facilities, planned to be carried out over several years. The smaller hall was renovated in 1998. A development programme to fund the work was started in the early 1990s to raise the sum of £150,000, to add to £36,000 already in hand. The sanctuary was rewired, new heating installed, with improved access for the disabled.

In 1885 Dundee UP Presbytery reported that two letters had been received on the subject of church extension in Downfield. One from Miss Jessie Taws offered to make over property to the Church in the village of Downfield, with the income to be used *in the propagation of UP principles in the district;* while the other from Mr David Irons offered the free use as a preaching station of a public hall he was about to erect.

The offers were accepted and the Downfield UP Mission was opened on 6 September 1885, when the Rev. John Brand, John Street Church, Glasgow, preached. Mr Brand had been convener of Presbytery's Church Extension Committee while minister of Bell Street Church, Dundee.[2] The Rev. James Drummond, the current convener of that committee, arranged for four of his elders at Ryehill UP Church to assist in the first communion service in June 1886. Mr Drummond and the Ryehill kirk session had been given the care of Downfield by Presbytery at their meeting in May. The mission station, which was referred to as *a daughter of Presbytery,* was raised to the status of congregation on 12 September 1886, with worship continuing in the village hall until the present church was built. Mr Brand, who clearly took an interest in the developments at Downfield, gave up his city centre charge in Glasgow on grounds of ill health in June 1886. However, in September of that year he accepted an invitation to become pastor of the new charge.

A site for a new church was obtained and Miss Jessie Taws gave £400 towards the building costs. The Home Board and Mr Brand promised £300 and £200 respectively, with the congregation fund-raising to meet the balance. At a ceremony on 16 March 1889, attended by most of the villagers, Miss Taws laid the foundation stone.

Downfield developed as a village in the nineteenth century with the arrival of the railway and the erection of villas and cottages for people wishing to move from the overcrowded city. From its beginnings the church, centrally placed geographically, was a focus for community, as well as congregational, activities, such as concerts and lectures. The congregation has, for most of its existence, encouraged and sponsored youth organisations. Shortly after Baden-Powell founded the Boy Scouts movement a troop was formed in Downfield and granted the use of the church hall. This connection lasted for many years, until the Scouts took over the village hall for their activities. The expansion of the area, with the building of private and local authority housing, particularly in the post Second World War period, resulted in the formation or expansion of other youth groups, including Boys Brigade, Girl Guides and Brownies. The demand on the accommodation in the 1950s resulted in the provision of the additional hall mentioned earlier.

Following the completion of the large hall in 1959, Mr Drummond, a teacher in the Sunday School and a student at Dundee Art College, gifted his painting of *The Last Supper* to be hung in the new hall. This work of art now hangs on the rear wall of the sanctuary. In 1961 Miss Greta Morrison gifted a silver communion bread tray in memory of her parents, Mr and Mrs Andrew Morrison. Mrs E Anderson gave an offertory pedestal in remembrance of her mother, Mrs Elizabeth Langlands. Communion linen was received from the

Woman's Guild, and the Misses Dora and May Davidson embroidered a communion tablecloth. Mr Dodds gave a pulpit bible, hymnary and New English Bible in memory of his wife. Further gifts over the years enhanced the sanctuary, including a font in memory of Mr and Mrs McAree, a lectern beautifully made by Mr James R Duncan, the senior elder, and dedicated to his father and mother, Mr and Mrs George Duncan. Miss Mabel Taylor and Mrs Harris donated wrought iron pedestals for floral decorations. Mr and Mrs Alex Sherrit gave a clock for the front of the gallery in 1980. A number of unspecified legacies had been made over the years and it was decided to place a permanent record of these in the vestibule in the form of a framed Legacy Roll, the intention being that it should be updated from time to time. In 1977 alterations to the choir area were carried out and a public address system was installed in memory of George Luke Grant. Mrs Dorothy Proctor gave a pulpit fall, which she had embroidered.

At a special service on 10 October 1993, a pulpit fall was gifted to the congregation by the Nicoll family in memory of the Reverend Charles Nicoll, Minister Emeritus, who died in 1991 while attending the General Assembly as a Commissioner. The fall, designed by Miss Morag Moyes, took as its format a circle of twining vines, surrounding and yet going out from a Greek Cross. The circle represents eternity and the twining vines the many strands and talents of the Christian community.

A centenary service to mark the anniversary of the laying of the foundation stone was held on Sunday, 12 March 1989. The opening of the church in 1889 was commemorated on Sunday, 24 September 1989, when the Rev. Dr Henry Sefton, Master of Christ's College, Aberdeen, was the guest preacher.

Following the settlement of a new minister in 1924, *Bellevue,* 289 Strathmartine Road, was purchased for £1,450 for a manse. The purchase was funded by borrowing, which was completely cleared by 1930. This property was sold in the 1970s when the minister bought his own dwellinghouse, this being an accepted practice within the Church of Scotland at that time. The funds realised were held in a manse fund until 1986, when they were used to purchase the present manse at 15 Elgin Street.

Downfield UP became Downfield UF in 1900 and Downfield South in 1929.

Ministers

1886	John BRAND	Formerly of Glasgow John Street UP. Died 1900 (Small I 346)
1901	Robert BOWIE MA	Ord. To Glasgow Pollock Street UF 1911 (FUF 383)
1912	William KING MA BD	Ord. To Edinburgh St Mary's UF 1915 (Died 1948) (FUF 383)
1916	Alexander S CRICHTON MA	From Troon Portland Street UF. To Inverurie UF 1924 (FUF 383)
1924	James MACKNIGHT	From Coldstream UF. Died 1949 (FUF 383, FES IX 507)
1950	Donald MORRISON MA	From Killean and Kilchenzie. To Greenock St Columba's 1959 (FES IX 393, 507, X 301)
1960	Charles NICOLL	From Strathkinness. Dem. 1985 (Died 1991) (FES IX 501, X 301, PM)
1986	Andrew J WILSON BA BD FSA (Scot)	From Elgin St Giles. Dem. 1990 (PM)
1991	Maurice Samuel BOND BA MTh	DipEd From Ballynahinch Co. Down. PhD (Trinity Dublin 1995) To Dumfries St Michael's and South 1999 (PM)
2000	Lezley Jane KENNEDY BD ThM Mth	Ord. (PM)

Notes

1. Broughton Place Church, Edinburgh, was a centre for the United Associate Secession Church, and then the United Presbyterian Church. The Synod of the UAS met there. It was used frequently for evangelical meetings, including one when Moody and Sankey visited Edinburgh.
2. In 1871 the Elders' and Managers' Association had urged the UP Presbytery to establish congregations in the new suburbs. As a result Victoria Street began in 1873 and Ryehill in 1876. Mr Brand was very involved in the formation of Ryehill.

Ian McCraw, *Downfield South Church Dundee 1885-1985,* Dundee 1985
Downfield South Church Record (congregational magazine)
DCA GD/X100/11

DUNDEE (St MARY'S)

Dundee Parish Church (St Mary's) occupies the eastmost part of the building known as Dundee City Churches. There are now two churches in the complex, but in 1815 there were four when Thomas Hood penned the lines,

And four churches together with only one steeple
Is an emblem quite apt for the thrift of the people.

In January 1841 a fire destroyed much of three of the churches, the Steeple Church escaping the conflagration. The architect, William Burn, proposed repairing the churches, a substantial portion having survived, but unemployment in the building trade supported complete reconstruction, which was the course favoured by the Town Council as heritors. Also destroyed in the fire was the Chapter House or Session House, containing the library of nearly 1,800 volumes, many of which were rare works dating from before 1590. The only articles saved were the silver communion plate and the records of Presbytery.

As a temporary measure the Town Council arranged for the congregation of St Mary's, or the East Church, as it was generally known, to worship in the former Original Secession Church in Reform Street. The bailies ensured they at least would have some measure of comfort, judging from this item of expenditure in the Burgh accounts: *By Thomas Simpson, covering and making cushions for Magistrates seats in Reform Street Church - £10:10s.* [This was a substantial sum in 1841] The Town Council decided to rebuild two churches, St Mary's and the South Church, to take the place of the three which had been destroyed. In time a building was purchased in South Tay Street for the use of St John's, also known as The Cross Church.

The foundation stone for St Mary's was laid on Thursday 19 May 1842, following a service in St Andrew's Church. Thereafter, the Town Council, Guildry, Trades and other organisations walked in procession to the Nethergate for the ceremony. The new St Mary's was completed in 1844 to the design of William Burn. It is decorated Gothic ashlar with a clerestoried nave and aisles. The south elevation has five buttressed bays with Gothic windows. The east elevation has a large traceried window over a basket arch door. The north elevation is similar to the south but without the buttresses.

Entering St Mary's by the south door one stands in the vestibule redesigned in 1960. A wall plaque lists the names of some of the vicars and all the ministers. The nave and aisles are on a round arched arcade and stout clustered piers. There are galleries on three sides, a horseshoe gallery to the west or rear on cast iron columns. The roof is timber hammer beam.

The magnificent organ is reputed to be the first used in any parish church north of the Forth and Clyde. It was installed by Forster and Andrews of Hull in the west gallery, and inaugurated on 5 January 1866. John R Miller, Dundee, carried out improvements in 1908; J W Walker & Sons, Ruislip rebuilt it in 1939 and again in 1969.

Hugh Ballingall and William B Robertson gifted the splendid stained glass of the east window in 1897, in honour of Queen Victoria's diamond jubilee. It was designed by Sir Edward Burne-Jones and executed by William Morris. Burne-Jones drew the figures of eleven of the twelve apostles, and Morris drew St Bartholomew. In the traceried upper portions of the window are figures of angels of praise, the theme being, *The Glorious Company of the Apostles praise Thee.* A window to the right by Small of Edinburgh, the gift of George Ower, shows *The Birth of Christ* and *The Flight into Egypt.*

Dundee Parish Church (St Mary's)
draped for Queen Victoria's Memorial Service, February 1901

To the left, a window gifted by the Larg family depicts *St Columba* and *St Cecilia.* To the right towards the south wall, one sees illustrated *The Baptism of Christ,* a window designed by Powell and Son, London. It is in memory of Thomas Bell of Belmont and his wife. The next window shows *The Good Samaritan,* the work executed by the Newcastle Stained Glass Company. It is in memory of John W Thomson, solicitor, and his wife. The window, *Gethsemane,* by Ballantine and Son, Edinburgh, is a memorial to the forbears of Sheriff George Thoms.

On the north wall, a modern window by A L Russell of Dundee represents *St Ninian, The Virgin and Child,* and *David, Earl of Huntingdon,* recalling the coming of the Gospel to Scotland, and the traditional founding of St Mary's. It was gifted by the congregation in memory of the Rev. Adam W Fergusson and the Rev Dr Alfred E Warr. Another Burne-Jones window on the same wall, in memory of the Rev. Dr Archibald Watson, depicts *Faith, Hope and Charity.* A window in the gallery was gifted by the Woman's Guild and is the work of T S Halliday. It was designed to complement the Burne-Jones window below it, the fish, the swallow and the pelican being the symbols of *Faith, Hope and Charity.* Below the gallery, at the west end, is a window with the subject of *The Resurrection,* by Cortier and Company of London, in memory of Thomas Smith. In the clerestory a light by William Morris has as its theme, *Enoch and Abraham*. It was placed in memory of Provost Lawson and his son.

In 1900 the Misses McLean gifted elders'chairs in memory of their uncle, Thomas Hunter Cox, an elder for fifteen years. In 1940 the church was reseated and pews of Austrian oak were installed. The organ bears the Saltire of St Andrew, encircled by the olive wreath of victory surmounted by the martyr's crown. The Town Council's pew is emblazoned with the coat of arms of Dundee. In the centre of the gallery is the emblem of the Church of Scotland, *The Burning Bush.*

An old reading desk or lectern, which had been formed from part of the 17th century pulpit of the old parish church of Dundee, was returned to St Mary's in 1987. The pulpit had been removed from the church in 1688, and was later installed in the Episcopal Chapel, Seagate, where it remained until 1812. When that congregation removed to Castle Street it was also transferred, but taken out in 1839. Thereafter, part of the wood was made into a desk by a Dundee cabinetmaker. The desk came to light in Dunfermline in 1987. Other panels from the pulpit had been distributed among various members of the Episcopal congregation, and in 1923 were collected by Provost A C Don of St Paul's Cathedral, reassembled and built into what is now the Lindores Cabinet in St Paul's. It is thought that the panels at one time may have adorned the choir stalls of Lindores Abbey.

The carved timber screen behind the pulpit was presented by the Woman's Guild in memory of the Rev. Dr John H Duncan. There are tablets on the east wall in memory of the Rev. Dr Archibald McLachlan and the Rev. Dr Charles Adie.

There is a memorial to the men of The Black Watch killed in the First World War, with the names of the fallen inscribed on silver sheets. Other war memorials include a brass plaque on a marble base which commemorates those men of the 1st (City of Dundee) Volunteer Battalion, The Black Watch, who fell in the South African War 1899-1902. The men of the 205th (1st Dundee Company) Royal Engineers, raised in Dundee in 1915 as a unit of the British Expeditionary Force, are honoured on a bronze plaque on a marble base. A bronze scroll, with the Dundee crest on a marble plaque, is a memorial to the fallen of the congregation in the war of 1914-1919, while a bronze plaque, with the Dundee crest on a marble base, remembers those of the congregation killed in the war of 1939-1945. To the left of the pulpit is a handsome memorial to the 4th (City of Dundee) The Black Watch Territorial Battalion, containing a fine metal allegorical statue and a copper plaque with 917 names.

In the 1990s substantial work was carried out on the building as part of the Dundee City Churches Restoration Project. The second of three phases was executed in 1996, including repair works to the south walls of the church and repairs to all windows. The third phase, scheduled for completion by March 2000, includes work on the roof and provision of protective window grilles. The whole project has cost in excess of £350,000, and has been assisted by a grant from Historic Scotland.

St Mary's can be regarded justifiably as the *Mither Kirk* of Dundee, although there have been disputes over the years regarding its status in relation to the other Burgh Churches. Civic occasions, such as the *Kirking of the Council* and Remembrance Day services are held in St Mary's. The minister who is chaplain to the School conducts the High School of Dundee services in the church. On the occasion of the octocentenary of the granting by King John of a charter to the burgesses of Dundee, entitling them to trade with England, the Guildry of Dundee presented the congregation with a framed copy of the charter on Sunday 24 October 1999. This was hung in the Huntingdon Aisle, alongside the stained glass window presented by the Guildry to mark the octocentenary of St Mary's.

The congregation has been active in the mission field. A mission at Drumgeith is mentioned in 1906, but may be earlier as there was involvement with Drumgeith School in 1866. It was carried on until 1955. Blackscroft Mission was conducted from 1864 until 1959. East End School and the mission house in Peep o' Day Lane may have been connected with Blackscroft, as well as St Mary's Rest, Ferry Road. The congregation took a lead in the early work to set up Douglas and Angus Church in 1953. The congregation has held an annual Christmas card and gift sale since 1963, raising well over £300,000, all disbursed to charities.

St Mary's Church is A-listed.

A number of properties have served as the manse. Wood's map of 1821 shows the glebe land to have been north of Ferry Road, east of Peep o' Day.[1] A house on the northern boundary of this land may have been the manse. In the 1870s the glebe land was feued to two individuals, except for a portion feued to the Trustees of St Matthew's Church, opened in 1875. A dwellinghouse at 69 Dalkeith Road, built in 1890, which bears the arms of Dundee carved in stone, was for long the Manse of Dundee. It was sold in the 1970s. In 1994 the manse at 371 Blackness Road was sold and a new manse purchased at 33 Strathern Road, Broughty Ferry.

The manse of Dundee Parish Church (St Mary's), Dalkeith Road. The coat of arms of Dundee is carved on the stonework of the manse, built in 1890

The medieval church of St Mary's is claimed to have been founded by David, earl of Huntingdon, brother of King William I (1165-1214). Earl David granted the church of Dundee and its tithes to the Tironensian Abbey of Lindores around 1200. The church was subject to the See of Brechin. The abbot of Lindores was parson or rector of the parish of Dundee. A Licence or Decree issued by Gregory, bishop of Brechin, about 1220, confirming the rights of the monks of Lindores to the church, gave consent to the appointment by the monks of a vicar to perform the duties of the church. Under the authority of that document vicars seem to have been appointed down to the Reformation.

According to the writer and historian, Andrew Jervise, the name *St Mary's* is not met with in writing until 1406. Early references mention it as being sited in a *field* or *fields,* suggesting that it was on the western edge of the burgh. However, Alexander Maxwell, the Dundee historian, has a reference to the church of St Mary in 1256. Edward I in 1296 burned the church, there being further destruction by the English in 1385. Except for the choir the church was completely destroyed by the English in 1548. The surviving great western tower of St Mary in the late decorated style of the fifteenth century suggests that the whole building was a splendid structure. Presumably, the east end as chancel would have been the first part of the building constructed. In size St Mary's was an outstanding parish church, its length of 286 feet rivalling Glasgow Cathedral and Arbroath Abbey. Its width of 174 feet at the transepts is the greatest for a Scottish church.

Contemporary records indicate that the burgesses of Dundee lavishly furnished the interior. For example, George Spalding in 1495 made a number of donations, including a bell for the tower. St Mary's was the first parish church in Scotland to be organised according to the Reformed faith.

Ministers

1558 Paul METHVEN
Arrived in Dundee in 1558 with John Willock. Largely through Methven's efforts *the toun of Dundie beganne to erect the face of a reformed church publiclie, in which the Word was preached openlie, and the sacraments truelie ministered.* To Jedburgh 1560 (FES V 315)

1561	John HAMILTON	Reader (FES VIII 486)
1563	James HAMILTON	Vicar (FES VIII 486)
1563	William KIDD	Reader 1563, pres. to vicarage 5 Aug. 1570 on forfaulture of John Hamilton. (FES VIII 486)
1569	William CHRISTISON	Pres. to vicarage by James VI 17 Nov. 1569 on forfaulture of John Hamilton. Mod. GA 1569. Had Ballumbie also in his charge in 1574. In 1589 he was nominated by the Privy Council one of the Commissioners for the defence of the True Religion in Angus. In 1597 he was unable, due to age, to discharge his duties. (Died 1603) (FES V 315, VIII 486)
1598	Robert HOWIE	Principal of Marischal College, Aberdeen, and min.of Third Charge Aberdeen. Elected by GA 14 Mar.1597 and adm. before 26 Sept. 1598. In 1605 Privy Council declared him *nowyse to be capable of any office, function or charge within the...town,* for aiding and abetting a faction in opposing the election of magistrates. Afterwards he had a charge in Strathbogie, and was Principal of St Mary's College, St Andrews, the buildings of which he almost completely remodelled. He was a scholar of distinction. DD(St Andrews)(FES V 315, R G Cant, *The University of St Andrews,* Edinburgh, 1970)
1606	David LINDSAY MA	Adm. before 1606. Consecrated Bishop of Brechin 1619 holding this parsonage until 1634 (FES V 315)
1623	Robert STIBBLES	Reader (FES VIII 486)
1626	Patrick PANTER MA	Probably asst. to David Lindsay. App. To Chair of Divinity, St Mary's, St Andrews 1627 (FES V 315)
1635	Andrew COLLACE MA	From Ecclesgreig before 24 July 1635. Dep. in 1639. Was officiating in Wapping, London in 1650. Allowed £2,000 from Vacant Stipends in 1661 and adm. to Duns in 1663 (FES V 315)
1642	Andrew AUCHENLECK MA	From Largo. Favoured the restoration of Charles II. At the siege of Dundee, Sept. 1651, was taken prisoner to London and detained there until spring, 1653. Died 1663 (FES V 315-6)
1664	Henry SCRYMGEOUR MA	Adm. Dem. 1690. Par. declared vacant by Com. Of Assembly for the North, 4 July 1694 (FES V 316)
1699	Samuel JOHNSTONE MA	From Southdean. Died 1731 (FES V 316)
1732	Thomas DAVIDSON	From Whitekirk. Died 1760. Ancestor of Randall Thomas Davidson, Archbishop of Canterbury (FES V 316)
1761	Robert SMALL	From Fourth Charge of Dundee. DD (St Andrews 1778) Mod. GA 1791. An excellent classical scholar and a highly interesting preacher, deeply versed in mathematics, natural philosophy and astronomy, and a patron of literature. With Robert Stewart, surgeon, founded in 1782 a medical dispensary for the poor, the forerunner of Dundee Royal Infirmary. Author of OSA Dundee. Died 1808 (FES V 316-7, W J Smith, *A History of Dundee,* Dundee, 1873)
1808	Archibald McLACHLAN	From Third Charge Dundee. DD (Marischal 1808) Died 1848 (FES V 317)
1848	Charles ADIE	From South Par. Dundee. DD (St Andrews 1833) Offered but declined Moderatorship of GA. Died 1861 (FES V 317)
1862	Archibald WATSON MA	From Glasgow St Matthews. DD (Glasgow 1862) Chap. to Victoria 1868. Mod. GA 1880. In 1867 he accompanied Norman Macleod to India with a Commission to visit all the mission stations. The Report drawn up by Dr Watson and highly praised was presented to the GA of 1868. Died 1881 (FES V 317-8)
1882	Colin CAMPBELL MA BD	From Partick St Mary's. DD (Glasgow 1892) Died 1931 (FES V 318, VIII 486)
1905	William Lyall WILSON MA	From Lesmahagow A&S. To Edinburgh St Cuthbert's 1911 (Died 1914) (FES V 318, KofE 116)
1911	Adam Wightman FERGUSSON MA BD	From Scots Kirk Melbourne A&S. Sen. Coll. 1933 Died 1943 (FES V 318, VIII 486, IX 508)

1933	Alfred Ernest WARR BD	From Glasgow Hillhead C&S. Died 1936 (FES IX 508)
1937	John Henry DUNCAN MA BPhil	From Kilmarnock Laigh. DD (St Andrews 1944) Died 1951 (FES IX 508)
1951	Hugh Osborne DOUGLAS MA KCVO CBE	From North Leith. Mod. GA 1970. DD (St Andrews 1958) LLD(Dundee 1971) Chap. to Queen1959. Dean of Chapel Royal 1974. Dem. 1977 (Died 1986) (FES IX 508, X 301, KofE 187, YB)
1978	William B R MACMILLAN MA BD LLD DD	From Bearsden South. Mod. GA 1991. Dem. 1993 (PM, YB)
1994	Keith F HALL MA BD	From Alloa St Mungo's (PM)

Note

1. Peep o' Day. A mansion house near the shore, east of Blackscroft, which appeared in Crawford's plan of 1777, was called Peep o' Day House. It was the town house of Walter Ogilvy of Clova, titular Earl of Airlie. According to A C Lamb, writing in 1895, it was later incorporated in the buildings of Dundee Gasworks.

I B Cowan, *Regional Aspects of the Scottish Reformation,* London, 1978

H O Douglas, booklet, *Dundee Parish Church (St Mary's)* n.d.

A C Lamb, *Dundee its Quaint and Historic Buildings,* Dundee, 1895

J A Rollo, *The Parish and the Burgh Churches of Dundee,* Dundee, 1897

E P D Torrie, *Medieval Dundee, A Town and its People,* Dundee, 1990 (Abertay Historical Society Publication No 30)

The Cathedral Church of Saint Paul Dundee, n.d.

Courier and Advertiser, 24 January and 11 April 1987, 17 November 1998, 23 October 1999, 7 February 2000

DCA   CH2/408, CH2/1218

DCA   *1840-41 State of the Affairs of the Town of Dundee from 27 September 1827 to 1 November 1841.*

DCC   Combined Statutory and Descriptive List

DPL   DNC Vol. 101, Lamb 391(35)

PM 1994, 1995

FAIRMUIR

Fairmuir church is situated at 329 Clepington Road and is a stone built building standing in its own grounds with a hall, which was added in 1938. The rear wall of the church is harled, reflecting the original intention to enlarge the building. A marble plaque commemorates the members of the congregation killed in the First World War, 1914-1919. Two stained glass windows were dedicated in 1950 as a memorial to those members who lost their lives in the Second World War. They are inscribed with the Beatitudes, *Blessed are they that mourn* and *Blessed are the peacemakers*.

In the late nineteenth century the development of the north of Dundee resulted in Mains and Strathmartine Parish Church having 200 more communicants than there were sittings. On 14 November 1897, the moderator advised the kirk session that he had met a deputation from the Dundee Office Bearers' Association of the Church of Scotland. The Association considered that church extension was required in the parish to serve the developing area of Fairmuir, which was then the northern boundary of the city. The kirk session agreed to meet representatives of the Association on the following Saturday and to hear their views. At that meeting the kirk session unanimously approved the proposal to erect a church in the Clepington Road area and appointed a committee to work along with the Association. In the following March it was reported that the sum of £1,130 had been subscribed for the erection of a church. A sketch of a building had been prepared; part of which to seat 400 could be built in the meantime. A site at the corner of Clepington Road and Neishfield Street was available. Grants of £800 from the Baird Trust, and at the rate of 10s per sitting from the Home Mission Committee, were approved and the construction work put in hand.

The minutes of Mains and Strathmartine kirk session for 25 March 1900 state: *Victoria Church Clepington Road was dedicated to the worship of Almighty God on Thursday 20th instant* [should be 22nd] *by the Right Reverend the Moderator of the General Assembly, John Pagan DD, Minister of the parish of Bothwell, who preached a sermon from Psalm 96 and 9th verse. He was assisted in the service by the Rev. R S Warren, Moderator of Presbytery, and the Moderator of Session who offered up the Dedication Prayer. Many members of Presbytery attended in their robes. This day the church was* [formally] *opened for Public Worship by the Rev. John McMurtrie DD, Convener of the General Assembly Committee on Foreign Missions and who was minister of the parish from Sept. 1858 to Jan. 1866. The Kirk Session are thankful to Almighty God that it has pleased Him to bring the building of Victoria Church to a successful issue and pray that it may be a blessing to the community.*

The mission station was under the care of Mains and Strathmartine kirk session. On 21 September 1900 the Rev. D Dewar MacDonald, assistant at St George's in the West, Aberdeen, was elected to the post of Missionary. Progress was evidently good, for it was soon reported that there were 381 communicants on the roll and that 400 scholars attended the Sabbath School. To raise funds the congregation held what was called the *Grand Delhi Durbar Bazaar* in the Kinnaird Hall, Dundee, on 24, 25 and 26 September 1903.

In 1903 the mission was raised to the status of Chapel of Ease, and on 20 December 1907 the parish was disjoined from St Mary's and Mains and Strathmartine, the name being changed from Victoria Mission Chapel to Fairmuir Church.

There is no manse.

Ministers

1903	Donald Dewar MACDONALD MA BD	Ord. Adm. first min. of par. 1907. Died 1926 (FES V 333, VIII 488)
1926	William Angus WALLACE	From Law. To Guthrie 1935 (FES IX 508)
1936	David Williams MAIN MA	From Greenock Wellpark, Died 1947 (FES IX 508)
1948	John BEAUMONT MA BD	From Shotts Erskine. Dem. 1971 (Died 1978) (FES IX 508, X 300, YB)
1972	Robert CLARK BD	Ord. To Gorebridge 1977 (Died 1982) (FES X 299)
1978	David C McLEOD BSc MEng BD	From Paisley Martyrs (YB, PM)

Victoria Church Bazaar Book 1903
DCA   CH2/256/3, CH2/1336
DPL   DNC Vol. 47
DPL   Lamb 174(11)
DYB   1900
Notes from Session Clerk received 17 April 1998

THE HIGH KIRK

The High Kirk stands on the side of Dundee Law at 119a Kinghorne Road. The church, designed by James Ireland of Ireland and Maclaren, architects, Glasgow, in a Gothic T plan style and opened on Thursday, 11 April 1878, is a distinctive landmark on the skyline when seen from the Tay. The square sectioned pinnacled tower was completed after 1881. The church has a gabletted entrance with a Celtic cross finial. The construction is in snecked rubble with ashlar band courses. A Gothic window with tracery is the principal feature of the front gable. The doorway is surmounted by a pediment with carved figures of two angels with hands clasped over the Bible. The building, which cost around £3,000, is in the Decorated style of architecture.

A gallery was added in 1881, and the building was enlarged in 1886 by the addition of transepts, and again in 1928 with the construction of two side galleries. A large hall was built in 1937, and a chapel formed in the lower hall in 1948. An organ was introduced in 1906. In 1954 the console was moved, a reredos placed behind the communion table, and elders' chairs added. Restoration work was carried out in 1982, when a screen was installed in memory of the former minister, Dr Roy R Hogg. The screen, which stands in the remodelled main entrance of the church, was made by Lord Roberts Memorial Workshops, Dundee, to the design of Mr Douglas Gray, an elder. Brass plaques commemorate members of the congregation killed in the wars of 1914-18 and 1939-45. A manse at 6 Adelaide Place was purchased in 1925.

In 1875 the Free Church Presbytery agreed to open a mission in Hospital Wynd, with the consent of the Chapelshade officebearers in whose parish it was. The mission seems to have grown, for a meeting of those favourable to the formation of a congregation to meet the needs of the developing area on the slopes of the Law was held in Butterburn Schoolroom, Harcourt Street, then called Well Road, on 12 June 1877. Twenty five people, mainly from the Free Church congregations of St Andrew's, St Paul's and Chapelshade, unanimously agreed to form *a congregation to worship in the hall to be erected at the top of Hospital Wynd by the Church Extension Committee of Dundee Free Presbytery.* The temporary use of two shops at the top of Hill Street was secured, and a dividing partition removed to make a large room for worship. Following a petition to Presbytery on 12 September 1877, it was recognised as a station to be designated the *High Church.* Presbytery approved plans for a building in the form of a Latin cross to accommodate 850, but initially only the centre of the cross was built to hold 400. The new church was erected in Hospital Wynd, later renamed Kinghorne Road. Behind the north gable was accommodation for the vestry and a large classroom.

On 13 February 1878 Presbytery recommended that the General Assembly raise the station to ministerial status and the charge was sanctioned as the *High Church* on 10 June 1878.

High Free became High UF in 1900 and High in 1929. However, it has for long been known as *The High Kirk.*

Ministers

1878	Gavin ANDERSON MA	From Edinburgh St Cuthbert's Free (Died 1899) (Ewing II 160, PM, KofE 164)
1899	Francis J MACLAUCHLAN MA	Ord. To Glasgow Victoria UF 1908 (Ewing II 160, FUF 383)
1908	John Howitt GRANT MA	From Elgin Moss Street UF. To Brodick UF 1925 (FUF 384)
1926	Douglas McRITCHIE MA BD	From Cromarty UF. To London Wimbledon 1930 (Died 1954) (FUF 384, FES IX 509)
1931	George Maclean WYLIE	From Ayr St Andrew's. To Methven 1942 (FES IX 509)
1942	Roy Ross HOGG MA	From Edinburgh Davidson Eyre Place. DD (St Andrews 1976) Dem. 1978 (Died 1978) (FES IX 12, 509, 736, KofE 156, YB)
1979	Henry M GIBSON MA BD PhD	From Aberfeldy linked with Amulree and Strathbraan. Dem. 1999 (YB, PM)

CC Barnett, *The Seven Churches of the Hilltown,* Dundee n.d.
DCC   Combined Statutory and Descriptive List
DPL   DNC Vol. 108
DPL   Lamb 170(11)
Letter received on 23 May 1998 from Mr J D Y Gray, Session Clerk

LOCHEE OLD AND ST LUKE'S

Lochee Old and St Luke's church is located at the corner of Bright Street and Methven Street, Lochee, just outside the entrance to the former Cox Brothers' Camperdown Works. It was built in 1829-30 to the design of David Neave, architect, Dundee, as a chapel of ease for the Established Church. The Rev. Dr Addison of Liff opened the church for worship on 7 February 1830. It is a rectangular neo classical building, with an ashlar façade and rubble sides. The south façade has two storeys of windows and shallow pilasters topped by a pediment. There is a central spire. The interior has a horseshoe gallery on Corinthian columns. Remodelling and repairs were carried out in 1883 by Alexander Johnston, architect, Dundee, at a cost of £5,000, paid for by Mr T H Cox.[1] The external masonry was redressed and repointed and the windows replaced. Porches were built at the east and west sides. The principal entrance was remodelled, and the sides of the doorway adorned with pilasters, mouldings and ornamental scrollwork. The original pews were replaced. A hall and an organ chamber were added. A marble tablet was placed as a memorial to the Rev. James Forsyth, minister from 1845 to 1882. The renovated church was reopened on 18 November 1883 by the Rev. A W Williamson[2] of St Cuthbert's, Edinburgh. Part of an aisle was altered to form a side chapel at the time of the union of 1985.

The church building is B-listed. The manse is at 16 Coupar Angus Road.

*Lochee Old and St Luke's was formed by the union of **Lochee Old** and **Lochee St Luke's** on 2 October 1985.*

Lochee St Luke's

When the UP congregation in Lochee moved to their new church, Messrs Cox Brothers purchased their former church, built in 1827. In consideration of the sum of £1,500 paid to the firm by Mr T H Cox, the building at 136 High Street was presented to Trustees of the Established Church to provide another place of worship in the expanding village. Dr Ritchie, Longforgan reopened it on 24 March 1874, as a chapel of ease. St Luke's parish was disjoined from Liff on 13 March 1876 and erected into a parish *quoad sacra* by the Court of Teinds. Extensive renovation was carried out in 1883, aided by Mr Cox. The interior was reseated, an organ installed, and a new vestry built on the south wall. The Rev. Professor Flint, Edinburgh reopened the church, on 6 May 1883. Further improvements were carried out in 1897. In 1910 the interior was modernised and electric lighting installed.

Ministers

1874	Peter MACLEOD	Ord. Pres. by Mr T H Cox, patron. Adm. first min. of par. 5 April 1876. To Neilston 1879 (FES V 335)
1879	William MAY MA	Ord. Dem. 1916 (Died 1925) (FES V 335)
1917	Evelyn GALL MA BD	From Logie, Fife. To Kirkcaldy 1927 (FES V 335, VIII 488)
1927	Matthew McPHAIL	From Castle Douglas. To Arbirlot 1929 (FES VIII 488)
1929	William BODIN MA	From Ardrossan New. Dem. to become Industrial Chap. 1948 (FES IX 509)
1948	James Alexander WATT MA	From Glasgow Gairbraid. Dem. 1960 (FES IX 509, X 302)
1961	John Powers BATES AA BA BD	From Asst. at Dundee Wallacetown having been ord. at Erie Chapel Chicago. To Dumfries St Michael's 1970 (FES X 302, YB)
1970	Joseph Logan LECKIE MA MPhil	From Presbyterian Church in USA. To Fowlis Wester with Madderty with Monzie 1984 (FES X 302, YB)

Lochee Old

Lochee East-St Ninian's was formed by the union of Lochee East and Lochee St Ninian's on 23 September 1959. The name of the congregation was changed to Lochee Old at the end of 1959.

Lochee Free, Lochee East UF, Lochee East

Lochee Free became Lochee East UF in 1900 and Lochee East in 1929.

At the Disruption of 1843 the minister and most of the congregation of Lochee *quoad sacra* parish *came out.* Initially, they retained the church building. The minister, Mr Stewart, complained of the strain of speaking in so large a building and he left, along with a number of the congregation, to become minister of

Dudhope church. However, he seems to have also been prompted by the knowledge that the church building could not be retained by the Free Church, the deed of constitution declaring it to be the property of the Church of Scotland. He had declined the proposal of the managers to keep possession of it, preaching instead from his parlour window with his audience seated on the lawn in front. After Mr Stewart's departure the majority of the congregation continued to use the church for two years, until required to vacate it by the Established Church in March 1845. They met for some time in a weavers' loft while their own church was being built.

The foundation stone was laid on 23 June 1845, and the new church opened on 18 January 1846. The original entrances to the church were by a central door and two side doors in Brown Street (later Methven Street) looking across to the Established Church. The cost was £1,500. A manse was built in Harefield Road in 1846 at a cost of £600. In 1890 the interior of the church, which was semicircular, was redesigned. The pulpit was removed to the centre of the east wall, the central door blocked up, and a new entrance opened onto High Street. A gallery was added and the tower completed. A public clock, made by James Rattray and maintained by the Town Council, was fitted in the tower. Side galleries were added in 1902. A harmonium was installed in 1895, but not used for regular Sunday services until four years later. A pipe organ, which cost £200, was inaugurated on 19 December 1900. Jubilee celebrations were held on Sunday, 19 January 1896.

Ministers

1843	William STEWART	Min. of Lochee Chapel of Ease. Joined FC. To Dudhope Free 1843 (Died 1852) (FES V 334, Ewing II 160)
1844	Thomas Boswall DODDS	Ord. Ret. 1889 (Ewing II 160, PM)
1888	David THOM MA	Ord. C&S Died 1928 (Ewing II 160, FUF 384, PM)
1929	George McGREGOR MA	From Aberdeen St Paul's. Dem. 1959 (Died 1972) (FUF 384, FES X 302)

Lochee Chapel of Ease, Lochee EC, Lochee St Ninian's
The name of the congregation was changed from Lochee to Lochee St Ninian's in 1929.

On 1 October 1828 the Established Presbytery received a petition *numerously subscribed...by several gentlemen from the village of Lochee craving...the erection of a chapel of ease in that village.* The proposal met with approval and agreement was reached with the heritors of Liff. A List of Subscribers was opened and contracts for the building work entered into by the managers, headed by James Cock senior. By November 1829 matters had progressed to the stage where the rules for the chapel were engrossed in the Presbytery minutes. A deputation of the managers was received at the Presbytery meeting in the following February. They advised that the chapel was now ready for divine service and asked that it be opened by the Rev. George Addison of Liff, who had agreed to preach at the morning and afternoon services, with Mr Tod of St David's officiating in the evening. The chapel achieved full status when the *quoad sacra* parish of Lochee was disjoined from Liff and Dundee St Mary's on 7 June 1880

At the Disruption of 1843 the minister and most of the congregation went over to the Free Church, retaining the building for about two years. During this time those members of Lochee Chapel of Ease wishing to remain within the Establishment seem to have worshipped in the Weavers' Hall, until they repossessed their church. The congregation seems to have recovered numerically, due to the growth of the village.

There was a long running dispute between the minister, the Rev. James Forsyth, and the Presbytery, due to his refusal to resign his office following the appointment of a colleague and successor. Mr Forsyth issued a series of pamphlets setting out his position between 1874 and 1880.

Ministers

1832	William STEWART	Ord. Joined FC in 1843 and after a few months as min. of Lochee Free became min. of Dudhope Free (Died 1852) (FES V 334)
1845	James FORSYTH	Ord. Adm. first min. of par. 9 June 1880. Died 1882 (FES V 334)
1871	William WRIGHT	Ord. C&S. Died 1915 (FES V 334)
1915	Thomas Downie MEREDITH MA	Ord. To Inchture 1920 (FES V 334)
1920	Richard GIBB MA	Ord. To Lochmaben 1925 (FES V 334, VIII 488)
1925	Hugh SHIRLAW MA BD	From Fogo. To Crail St David's 1949 (FES VIII 488, IX 509)
1949	John MACDONALD AE MA	Ord. Min. of united charge 23 Sept. 1959 (FES IX 509, X 302)

Lochee East-St Ninian's

After the union of 1959 the Lochee St Ninian's building was chosen for worship. The former Lochee East church was sold in 1960 to Woolworths who demolished it and erected a store.

Minister

1959 John MACDONALD AE MA   Min. of Lochee St Ninian's. Dem. 1985 (FES X 302, YB)

Lochee Old and St Luke's

After the union of 1985 the Lochee Old building was chosen for worship. The manse of Lochee St Luke's at 16 Coupar Angus Road became the manse of the united charge.

Ministers

1985 Roy MACKENZIE LTh   From Alves and Burghead. Died 1994 (PM, YB)
1995 Elisabeth G B SPENCE BD   Ord. (PM)

Notes

1. Mr T H Cox was a partner of Cox Brothers, of Camperdown Linen Works, Lochee. He was a very active churchman and, apart from his generosity to and active involvement with Lochee churches, was concerned with church extension in Dundee. In 1872 he was a member of a deputation to Presbytery called *Subscribers towards the erection of additional churches in Dundee* which was interested in the opening of Logie and Rosebank churches.
2. The Rev. Andrew W Williamson MA BD became minister of St Giles', Edinburgh, in 1910. He was Moderator of the General Assembly in 1913, and Dean of the Thistle and Chapel Royal.

A Elliot, *Lochee: As it was and as it is,* Dundee, 1911
George McGregor, *A Short Sketch of the History of Lochee Free Church now Lochee East Church of Scotland 1846-1946,* Dundee, 1945
C McKean and D Walker, *Dundee, An Illustrated Architectural Guide,* Edinburgh, 1993
DCC Combined Statutory and Descriptive List
DPL Sp 1/66, 2/39, 4/236, 5/187
DPL Lamb 173(1, 7), 369(26, 27)
DCA CH2/103/17, CH2/940, CH2/1218/56, CH2/1268, CH3/378

LOCHEE WEST

Lochee West church is located at 191 High Street, Lochee, standing on a prominent site within its own landscaped grounds. The church, with sittings for 1050, was built in 1871 to the design of James Maclaren, architect, Dundee, the total cost being £7,000. The building costs had been estimated at £3,775, and funds to meet this seem to have been available. However, the congregation over a period, raised the balance of £3,000 with substantial assistance from Messrs William, James and George Cox, local manufacturers.[1]

The church has a Gothic south façade and spire. There is a large 5 light traceried pointed arched window in the central buttressed gable. The jambs of the main doorway are deeply moulded and contain a shaft of serpentine marble. The building is constructed of coursed rubble with ashlar dressings. Lochee stone was used for the body of the walls, and Dunmore stone for the hewn work. Inside there is a 5 bay timber collar beam roof on timber spandrels and slim cast iron columns, which also support the gallery. William, George and Edward Cox gifted a pipe organ by Hill of London in 1890. It was installed beneath the pointed chancel arch. The attractive wheel window above the organ was the gift of Mr William Cox. A peal of bells, which could be rung as a peal or a chime, was hung on 14 April 1872, inscribed, *Presented by Cox Brothers, Camperdown Linen Works, Lochee, 1872.*

Mrs Cox presented a stone font and silver bowl in 1895 in memory of her husband, William Cox. Tablets in Sicilian marble were placed in the church on 28 January 1906, in memory of the Rev. David Marshall and Dr A B Connel. The communion table was dedicated in 1916 as a memorial to the Rev. H D Morton. The members of the congregation who lost their lives in the two World Wars are commemorated in a three panel wooden plaque.

The present church was opened for worship on Sunday, 24 September 1871 by Dr John Eadie[2] of Lansdowne Place Church, Glasgow. The opening collection was over £1,000. The hall, which is adjacent in Nicoll's Lane, was built in 1883 to the design of James Maclaren, and opened on 22 May. It is also Gothic in coursed rubble with ashlar dressings.

A scheme of renovation and redecoration of the church building began in 1956, and was phased over five years. The grounds surrounding the church were landscaped in the 1960s. An appeal to raise monies to restore the spire was launched in 1968.

The congregation opened a mission in their school premises in Balgay Street in April 1869, under Andrew Chapman, student.

The church building is B-listed and the hall is C-listed.

The Seceders in Lochee came together as a group, when a small number of people met in a house at the corner of North Church Street and South Road. The text of the first sermon delivered here is recorded as, *Be not afraid, for I have much people in this place.* At a soiree held in 1871 mention was made of the *Myre Kirk*, presumably Liff Burgher congregation. Mr Connel, minister of the day, said that an old member remembered going to the *Tent Kirk,* the minister being Mr Black. The last minister to preach in the Myre Kirk was said to have been Mr Offenbach. Dr Marshall, minister emeritus, said that in 1825 there was no place of worship [in Lochee] except the *little kirkie,* a two-storey house with an outside stair. Mr Thomson and then Mr Pringle preached the gospel to those of an Independent persuasion. A few seceders met in the Weavers' Hall, led by Mr Scott.

On 2 November 1824 a petition for sermon, subscribed by twenty people in Lochee and its neighbourhood, was presented to the United Associate Secession Presbytery of Forfar. They had fitted up a hall as a place of worship, and the Rev. Matthew Fraser of Overgate Church, Dundee, reported that he had preached there on the evening of the third Sunday of September, and as Clerk of Presbytery had arranged supply for the subsequent Sundays. The congregation can trace its origins to the establishment of this preaching station. Lochee was a growing village and there were a number of Secession families, mainly belonging to School Wynd Church, Dundee, including those who had formerly been connected to Liff congregation which had been dissolved. At the Union of 1820 the two congregations in Dundee continued under different presbyteries, School Wynd belonging to Cupar, and Overgate to Forfar. The minister of School Wynd raised the matter at Cupar Presbytery. While approving of the new station, he considered that Forfar Presbytery should have consulted his officebearers beforehand. Forfar Presbytery agreed to give notice to both Dundee kirk sessions before raising the preaching station to a congregation. When the petition to be congregated came from Lochee in 1826 no objections were raised and, according to *McKelvie,* the station was granted its new status on 15 June. Communion was first celebrated on 1 September 1826 in the open air.

A church, with sittings for 567, was opened on 1 February 1827, at 136 High Street, the cost being about £800. In 1835 there was still a debt of £500 on the property. Efforts to obtain monies from other sources had little success. Other congregations approached claimed they were unable to help because of the depressed state of trade, and the Synod Fund refused assistance.

Ten years into the first ministry a membership of 400 communicants was reported, some coming from nearby parishes such as Mains and Lundie. Eleven families travelled more than four miles, while the people were described as *nearly all of the poor and working classes*. The increase in numbers meant the church became inadequate, and in 1856 it was enlarged and remodelled at a cost of about £1,200. The outside entrance to the gallery was taken down, and the pulpit removed to the west gable. A new front formed part of the extension, with a large vestibule from which stairways on either side led to the gallery. When a further rise in membership resulted in the new church at the junction of High Street and Coupar Angus Road being built in 1871, the vacated church was bought by Messrs Cox Brothers and given to the Established Church, it becoming St Luke's Church.

The centenary of the opening of the present church was marked by celebrations from 26 to 29 September 1971. A Service of Thanksgiving and Rededication was held on Sunday, 29 September, when the preacher was the Rev. Professor John Mauchline, Trinity College, Glasgow.

A large stone built dwellinghouse at 3 Coupar Angus Road, adjacent to the church, was for long the manse. At one time it was known as Churchmount. This was probably the manse which Provost James Cox of Cardean assisted the congregation to purchase in the mid 1880s. At the time of writing it is not used as the manse of the charge.

Lochee UAS became Lochee UP in 1847, Lochee West UF in 1900 and Lochee West in 1929.

Ministers

1827	David MARSHALL	Ord. From Auchtergaven. Died 1873 (Small I 339-40)
1867	Archibald Browning CONNEL MA	Ord. A&S. Sole min. 1873. DD (St Andrews 1890) Min.Emeritus 1900 (Died 1904) (Small I 340, FUF 384)
1901	Hugh Dykes MORTON	From Cumbernauld Baird UF. Died 1914(FUF 384)
1915	Henry Angus WILLIAMSON MA BD	From Kirkcaldy Victoria Road UF. War service with YMCA in France 1918. Dem. 1947 (Died 1957) (FUF 384-5, FES IX 510, X 302)
1948	John Rogers COLQUHOUN MA	From Stewarton Cairns. To Killin 1955 (FES IX 510, X 302)
1956	Henry Lyall ORR	From East Kilbride Moncrieff. Dem. 1959 on app.as Secretary Scottish Epilepsy Society (FES X 302)
1959	David Davidson MITCHELL	From Greenock East. To Strone and Ardentinny 1973 (FES X 302)
1973	James Alexander ROY MA BD	From Stonehaven Dunnottar (FES X 302)

Notes

1. The Cox Brothers (the name was originally Cock but changed in 1845) were owners of the huge Camperdown Works in Lochee. The family were benefactors of other churches in Lochee and Dundee.
2. Dr John Eadie, minister of Cambridge Street Church, then of Lansdowne Church, both Glasgow, was one of the leading figures in the United Presbyterian Church in the mid nineteenth century, being Moderator of the UP Synod in 1857. He had a remarkable memory and, according to his biography, at one time knew by heart the whole of Milton's *Paradise Lost*. He was a distinguished scholar, editing an edition of Cruden's *Concordance*.

A Elliot, *Lochee:As it was and as it is,* Dundee, 1911

C McKean & D Walker, *Dundee, An Illustrated Architectural Guide,* Edinburgh, 1993

H S Young, *Lochee West Parish Church 1871-1971,* Dundee, n.d. (in DCA CH3/334/39)

DCA   CH2/103/49 Presbytery Benefice Register 1949

DCC   Combined Statutory and Descriptive List

DPL   Lamb 369(28)

DNB   Vol. XVI

DPL   Dundee Obituary Book Vol. I

LOGIE AND ST JOHN'S (CROSS)

*The congregation of **Logie and St John's Cross** was formed by the union of **Logie** and **St John's Cross** on 31 August 1982.*

Logie and St John's (Cross) church is situated in Blackness Avenue, and has been described as *a bold architectural witness*. It was built in 1911-14 to a design by Frank Thomson, architect, Dundee, to accommodate 1,000. The foundation stone was laid on 21 September 1912. It is a substantial Romanesque cruciform building, with a tower at the southeast corner, but no spire as originally intended. It is constructed in snecked rubble with polished ashlar dressings and pilaster buttresses. The large interior, with two bay transepts, is concrete faced with ashlar dressings. The tall wide nave, with timber clad barrel vaulted roof, is separated from narrow aisles by an arcade of stout piers with cushion capitals. There are taller piers to the transepts. While the pipe organ is still *in situ* in the south transept, it has been replaced in worship by an Allen organ. The wooden furnishings and the organ have an interlaced Celtic theme. There are stained glass windows in the aisles, post World War II, with some by A L Russell. The hall is 5 bay and barrel vaulted. An extension built in 1974 to the design of Robbie and Wellwood, architects, Dundee, is in brick. In 1957 a memorial plaque was placed in the church in remembrance of two former ministers, Dr Marshall Lang and the Rev. G Mackay Thom.

The church and the hall elevations to Shaftesbury Road and Terrace are B-listed. The manse is at 7 Hyndford Street.

Logie

Prior to the Reformation the church of Logie Dundee belonged to the Abbey of St Andrews. William the Lion confirmed the granting of the church to Scone Abbey by William, Bishop of St Andrews [1202-12]. According to the historian Andrew Jervise, Alexander I [1107-1124] gave the kirk of Logyn-Dundho to Scone Abbey. The church was dedicated (or rededicated) by Bishop David de Bernham on 25 August 1243. In a papal confirmation of 1395 it is mentioned as being in the patronage of the Abbot and Convent of Scone. According to Alexander Maxwell, *Dan Andro Gornar, ane o' the brether o' the Abbey of Scone* in 1551 was *Vicar of Loge, Lif and Innergowry*. Sometime before 3 September 1613, the parish was united to Liff by the Commissioners of Parliament, but was served *quoad spiritualia* by the parson of Dundee. This church was located in Logie Den and all that remains is the burial ground, the monuments of which are later in date.

On 6 November 1872 Presbytery received a deputation from *Subscribers towards the erection of additional churches in Dundee*. They presented a petition from 146 members and adherents of the Church in the Logie area, asking that the Rev. G B Lunan, who had been working as a missionary for about eighteen months, be appointed minister. This takes the origins of the mission, which was started in a shop, back to mid 1871, with Mr Lunan being admitted minister of Logie Chapel on 13 January 1873. On 5 August 1874 the Established Presbytery formally constituted Logie as a chapel of ease, and on 5 July 1877 the parish was disjoined again *quoad sacra* from Liff, Benvie and Invergowrie. A church, which was mentioned as being in the course of erection in the petition of November 1872, was built in Scott Street with sittings for 600. Designed by Alex. Johnston, architect, Dundee, it was opened on 8 December 1872. The church had transepts at the north end and a vestry and classrooms at the back. With an increase in membership a gallery was constructed. There was a memorial stained glass window in the three light window in the south gable. A member gifted a belfry with a peal of bells. An organ was installed and inaugurated on Sunday, 20 October 1904. A hall was erected in 1888.

Ministers

1574	William HAITLIE	From Abernyte with Liff, Invergowrie, Abernyte and Lundie also in his charge. To Benvie before 1576 (FES V 335)
1574	Andrew HANY	Reader here and at Liff (FES V 335)
1576	John CHRISTISON	Adm. before 1576, with Liff and Invergowrie also in his charge. Died 1615 (FES V 335)

-o-o-o-o-o-o-o-o-

1873	George Bell LUNAN MA BD	Ord. To Newtyle 1874 (FES V 335)
1874	George Bruce Scoular WATSON MA BD	Ord. To Cavers 1876 (Died 1923) (FES V 335)

1877 Stewart GALLOWAY	Ord. Adm. first min. of par. 3 Oct. 1877. Died 1909 (FES V 335)
1909 Richard Mackie CLARK MA	Ord. CF World War I. To Wamphray 1922 (FES V 335)
1922 James Wilson MUGGOCH MA BD	From Hurlford. To Paisley Martyrs 1928 (FES V 336, VIII 489)
1928 Henry Matthew BARTLETT MA BD	Ord. Clerk of Presb. 1952. Dem. 1969 (Died 1980) (FES VIII 489, XI 510, X 302, YB)
1970 Frank DEY FPhS BEM	From Finzean with Strachan. Dem.1982 (FES X 302)

St John's (Cross)

The north transept of St Mary's Church is stated by the local historian, Andrew Jervise, to have been destroyed by Edward I in 1303, and to have lain in ruins until 1588-90, when the magistrates decided to have it *buildit and repairit* as a church. Those who gave to the repair of the building were allowed to have monuments erected to themselves within the church, intimating the extent of their liberality. This church, called the Cross Church, also referred to as the North Church, was destroyed by fire in 1645 and used as a stable by General Monck's cavalry in 1651 and again in 1745 by the forces of Princes Charles Edward. In 1759 it was repaired and fitted out for divine service as the Fourth Charge of Dundee. The Court of Teinds erected it as a chapel on 23 July 1788. St John's parish was disjoined from St Mary's on 3 July 1834.

The church was rebuilt in 1839 but, on 3 January 1841, the Cross Church was one of three burgh churches destroyed by fire. The Town Council arranged temporary accommodation for the congregation in the new Gaelic Chapel in South Tay Street. Lindsay Street Congregational Chapel was also provided for the Cross congregation, it being used from Sunday, 1 January 1843, when there were *crowded audiences both forenoon and afternoon.* As the Gaelic congregation were unable to maintain their new church, the South Tay Street building was purchased for £1,600 in July 1845 by the Town Council, acting a patrons, and allocated to the Cross Church congregation.

At the Disruption of 1843 the minister, the Rev. John Roxburgh, and a substantial number of the congregation left and formed Free St John's. (See Roseangle Ryehill under West) Mr Roxburgh appears individually and in the group photograph of Dundee Free Church ministers taken at Glasgow on 22 October 1843, reproduced in the catalogue of Hill and Adamson's calotypes. These photographs were used by David Octavius Hill RSA for likenesses in his large painting entitled, *The First General Assembly of the Free Church of Scotland Signing the Act of Separation and Deed of Demission at Tanfield, Edinburgh, May, 1843.*

In 1909 the congregation decided to take advantage of the Town Council's proposed Tay Street improvement scheme and either erect a new church in that street or in the west end. In the event they decided to move, and a new church was built in Blackness Avenue, with a portion of Liff and Benvie parish being added *quoad sacra.* The dedication service was held on 3 September 1914, and on the following Sunday the opening service was conducted by Dr W Williamson. The building in South Tay Street became a cinema, but was subsequently demolished.

In the 1830s the minister, the Rev. John Roxburgh, and his elders were the movers behind a plan to build a new church, St Peter's. Mr Roxburgh, who came to the charge in 1834, had found that his parish had a population of 6,000, in addition to his own congregation, showing the need for church extension. As a result, in 1835 the kirk session of St John's appealed for subscriptions for the purpose of *erecting a chapel in the north west end of the Hawkhill.* The congregation at one time ran a Sunday School in Balfour Street.

Ministers

1759 Robert SMALL	App. Preacher by Town Council. Ord. to First Charge of Dundee 1761. DD (St Andrews 1778) (Mod. GA 1791) (Died 1808) (FES V 316, 328)
1761 James THOMSON	Elected. He was very eccentric. He bitterly attacked the magistrates of Dundee *for their unchristian usage of him, severely reproaching the provost for sending a whole company of soldiers to annoy him by exercising in his dining room in South Tay Street.* Supposedly, the last time he preached, a black cat walked several times round the pulpit. He considered this was the Devil come to put an end to his usefulness, as it put an end to his sermon. Dem. 1785. (Died 1791) (FES V 328)
1785 William REID	Elected preacher. Ord. 1789. Died 1794 (FES V 328)

1795 Patrick MACVICAR	Ord. Pres. by Town Council. To Third Charge of Dundee 1808. DD (St Andrews 1827) (Died 1842) (FES V 328)
1809 Alexander PETERS MA	From Logie Pert. Pres. by Town Council. DD (Marischal 1809) Died 1836 (FES V 328-9)
1834 John ROXBURGH MA	Ord. A&S. Pres. by Town Council. Joined FC. Min. of Free St John's 1843-7. DD (Glasgow 1849) (Mod.Free GA 1867) (Died 1880) (FES V 329)
1844 John ANDERSON	Ord. Pres. By Town Council. To Perth East 1845 (FES V 329)
1846 Andrew JOHNSTONE	Adm. Pres. by Town Council. To Paisley High 1846 (FES V 329)
1847 James CAESAR MA	Ord. Pres. by Town Council. To Panbride 1851 (FES V 329)
1851 Peter GRANT	Ord. Pres. by Presb. *jure devoluto* as Town Council as patrons declined to fill the vacancy. DD (Queen's College, Canada 1868) Died 1905 (FES V 329)
1902 George CHRISTIE MA BD	From Renton A&S. To Edinburgh St Andrew's 1908. DD 1927 (Died 1937) (FES V 329, KofE 122)
1909 Marshall Buchanan LANG MA BD TD DD	From Old Meldrum. Son of John Marshall Lang, Principal of Aberdeen University and Mod. GA 1893, and brother of Cosmo Gordon Lang, Archbishop of Canterbury. CF during World War I. To Whittingehame 1918. (Mod. GA 1935) (FES V 329-30)
1919 John Anthony MACRAE BA	Adm. Resigned from Edinburgh Bonnington Chapel in 1917. To Partick 1928 (Died 1957) (FES V 330, VIII 487, KofE 465)
1928 McIntosh MOWAT	From Ruthrieston. To Campsie High 1941 (Died 1948) (FES VIII 487)
1941 George Mackay THOM BA	From Hamilton West. Died 1950 (FES IX 515)
1951 Alastair Gilbert Steven RAE MA	From Edinburgh Presb. Youth Service Organiser and Warden of Simpson House. To Gullane 1958 (Died 1979) (FES IX 515, X 306, KofE 286)
1958 Robert John REID MA BD	Ord. To Loughcree, Ireland 1963 (FES X 306)
1964 George Ramsay Rattray MACKENZIE MA BD	From Glasgow Ibrox. Min. of united charge 31 Aug.1982 (FES X 306, PM)

Logie and St John's (Cross)

After the union of 1982 the St John's (Cross) buildings were retained and the Logie buildings sold.

Ministers

1982 George Ramsay Rattray MACKENZIE MA BD	Min of St John's (Cross) Dem. 1987 (PM)
1988 David Dominic SMART BSc BD MTh	Ord. To Aberdeen Gilcomston South 1998 (PM)
1999 David S SCOTT MA BD	From Invergordon (PM)

A Elliot, *Lochee, As it was and as it is,* Dundee, 1911

A Jervise, *Memorials of Angus and Mearns,* Edinburgh, 1861

E McGurk (ed.) *Calendar of Papal Letters to Scotland of Benedict XIII of Avignon 1394-1419,* Edinburgh, 1976

C McKean and D Walker, *Dundee, An Illustrated Architectural Guide,* Edinburgh, 1993

J A Rollo, *Dundee Historical Fragments,* Dundee, 1911

Sara Stevenson (ed.) *David Octavius Hill and Robert Adamson,* Catalogue of their Calotypes taken between 1843 and 1847 in the Collection of the Scottish National Portrait Gallery, Edinburgh, 1981

DCA CH2/103/18, CH2/1218, CH2/1223

DCC Combined Statutory and Descriptive List

DPL Dundee Photographic Survey, 1916, Lamb 172(7), Sp 5/203, DNC Vol. 106

DYB 1904, 1910, 1912, 1914

MAINS

Mains congregation has worshipped in the hall church in Claverhouse Road, adjacent to the former church, since 1994 when the church building was declared unsafe. Necessary repair work was estimated at £100,000, a sum that was beyond the resources of the congregation. The halls, in a harled brick building, were built in two stages in the 1970s and 1980s. Substantial internal alterations were carried out, with a chancel being built onto the east end, following the move in 1994.

The church, which was given up in 1994, was erected in 1800 and opened on 19 October after the parish of Mains was joined with the neighbouring parish of Strathmartine. The union was at the instance of the heritors, and the new church, a plain stone building, was centrally situated in the united parishes. It was constructed in rubble with ashlar dressings with four tall round arched windows on the south elevation. The interior had a gallery on Tuscan columns. The church contained a tablet in memory of Charlotte, Lady Ogilvy, widow of Sir John Ogilvy of Inverquharity. The Ogilvys resided at nearby Baldovan House, at one time known as The Bank. A stained glass window in memory of the men of the parish killed in the First World War was unveiled on 14 May 1922. A plaque on the north wall remembered Mr J M Coutts Duffus, a benefactor of the church. The communion table and chairs were gifted in 1938 as a memorial to Mrs Hannah W Sinclair, wife of the minister, who died on 21 September 1935. Memorial plaques were placed on the south wall to the Rev. R Spencer Ritchie, and on the east wall to the Rev. William Boyd and members of his family. In the 1890s major renovations were carried out, when a new pulpit and probably new pews were installed.

In 1996 the old church building was sold and converted to five flats. As a result the gallery has been removed, the four arched windows have been reglazed, and the stained glass window sold. The plaques have been removed and installed in the hall church, except for the plaque in memory of Mr Ritchie, which has been stored, being too heavy for wall mounting. It was intended that the plaque in memory of Lady Ogilvy be relocated. The communion table, font, communion chairs and organ were removed to the hall church. A large brass offering dish, now used in the hall church, was presented by the Rev. Alexander Stewart, a former minister and Moderator of the General Assembly in 1911.

The former church building is B-listed. There is a churchyard to the south. The Mains Old Churchyard site is C-listed. The old manse, dating from 1760, stood near the church and was a south facing, two-storey building. It was demolished many years ago. The present manse is at 9 Elgin Street.

Mains and Strathmartine

Mains and Strathmartine was formed by the union of the parishes of Mains and Strathmartine on 21 November 1795.

The foundation of **Mains Church** dates from 1201-7 when it was granted to Arbroath Abbey by Gilchrist, earl of Angus. The old name of the parish was Strathdichty, or Earl's Strathdichty, and the church was dedicated to St Ninian. The name was changed to Mains of Fintry, after the local proprietors, the Grahams who came from Fintry in Stirlingshire. The old church was situated in what is now Caird Park, near to Mains Castle which it predated. A well nearby was known as *Sinavey's Well*, most likely a corruption of *St Ninian*. In 1242, the church was consecrated, or reconsecrated, by Bishop David de Bernham. Robert Graham of Fintry had a dispute with his stepmother about the disposal of some ecclesiastical vestments and ornaments, which his father had given to the church. He did, however, return them to the church and founded a perpetual chantry to the honour of God Almighty, the Blessed Virgin, and St Joseph. Following the union of the congregations of Mains and Strathmartine, the old church of Mains fell into a ruinous condition. The pre-reformation font remained in place. In the north wall there was an aumbry with an iron door. The burial vault of the Grahams projected from the south side of the church. In 1869 a carved stone representation of the Annunciation was unearthed, showing the Virgin, a descending dove, and an angel with a scroll and a pot of lilies. It was built into the wall above the three lance windows of the vault. There was a carved sundial in the southwest corner, similar to those at Linlithgow and Melrose.

Ministers

1563	Ninian HALL	Exhorter in 1563 (FES VIII 493)
1568	William AUCHMOUTIE MA	Min. in 1568 with Lundie also in his charge. To Strathmartine 1572 (FES V 357, VIII 493)
1572	Ninian COOK	Reader (FES V 357)

1574	Alexander TYRIE	From Meigle. Strathmartine, Auchterhouse and Tealing also in his charge. To Auchterhouse before 1582 (FES V 357)
1575	Alexander GRAHAM	Vicar. Died ca. 1588 (FES VIII 493)
1585	William BRUCE	Reader in 1585. Pres. to vicarage 1588-9 (FES V 358, VIII 493)
1590	William RAIT	Min. in 1590. To Lundie 1593. To Strathmartine 1594, returned to Mains 1594. Had Strathmartine also in his charge in 1612. Died ca. 1630-3 (FES V 358, VIII 493)
1633	Henry FITHIE	Pres. by Charles I. Dep. with seventeen others by Committee of GA for Visitation. Died before 1655 (FES V 358)
1652	Henry AUCHENLECK MA	Ord. To Second Charge Perth 1662 (FES V 358)
1663	James FITHIE MA	Ord. Son of Henry Fithie. Died 1672 (FES V 358)
1673	Patrick STRACHAN MA	Adm. Dep. 1701 for contumacy but continued to perform clerical duties in parish till 1707. Died after 1710 (FES V 358, VIII 493)
1707	James HODGE	Ord. To Longforgan 1709 (FES V 358)
1710	Andrew RONALDSON MA	Ord. Died 1722 (FES V 358)
1723	John KER MA	Ord. Died 1759 (FES V 358)
1760	John GIBSON	Ord. Pres. by George II. Died 1795 (FES V 358)

Strathmartine Church was dedicated, or rededicated, by Bishop David de Bernham on 18 May 1249, but is a much older ecclesiastical site. A number of Pictish symbol stones have been uncovered in the churchyard. The church was dedicated to St Martin, with the old name of the parish being Strathdichty Martin. The ruins of the former church are in the small village of Kirkton of Strathmartine, also known as Bridgefoot.

Ministers

1562	Thomas CUMMING	Vicar 1562-6 (FES VIII 494)
1567	James WEICHT or WIGHT	Served as co-parson before Reformation. Exhorter 1563, min. in 1567. Died 1572 (FES V 360, VIII 494)
1568	Thomas MORRISON	Pres. to vicarage. (FES VIII 494)
1572	William AUCHMOUTIE MA	Adm. Pres. by James VI to prebend of quarter of parsonage on death of Sir James Weicht (FES V 360, VIII 494)
1572	David TYRIE	Reader (FES V 360)
1594	William RAIT	From Lundie. Also min. of Mains (FES V 360)
1620	William ROLLOCK MA	Adm. (FES V 360)
1626	David JAMESON MA	Adm. Died after 1637 (FES V 360)
1638	Alexander RAMSAY MA	Adm. Dep. 1649 with seventeen others by Committee of GA app. for Visitation (FES V 360)
1653	James FRASER	Adm. To Arbroath 1653 (FES V 360)
1655	John MOW	Adm. (FES V 360)
1664	David FERGUSSON MA	Adm. Died before 29 June 1696 when par. declared vacant (FES V 360)
1697	Thomas OGILVIE	Ord. To Coupar Angus 1703 (FES V 361)
1706	James GOODSIR	Ord. To Monikie 1717 (FES V 361)
1718	William THOMSON	Ord. Died 1743 (FES V 361)
1744	Hugh MAXWELL MA	Adm. Pres. by George II. Died 1751 (FES V 361)
1751	David MAXWELL	Adm. Son of preceding. He was proprietor of chief part of the parish. Died 1774 (FES V 361)
1775	Alexander STRACHAN	Ord. Pres. by George III. Min. of united par. of Mains and Strathmartine in 1795 (FES V 361)

Mains and Strathmartine

After the union of 1795, a new church was provided by the heritors at Trottick and opened on 19 October 1800. The churches at Strathmartine and Mains were abandoned. The name of the congregation was changed to Mains in 1929.

At the Disruption of 1843, a number of the congregation left to form a Free Church at Downfield, but the minister remained in the Establishment, becoming moderator of Presbytery. (See **Strathmartine**).

Victoria Chapel, later Fairmuir Church, was a daughter charge of Mains and Strathmartine. (See **Fairmuir**). Mains opened a mission station at Downfield around 1885, which became the *quoad sacra* charge of Downfield in 1912. (See **Strathmartine**). West March hall church, Helmsdale Avenue, was opened around 1950, under the supervision of Mains, to serve the Kirkton and West March post war housing developments. It was closed in the 1970s and the building, which had suffered greatly from vandalism, disposed of.

Ministers

1795	Alexander STRACHAN MA	From Strathmartine on union of parishes. Died 1799 (FES V 359)
1799	Francis NICOLL MA	From Auchtertool. Pres. by George III. Mod. GA 1809. To St Leonard's St Andrews 1820 (FES V 359)
1820	David CANNAN	From Murroes. Pres. by George IV. DD 1828. Dem. 1848 (Died 1854) (FES V 359)
1848	John ROBERTSON DD	Ord. Pres. by Victoria. To St Mungo's Glasgow 1858[1] (FES V 359)
1858	John McMURTRIE BA MA	Ind. Pres. by Victoria. To St Bernard's Edinburgh 1866 (Died 1912) (FES V 359, KofE 153)
1866	William BOYD MA	Ord. Pres. by Victoria. Died of malaria at Florence 1873 (FES V 359)
1873	Alexander STEWART MA DD	Ord. Pres. by Victoria. Dem.on app. as Professor of Systematic Theology, Aberdeen 1882 (Mod. GA 1911) (FES V 359)
1888	Richard Spencer RITCHIE	From Sorn. Died 1917 (FES V 360)
1918	Alexander ANDERSON MA BD	From St James' Kirkcaldy. Dem. 1925. Adm. to Glasgow Robertson Memorial 1928 (FES V 360, VIII 493)
1926	John SINCLAIR MA BD	From Lundie. Dem. on app. as Asst. Clerk to Presb. of Glasgow 1945. DD (Edinburgh 1952) (FES VIII 493, IX 511)
1946	John Campbell STEWART MA BD	From Kirn St Margaret's. To Coatbridge Gartsherrie 1952 (FES IX 511)
1953	David William ROSS MA BD	From Lochgelly Macainsh. To Cluny, Lethendy and Kinloch 1968 (FES IX 511, X 303)
1969	John Clark SCROGGIE	From Flisk with Kilmany. Dem. 1985 (FES X 303, YB)
1985	Kenneth R THOM	Ord. To Chap. RAF 1990 (PM)
1991	Michael Stewart GOSS BD DPS	Ord. (PM)

Note

1. St Mungo's is Glasgow Cathedral. Dean Ramsay in his *Reminiscences of Scottish Life and Character* tells a story of the Mains beadle, Walter Nicoll, and Dr Robertson. After removing to Glasgow Dr Robertson invited Walter (Watty) to Glasgow. He showed him over the Cathedral and asked him what he thought of it and if it was not better than Mains Church. Watty shook his head and said, *Aweel, sir, you see she's bigger, but she has nae laft, and she's sair fashed wi' thae pillars.*

G Kiernan, *A History of Mains Parish Church,* Dundee, 1978
Letter of 1 July 1998 from Rev. M S Goss
DCA CH2/256
DCC Combined Statutory and Descriptive List.

MAINS OF FINTRY

Mains of Fintry church stands at the corner of Fintry Road and Fintry Drive, in the local authority housing estate of Mains of Fintry.

The congregation traces its origins to 1952, when Presbytery erected a prefabricated hut accommodating 120 people. The *Hut Hall* was opened on 1 June 1952. A deaconess was appointed, and services in the hall were at first conducted by ministers of Presbytery in rotation on Sunday afternoons, until the first minister was inducted on 25 February 1953. The foundation stone of the church was ceremonially laid on 29 September 1954. The church was built at a cost of £20,000, and opened on 4 September 1955. The church building was reconstructed, and a new hall opened in April 1968. The congregation achieved full status in May 1959.

Following their union in June 1953, St Luke's and Queen Street Church, Broughty Ferry, presented chancel furnishings of communion table, chairs, lectern and font.

Due to structural problems, the church tower was demolished in 1996. Major alterations to the church began in 1998, with the first two phases of the work completed in 1999 at a cost of £52,000. The sanctuary was converted from bare floorboards and wooden pews into a bright carpeted area with comfortable chairs. A new lounge area was created. A rededication service was held on Sunday, 21 November 1999. The next stages of work will seek to improve the hall and the ground surrounding the church.

The manse is situated at 4 Clive Street.

Ministers

1953	John CORDINER	From Lundie and Fowlis Easter. To Dumfries Lincluden with Holywood 1961 (FES IX 511, X 303)
1961	Donald John BARRON	From Foveran. To Macduff Gardner 1968 (FES X 303)
1968	Henry Finlayson Calder NIVEN	Ord. To Dumbarton Riverside C&S 1974 (FES X 303)
1974	Ewen Sinclair NICOL MA BD	From Glasgow Cathedral (Ord. Asst.) To Carlisle 1976 (FES X 303)
1977	Peter M HUMPHRIS BSc BD	From Asst. Nairn Old (YB)

Mains of Fintry congregational magazine of September 1992 (40th anniversary edition)
Notes from Session Clerk 15 April 1998
DPL   Sp. 3/2
PM   1996
Courier, 22 November 1999

MEADOWSIDE St PAUL'S

Meadowside St Paul's church is situated in Nethergate next to the Inner Ring Road of South Marketgait. Built in 1852 as Free St Paul's, at a cost of £6,400, the building was designed by Charles Wilson of Glasgow, celebrated as the designer of the terraces overlooking Kelvingrove Park. It has a Gothic Revival façade of sandstone ashlar, and a three stage centred tower with angle buttresses 80 feet high, a tall thin spire 80 feet high, topped by a copper crosslet, making a total of 167 feet. There is a pointed arch entrance. Originally inserted on a restricted site, the church was intended to be an integral part of terraced buildings facing onto Nethergate. Two shops are incorporated in the front. The church is listed under Scotland's Churches Scheme of *Churches for You to Visit.*

The former St Paul's building was adopted in 1982 as the place of worship of the united charge of Meadowside St Paul's. It now occupies, thanks to road development, the prestigious site at the corner of the ancient Nethergate and the modern Marketgait, which is effectively the gateway, past the church garden with its enclosing wall, to the new waterfront development and the Discovery Centre, all within its parish.

The garden was designed by the landscape architect, Brian Snell, and the wall created by the artist, David Wilson. The wave theme of the wall is picked up again by the metal sculptures in the garden, and also in the railings that lead from the hall to the Nethergate. There are seven carved stones, repeating broadly the same theme which is continued in the logo on the west wall of the hall, based on the Christian ichthys or fish symbol (the acrostic *Jesus Christ, Son of God, Saviour*) and in the two pavement mosaics at the front of the church. These were designed by the artist, Elizabeth McFall.

The church was formally opened on Sunday, 12 December 1852, by two of the foremost ministers of the Free Church, Dr R S Candlish[1] and Sir Henry Moncrieff[2] suggesting its inauguration was considered an important event in the young denomination. A contemporary magazine, *The Builder,* claimed that the new building was *of no great merit.* The sanctuary has, of course, since been embellished with good quality stained glass windows and other furnishings. However, the writer was probably not judging it in the context of the Dundee Free churches of the mid nineteenth century, and it may be regarded as the finest of that group. Those Free churches erected in the 1840s, such as St Andrew's, St David's, and the original St John's in Small's Wynd, were plain buildings, while the churches taken over from the Establishment, because of outstanding debt, had been built, like Dudhope in 1840, with the *utmost economy that may be consistent with the neatness and respectability of a house devoted to the worship of God,* or St Peter's in 1836, as *plain and substantial, so as to secure at once both quantity and cheapness of accommodation.* Clearly, St Paul's was an adornment to the ecclesiastical architecture of Dundee, as is testified by a more recent comment (McKean and Walker, Dundee, 1993) to the following effect, *The tall thin spire...and its Gothic Revival façade lend quality and interest to the locality.*

The interior is galleried with a timber collar and hammerbeam roof. The progressive lightening of the woodwork in 1936 and 1958 was continued in the redecoration carried out in 1982 after the union. Lighting was originally by gas, electric lighting being installed in 1897. Interestingly, James Bowman Lindsay, who discovered the lighting possibilities of electricity as early as 1835, was a member of the congregation.[3] In 1888 the contributor of a magazine article on St Paul's made reference to the poor lighting.

The Cross on the north wall was part of the 1958 redecoration. The oak pulpit is part of a development in 1902 designed by architects, Thoms and Wilkie, to incorporate, in the absence of an organ chamber, the pipe organ installed by Walcker of Ludwigsburg, Wurttemberg. The organ console was moved to its present position in 1971, when electrical operation replaced mechanical and the organ was overhauled by Rushworth and Dreaper, Liverpool.

There are a number of fine stained glass windows. The first group are those in the upper church. The three windows behind the organ were the first to be installed in 1898 and represent *Faith, Hope* and *Charity.* On the same wall are two windows, one on each side, fitted in 1910, with the respective themes of *Moses* on the left and *Isaiah* on the right.

Outside these windows on the south wall are two windows dedicated in 1949 to the memory of the Very Reverend Dr James Weatherhead, former minister and Moderator of the United Free Church General Assembly. The subject of the window on the extreme left left is *St Columba,* and on the extreme right, *St Andrew.*

On the east wall of the east transept is a window dedicated to the memory of the Rev. Dr William Patrick, former minister, with a twofold theme, *Christ leaving the Judgment Hall* and *The Last Supper.* In the back gallery on the east wall is a window depicting *The Nativity,* and on the west another depicting *Jesus at Bethany.*

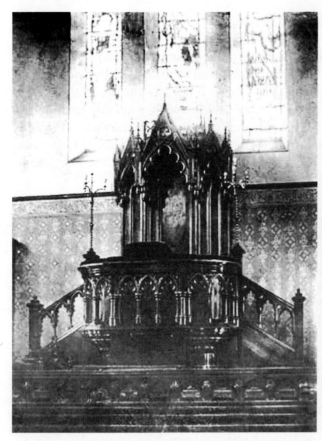

St Paul's UF, Nethergate before and after the alterations of 1902 when a new pulpit and a pipe organ were installed

On the west wall of the west transept the window shows six incidents in the life of Jesus; on the top half, *The Adoration of the Magi, Ascension at Bethany,* and *John the Baptist;* and on the lower half, *Jesus as a Boy in the Temple, The Road to Calvary* and *Cana of Galilee.*

With one exception, all the stained glass windows in the lower church were installed in the same year, 1910. The symbols in the three small windows on the east wall are respectively, *Alpha, A Dove,* and *Omega,* and in the corresponding windows on the west wall, *IHS, A Lamb* and *XP.*

The subjects of the three windows on the east wall of the east transept are, *Eunice, Jesus and Dorcas,* and of the window on the south wall, *Purity.* The themes of the three windows on the west wall of the west transept are, *St John, St Paul,* and *St Peter,* and of the window on the south wall, *Fortitude.* The one window in the lower church ,installed later in 1914, on the back wall under the gallery has as its motif, *Blessed are the Peacemakers.*

Three windows are definitely known to be by Jones and Willis of Birmingham, and it would appear from the style and date of the windows that, apart from the *St Columba* and *St Andrew* windows, the others are likely to be from the same studio. The two exceptions were executed by Alex. Russell of Dundee College of Art, now part of Dundee University.

The communion table was commissioned from Lord Roberts Workshops, Dundee, in 1982, to mark the union of St Paul's and Meadowside, the cost being met from the sale of the Meadowside organ. St Paul's communion table was placed in the vestibule of the church. The three communion chairs at present in use were transferred from Meadowside Church, and the three St Paul's chairs are retained in the lower hall. The baptismal font was presented to St Paul's in 1902.

A Book of Remembrance prepared by the artist, Ian Turner, replaced the separate war memorials of the various churches now merged into Meadowside St Paul's in 1984. It lists the names of the fallen by churches for each of the wars and, in addition, includes a photographic record of the original memorials which have been deposited with the City Archivist. Details have also been recorded in the National Register of War Memorials. The Memorial Book is kept before the congregation on a lectern transferred from Meadowside Church, while the St Paul's lectern remains in its original position.

There are two main sets of pulpit falls; the four St Paul's falls prepared to fit the reading desk in the pulpit are in use each Sunday according to the Christian calendar. In keeping with St Paul's Church origin as the Mariners' Church, as well as with early Christian symbolism and the concept of the Trinity, each of the falls includes in its design three fish. On the white fall three stars also represent the Trinity, and one a symbol for

St Paul. The blue bears a star representing the Nativity, a cross for the Crucifixion and the letters *Alpha* and *Omega*. The green fall bears *IHS,* while the red fall has a Dove and Tongues of Fire, representing the Holy Spirit, as well as *XP.* The two Meadowside falls, which fit the lectern, are used at appropriate seasons of the Christian year. The white fall bears a Cross and Doves, while the blue fall has the Burning Bush. There are four tapestry kneelers bearing symbols, which were presented in 1988 and later.

The floor of the vestibule is of Norwegian slate, and the panelling of Austrian oak. The panelling was a gift in 1938 in memory of Sir George and Lady Ritchie. A brass plaque in the vestibule commemorates the jubilee of the Boys Brigade in Dundee in 1936, St Paul's having provided four Battalion Presidents, and being where the 1st Dundee Company was founded in 1886. A second brass plaque draws attention to the Book of Remembrance in the chancel. There are also memorials to two former ministers, the Rev. James Ewing of St Andrew's, and the Rev. Dr James Cosh of St George's.

Twice in over fifty years the church building was threatened by fire. In 1944 the furniture premises of Methven Hyslop to the west were burned down. A proposal to build halls on this site suffered planning blight, and it was not until 1988 that a new hall complex could be built on cleared ground to the south of the church. On 27 August 1995 the church was again endangered when Green's Playhouse to the west was destroyed by fire. Again damage to the church was minimal.

A new hall complex, designed by Reid and Greig, architects, Dundee, was opened officially by Her Majesty, Queen Elizabeth the Queen Mother on 19 October 1988. The complex was linked directly to the church in 1990, thus making it possible to realise the vision of the united charge to establish a church centre with the church itself as the centrepiece. Of the two shops, one is used as the Cornerstone Coffee House staffed mainly by volunteers to provide a quiet place of meeting in a Christian environment, and the other is used as a Christian bookshop under the auspices of Wesley Owen. The original vestry below the church houses the Presbytery Resource Centre. The other accommodation, consisting in the crypt of a small hall, and in the complex of a large hall, two committee rooms, vestry, kitchen and storage, is used not only to meet the requirements of the congregation's organisations, but also to provide suitable venues for the Presbytery and other committees. In addition, the facilities are made available for community activities of various kinds.

The focus of the hundred years of mission work in the Overgate lost its *raison d'être* with the demolition, not just of the mission buildings, but of the Overgate itself. When, therefore, the new hall complex was completed in 1988 the drive was towards outreach from the Church Centre. As part of the outreach the congregation regularly presents the Christian message through open weeks. Sometimes these coincide with the great Christian festivals such as Easter; sometimes they are a prelude to the winter session with themes such as Festival of Flowers, Maritime Year, Year of the Bible, Remembrance 1939-89, Ecclesiastical Embroidery; sometimes they have marked stages in the attainment of the vision of the Church Centre. During the season of Advent the congregation can be found conducting open-air services in City Square. It takes part in local festivals and street processions, offering hospitality to spectators on such occasions. The congregation regularly takes part in ecumenical activities and services in the City Centre and provides chaplaincy services to two primary schools, Dundee College, and the University of Dundee, all within its parish. It maintains contact with local businesses.

The church, with the two adjacent shops, is B-listed. The manse is at 36 Blackness Avenue.

The present congregation was formed by the union of **St Paul's** *and* **Meadowside** *on 4 December 1981.* **St Paul's** *(as it was in 1981) was formed by the union of* **St Paul's** *and* **Tay Square** *on 4 July 1952.*

Mariners', St Paul's

Mariners' congregation had its origins in a meeting called by the Rev. Robert Murray McCheyne on 10 October 1838, in the aftermath of the wreck of the Dundee steamer, *Forfarshire,* of Grace Darling fame[4], to consider the formation of a society to care for the spiritual interests of sailors. As a result, the Dundee Seamen's Friends' Society had been formed and a mission established, meeting in the Caledonian Hall, Castle Street. The Rev. James Law, who had been chaplain to the Seamen's Mission before the Disruption of 1843, had gathered a large congregation, at whose request the Free Church Presbytery had ordained him in July 1843. However, in 1844 Mr Law returned to the Established Church, together with many of his followers. While the remnant congregation was vacant the Central congregation came to worship with them.

A calotype photograph of a group of Dundee Free Presbytery, taken at Glasgow on 22 October 1843 by Robert Adamson, probably includes the Rev. James Law, some of the figures being unnamed. The Mariners' Church minutes show he received the sum of £5 for his expenses in attending.

Before the schism in the Church of Scotland, the substantial sum of £1,000 had been subscribed for a Seamen's Chapel but no building had been acquired, and, in the circumstances, of the Disruption, it was considered appropriate to return the money to the subscribers. However, most of the money was immediately re-subscribed for the Free Church and a hall in Reform Street was purchased at a cost of £825 for the congregation's use as a church called **Mariners'.** This was the former Original Secession Church that had been used temporarily by the East Church congregation (St Mary's) until their church was rebuilt in 1844, following the fire which destroyed three of the Burgh Churches in 1841. The minutes of Mariners' Church disclose that on 9 October 1843 consent was given for the East Church to continuing worship in the Reform Street building *until the middle of December or the last Sabbath of the year.* At this period Mariners' congregation was using the Thistle Hall in Union Street.

In 1844 there was an accession of new members from Dundee Central Church, the erection of which charge had been abandoned. At the Disruption many former elders, members, and adherents of those Burgh Churches, the ministers of which remained in the Established Church, requested the Free Presbytery to organise them into a congregation. A temporary place of worship was arranged in the Caledonian Hall, Castle Street.[6] At the end of 1843 they were recognised as a regular charge under the name of Central Church. In January 1844, the congregation at a meeting in the Caledonian Hall elected James Gibb Duncan to be their minister, and the call was sustained by Presbytery. However, in March Mr Duncan withdrew, due to illhealth. There was an unsuccessful attempt to unite them with Chapelshade congregation, which had become vacant. There are two echoes of the Central Church in the minutes of Mariners'. In January 1845, some of the subscribers to the building fund of Central asked that the monies they had donated be applied to renovation work required in Mariners' Church. In July 1850, before St Paul's was proposed to Presbytery by the Kirk Session as the name to replace Mariners', Central was considered as a possible alternative.

The dual nature of Mariners' Church as a seamen's mission and as a regular pastoral charge created problems for the infant congregation. Whereas the approved national system of support for the ministry of the Free Church, through the Sustentation Fund, was based on weekly payments collected by districts, the Deacons' Court of Mariners' averred that the constitution of the Free Church allowed each congregation to act for itself in this matter. However, since the seamen received each month half pay only, with the balance of their wages paid in two instalments in July and December when they returned to port, they would be well able to support the minister through seat rents which were paid twice a year. They claimed that more could be raised in this way than by *weekly pennies.* The General Assembly of 1844 rejected their claim that the constitution of Mariners' Church be thus amended.

A division was thereby created in the Mariners' congregation, which is illustrated by a petition presented to the Established Presbytery on 1 May 1844, by *elders, deacons, members and others connected with the Mariners' congregation.* They complained *that your petitioners are tired and worn out with the ever changing, neglectful and oppressive treatment they have underwent* [sic] *in the Free Church. They express deep regret and sorrow from having ever withdrawn from the established Church of Scotland and now desire most sincerely to be admitted into her communion...* The petition was subscribed by 382 names. While they were received back into the Established Church, they were not granted their request *to meet in a separate place of worship under their late pastor.*

Later, on 22 November 1847, the Kirk Session submitted a plea to Presbytery to sanction the appointment of a missionary to seamen, thus leaving the minister of Mariners' to devote his attention to members of his congregation. Since the money to buy the church had been subscribed in order to provide care for the seamen frequenting the port, a further resolution was passed on 6 February 1848, asking that Mariners' constitution be amended to permit it to become an ordinary pastoral charge. The Mariners' Church was to be sold to the newly sanctioned charge and the proceeds used to establish a seamen's mission nearer to the docks, with its own missionary in charge. The constitution as approved by the General Assembly of 1844 had specifically tied Mariners' congregation to the welfare of seamen, and this tie could only be loosed by a further decision of the General Assembly. In the event, the Reform Street church was leased to the newly sanctioned charge until 1852, when the church in Nethergate was opened under the name of **St Paul's** approved subsequently by the General Assembly of 1850. The Reform Street church was sold to the Evangelical Union, the proceeds being set apart for the benefit of seamen. A manse was bought in 1870.

The congregation had a fine mission record, Dr William Wilson, minister for thirty years from 1848, being Convener of the Assembly Home Mission Committee for ten years. The congregation conducted a mission in the Overgate area, using the old Gaelic Church in Long Wynd for ten years, and thereafter at 145 Overgate, which was opened on 25 November 1866. It was reported in 1867 that £2,659 had been subscribed, sufficient to buy the site and erect the hall. Until 1917 the mission was run by assistant ministers, but thereafter by two outstanding lay missionaries, Mr Frank Hunt appointed in 1917 and Mr J K Robertson in 1945. For five years from 1876 the mission enjoyed a brief period of independent existence as **Wilson Church** (q.v.)

From 1846 to 1848 a school was organised in a rented hall behind the premises of the Dundee, Perth and London Shipping Company, Dock Street. In 1855 a school in Wallacetown, opened in the 1840s by a committee of ladies, was transferred to the care of St Paul's which was responsible for it until 1878. A school in the Overgate Mission remained in the control of St Paul's from 1862 to 1888. The departure of the school in 1891, the last three years being under Dundee School Board, allowed the mission building to be redeveloped entirely for mission purposes. Despite a threat to its existence in 1912 from the City Improvement Scheme, the premises served the church and community for another forty years until 1953. Apart from normal mission activities the premises were used during the First and Second World Wars as a social club and canteen for the troops, and during the Depression of the 1930s by the Committee for Service to the Unemployed and by the Committee for Social Service to Unemployed Women.

The congregation was equally supportive of its ministers who were conveners of earlier committees for the maintenance of the ministry, e.g. Dr William Wilson appointed Convener of the Free Church Sustentation Fund in 1877, and Dr James Weatherhead as Convener of the United Free Church Central Fund in 1918. Thus contributions of over £1,000[5] to the Sustentation Fund placed St Paul's as the third highest contributor in the Church, and a contribution of £1,354 to the Central Fund was the equivalent of five minimum stipends.

Ministers

1843 James LAW	Ord. An Episcopalian who became an Original Seceder, before joining EC. App. Chaplain to Seamen's Mission, joining FC in 1843. Disciplined by FC but dem. 1844, returning to EC. Thereafter suspended by EC following attempt to take orders in Church of England. Reinstated by EC and served in Kirriemuir and Arbroath (Ewing II 162, PM)
1845 Thomas ROBINSON	Ord. To Salford 1847 (PM)
1848 William WILSON	From Carmylie Free. Was interim Professor of Theology in College of English Presbyterian Church in 1847. To Secretary and Joint Convener Sustentation Fund Committee 1877 while remaining Senior Colleague. DD. Mod. Free GA 1866.Principal Clerk Free GA (HN, PM)
1878 Richard A WATERSTON BA	From Glasgow Union Free C&S. Died 1892 (PM)
1892 William PATRICK	From Kirkintilloch Free. DD. To Winnipeg Presbyterian College as Principal 1900 (Died 1911) (HN, PM, DYB 1911)
1900 John MARTIN	From Nairn Free. To Callander UF 1905 (FUF 388)
1906 James WEATHERHEAD MA BD	From Giffnock. DD (1924) Mod. UF GA 1927. Sen. Min. 1937. Died 1944 (FUF 389, FES IX 516)
1937 James MUNN MA	From Saltcoats Erskine. To Glasgow Newlands South 1951 (FES IX 516)
1952 Basil Gathorne HARDY MA BD	From Peterhead East. Min. of united charge 4 July 1952 (FES IX 516)

Tay Square, as it was in 1952, was formed by the union of Tay Square and Hawkhill on 22 March 1903.

Tay Square

In 1832 there was a schism in the School Wynd congregation over a call and, following a meeting held in Caledonian Hall, Castle Street[6] on 30 August, 235 members applied to the United Associate Presbytery of Cupar for sermon. On 6 November they were congregated and the seven elders among them constituted into a session. At first the new congregation worshipped in the Caledonian Hall, but the accommodation was insufficient, and in February they exchanged halls with the Reformed Presbyterian Church who had been using Thistle Hall, Union Street[7]. By the end of 1833 the church in Tay Square, with accommodation for 1,000, was in course of erection. It was opened in 1834 and membership increased rapidly to a roll of 900 in 1837. There may have been a decline in the following decade for the membership was stated at 700 in 1848. The building had cost £2,300, two thirds of which remained as debt four years later. However, there was a substantial income from seat rents, part of which was available to reduce the loan on the property.

A visitor in 1888 wrote that *the rather heavy exterior altogether* [belied] *the bright interior of the building. The pews in the area of the church are neat, comfortable, and well appointed. The full sweep of the gallery, the gracefully proportioned pillars, the beautifully designed and decorated organ, and the abundance of light, all tend to give the church a lightsome appearance.*

The congregation conducted mission activities centred on West Port, Artillery Lane and Hawkhill. The Hawkhill mission led to the founding in 1876 of **Hawkhill UP** congregation (see below). The minister of Tay Square, the Rev. John Mansie, when Convener of the Assembly Committee on Social Problems, was largely responsible for the establishment in 1931 of Belmont Castle Church of Scotland Eventide Home.

Originally, the congregation was known officially as the Third United Secession Congregation Dundee. Their popular name was adopted from their location, so what was usually called Tay Square United Secession became Tay Square UP in 1847 and Tay Square UF in 1900.

Ministers

1833 James Reid McGAVIN	Ord. DD (Princeton 1858) Mod. UP Synod 1875. Ret. from active duty 1878. Died 1887 (Small I 303- 4. HN)
1879 Charles JERDAN LLB DD	From Dennyloanhead UP. Ind. C&S. To Greenock Sir Michael Street UP 1884 (Principal Clerk UF GA) (Small I 304-5, *Five into One*)
1884 John REID MA	From Milnathort UP C&S. Min. of united charge 1903 (FUF 379)

Hawkhill

The congregation was the result of mission work carried out in the West Port district for a number of years by Tay Square UP Church. On 11 April 1871, Presbytery agreed that the members should have *sealing ordinances* and on 7 December 1875 the station was erected into a congregation. The Rev. John Taylor was ordained on 7 March 1876 as first minister of what became known as West Port UP Mission Church, then meeting in Temple Lane. The former Hawkhill Free Church was purchased at a cost of £1,850, and was used as the place of worship of what became Hawkhill UP Church from 3 February 1878.

This church, with seating for 400, had been erected in 1855 for the Reformed Presbyterians but had passed over to the Free Church at the union of 1876, following which it assumed the name of Martyrs' Church. Martyrs' congregation had vacated it, having opened a new church in Annfield Road at the end of 1877. (See **Balgay**)

The acquisition meant that the congregation was burdened with debt for many years, despite a grant from the Home Board and a substantial bequest. A sale of work in 1887, promoted by the other Dundee congregations, brought in almost £650 clearing the sum outstanding. Because of the first minister's poor health during his latter years in the charge the membership declined. The second ministry was cut short by the death of the Rev. Robert H Wyllie in 1900. The vacant charge was served by the Rev. J M Richmond, a probationer, until 22 March 1903 when it was united with Tay Square under their name and minister.

Hawkhill UP became Hawkhill UF in 1900.

Ministers

1878 John TAYLOR	Ord. after missionary work in West Port. Dem. 1889 (Died 1893) (Small I 311-2)
1889 Robert H WYLLIE	Ord. From Kilmarnock King Street. Died 1900 (Small I 312)

Tay Square

After the union of 1903 Tay Square church became the place of worship. Tay Square UF became Tay Square in 1929.

Ministers

1903 John REID MA	Min. of Tay Square. To Inverness Ness Bank UF 1904 (FUF 389)
1905 John MANSIE MA	From Alexandria. War service YMCA 1915, Scottish Churches Huts 1918-9. Died 1934 (FUF 389, FES IX 517)

| 1935 | Andrew Morris MOODIE MC MA | From Paisley Oakshaw East. To Buchlyvie 1949 (FES IX 517) |
| 1950 | Charles FRASER | Introd. Dem. 1952. Ind. Flotta and Fara 1953 (FES IX 517) |

St Paul's

After the union of 1952 St Paul's church was used for worship and the Tay Square buildings were converted into halls for use by congregational organisations and let to others including Presbytery.

Minister

| 1952 | Basil Gathorne HARDY MA BD | Min. of St Paul's. On union with Meadowside as Meadowside St Paul's introd. as min. of united charge on 4 December 1981 (FES IX 516, PM, YB) |

Meadowside

Formerly called **Albert Square and St George's, Meadowside** was formed by the union of **Albert Square** and **St George's** on 5 March 1955. St George's church was used for worship. The former Albert Square church was converted in 1956 to provide hall accommodation. In 1973 the hall in Meadow Street, originally acquired by Free St Andrew's in 1846, was demolished to make way for the Wellgate Shopping centre. In exchange the congregation received the vacant building of the former **Euclid Crescent Church** (q.v.), whose congregation had been dissolved in 1968. The building was converted into halls. This property was sold in 1987 to Dundee High School and converted, along with the adjacent former Panmure Street Congregational Church, into the school's Trinity Hall.

Minister

| 1956 | John Brown COUPAR | From Airdrie Wellwynd. Dem. 1980 (Died 1987) (FES X 303, YB) |

St George's

The congregations of **Chapelshade UF** and **St Andrew's UF** were united on 12 January 1916 as **St Andrew's and Chapelshade UF**. The Chapelshade church at the corner of Bell Street and Constitution Road was sold to White, Milne and Company, mill furnishers. The St Andrew's church in Meadowside was used as the place of worship and the hall in Meadow Street was retained for mission and congregational purposes. The Chapelshade manse was retained. At the union of 1929 the name of the congregation was changed to **St George's**.

Minister

| 1916 | James COSH MA BD | From Irvine Mure UF. DD (St Andrew's 1954) Dem. 1954 (Died 1961) (FUF 387-8, FES IX 514, X 305) |

St Andrew's Free and UF

At the Disruption of 1843 the Rev. James Ewing, minister of St Andrew's church, and many of the congregation *came out,* worshipping at first in Shaw's Mill in King Street provided by Baxter Brothers. A church with sittings for 1,300 was built in Meadowside to the plans of Mr Davidson, architect, and opened on 2 February 1845. The contributor of a magazine article in 1889 described it as the largest Free kirk in the city.

Mr Ewing appears in the group photograph of Dundee Free Church ministers previously mentioned. Some of these photographs were used by David Octavius Hill RSA, for likenesses in his large painting entitled, *The First General Assembly of the Free Church of Scotland Signing the Act of Separation and Deed of Demission at Tanfield, Edinburgh, May, 1843.*

A schoolroom, bought in 1846, was organised by Mr Ewing, under Alexander Hood, schoolmaster. It was subsequently used as a church hall. Ground for a new church was acquired in 1875, but the plans for this building were not proceeded with. The congregation began a mission in 1850, which was the origin of Wellgate Free Church. (See **St Stephen's** dissolved in 1906) Elders of the congregation, under the supervision of Mr Ewing, began prayer meetings in the 1860s from which developed Ogilvie church (See **Stobswell**).

St Andrew's Free became St Andrew's UF in 1900.

Ministers

1843 James EWING	Min. of St Andrew's. Joined FC. Father of Sir James Alfred Ewing, Principal of Edinburgh University. Died 1886 (Ewing II 161)
1886 Charles SHAW	From Kinghorn Free. Dem. 1915. Was Asst. to Dr Wilson of Free St Paul's early in his career. He played a leading part in raising monies to erect a monument at Kinghorn to Alexander III (Died 1928) (Ewing II 161, FUF 387, Po'D)

Chapelshade Free and UF

At the Disruption of 1843 the minister and almost the entire congregation of Chapelshade church *came out*. They worshipped at first in Lindsay Street chapel. Their own church, built at the corner of Bell Street and Constitution Road, was opened on 2 January 1848 when the Rev. Samuel Miller, formerly of Monifieth and then of St Matthew's, Glasgow, was the preacher.

A contemporary newspaper account stated that *the church was crowded during all the services, especially in the evening when there could not have been fewer than 1,400 persons present, and several hundreds went away who could not procure admission ... This substantial, neat, and commodious place of worship does great credit to the architect, Mr William Scott.* William Scott, the Town's architect, also designed the former National Bank, later Royal Bank, building at 71 Reform Street, and Murroes Church.

In 1876 the congregation undertook to support a proposed Church Extension mission in the north of the Town. This may have been the mission in Hospital Wynd, which became the High Kirk.

Chapelshade Free became Chapelshade UF in 1900.

Ministers

1843 William REID	Min. of Chapelshade. Joined FC. To Collessie Free 1844 (Died 1854) (Ewing II 159, PM)
1844 John MACDOUGALL	Ord. Dem. 1865 (Ewing II 159, PM)
1866 Andrew CRICHTON BA	From Edinburgh New North Free. According to his obituary *His brief ministry in Dundee was a marvellous success. Crowds flocked to hear him, and hung upon his lips. He became the most popular preacher in the town. At the seat letting in May 1867 hundreds of applicants for sittings were disappointed, numbers of whom went away in tears.* Died 1867 (KofE 92, Ewing II 159, Norrie)
1867 George LAING	From Penpont Free. Dem. 1881 (Ewing II 159)
1882 Alexander ADAMSON BD	From Cumnock Free. Ret. 1915. Sen. Min. Died 1937 (Ewing II 159, FUF 382)

Gaelic Free, Albert Square Free and UF

While Gaelic church services had been given in Edinburgh from 1709, it was much later in the eighteenth century before chapels of ease for Highland congregations were erected in the principal Lowland towns. A Gaelic chapel was opened in Castle Wynd, Edinburgh, in 1769, and a chapel in Perth was planned in 1786.

When moves to erect a chapel in Dundee began is unclear, but the church in Long Wynd, formerly Seres Wynd, was opened in 1791 under the jurisdiction of the Established Presbytery. Two of the first four ministries were very short but the Rev. Malcolm Colquhoun (1796-1819) was praised for his *faithfulness, diligence and success among his congregation.* Charles MacAlister (1822-54) was held in high regard. It is recorded that *he laboured with very great devotedness and zeal among his flock, who manifested the warmest attachment to him...He never ceased to impress upon his hearers the necessity of doing justly, loving mercy, and walking humbly.* His regular visitations allowed him to become intimately acquainted with the state and circumstances of all his parishioners.

Mr MacAlister had started a fund towards the erection of a new chapel in May 1835. There were special collections, subscriptions and lectures to raise monies, but insufficient was raised to meet the cost. However, the building work went ahead. A writer in the *Dundee Advertiser* of 23 November 1838 noted that, *It is indeed lamentable to observe the state of the Gaelic Chapel. The mason and slater work are completed, and the inside fittings are all that are required to render the church ready for the poor congregation.* Their fine new church in Tay Street was completed in the early 1840s, but the cost proved too great a financial burden.

The Town Council, which had to provide a building for St John's (Cross) congregation, made homeless by the fire of 1841, purchased the building, and worship resumed in the Long Wynd church. Mr MacAlister and almost the entire congregation *came out* at the Disruption of 1843.

The charge was reduced to a station but was granted full status again in 1854, in which year they were reported as worshipping in Lindsay Street Hall. In 1855 they bought an old Secession chapel in Meadowside and worshipped there for a time. When the Rev. Neil Taylor came to the charge in 1860 he set to work to achieve the ambition of the congregation to build a new place of worship. In 1866 they bought the whole site on part of which this chapel stood, pulled down the tenements which occupied it, and erected a new church which was opened in 1869. Henceforth the congregation was known as Albert Square Free.

The communicants roll in 1859 stood at 308, but there were many more Highland born people in Dundee who did not attend for one reason or another. Gaelic became less used in the services later in the century. The Rev. George MacPhail was required to give *not fewer than one Gaelic service once in four weeks*. All ministers up to and including Mr MacPhail were Gaelic speakers. At one time an annual service was held in French.

The Gaelic Church was active in mission work. In 1865 it was reported that they had responsibility for a mission in Seagate. In 1861 members were conducting a meeting in Scouringburn, which was taken over by Chalmers Church in 1863. There were Highland people working in the bleachfields along the Dighty Water and the Gaelic Church had stations at Claverhouse, Douglasfield, Balunie and Broughty Ferry.

David MacKenzie, architect, Dundee, designed the Albert Square building in sandstone ashlar. It has segmented arch windows with stilted architraves. To Chapel Street the door is to centre with a keystoned round headed doorcase and fanlight. The ground floor was a hall and the first and second floors the galleried church. Considerable alterations were carried out in 1923-4. A pipe organ was installed in 1906.

Albert Square Free became Albert Square UF in 1900 and Albert Square in 1929.

Ministers

1791	Mungo McFARLANE	App. Died 1794 (FES V 333)
1796	Malcolm COLQUHOUN	Ord. Died 1819 (FES V 333)
1819	Alexander MACLEOD	Ord. To Gaelic Chapel Cromarty 1821 (FES V 333)
1822	Charles MACALISTER	Min. of Gaelic EC. Joined FC. Died 1854 (Ewing II 159)
1854	John LOGAN	From Lawers Free. To Duthel Free 1859 (Ewing II 159, PM)
1860	Neil TAYLOR	Ord. He was described as *a model pastor, taking a kindly and thoughtful interest in the members of his congregation, preaching every Sabbath, in Gaelic and English thoughtful and carefully prepared sermons, notable for their clear, concise and polished diction.* To Dornoch Free 1882 (Died 1889) (Ewing II 159, PM)
1882	Dugald MATHESON	From Killearn Free. To Tarbat Free 1887 (Ewing II 159, PM)
1887	George Ross MACPHAIL MA	Ord. War service with YMCA in France 1917. Dem. 1932 (Died 1940) (Ewing II 159, FUF 380-1, FES IX 502)
1932	Robert William MATHESON MA	From Halkirk West. App. To Indian Ecclesiastical Establishment 1933 (FES IX 502)
1934	Frederick Charles ANDERSON MA	From Tarbolton Erskine C&S. To Dunino 1950 (FES IX 502)
1951	John Hemingway COMBES	Introd. From Nelson N.Z. Appt. terminated 1956 (FES IX 503, X 298)

Meadowside St Paul's

After the union of 1981 the St Paul's buildings were retained and the Meadowside buildings sold. The former Meadowside church became licensed premises. Student accommodation was erected on the site after the building was destroyed by fire and demolished. The Albert Square building, converted into halls in 1956, was sold in 1983 to TSB for conversion into banking offices. With the provision of the new hall complex at the Meadowside St Paul's location the Tay Square property was disposed of. After a period of use by Dundee Repertory Theatre the site was redeveloped for housing.

Ministers

1981 Basil Gathorne HARDY MA BD   Min. of St Paul's. Dem. 1984 (PM, YB)
1984 Maudeen I MACDOUGALL BA BD   From Livingston Ecumenical Experiment (YB)

Notes

1. Dr Robert Smith Candlish was one of the most outstanding figures in the Free Church, being its acknowledged leader from the death of Dr Thomas Chalmers in 1847 until his own death in1873. He was minister of the prestigious St George's, Edinburgh, leaving at the Disruption, of which he was one of the moving spirits, to form Free St George's (later St George's West). He was Moderator of the General Assembly in 1861 and Principal of New College, Edinburgh. He was a notable educationist, advocating that, on the passing of the School Board Act, Free Church schools should be transferred as free gifts to the Boards. His parents, both of whom came from Ayrshire, had interesting connections with Burns. Burns referred to his father, James Candlish (the surname had originally been McCandlish) in a letter as *the earliest friend except my only brother that I have on earth.* His mother, Jane Smith, was one of the Mauchline Belles immortalised in the poems, *O Leave Novels* and *The Belles of Mauchline.*

2. Sir Henry Wellwood Moncrieff, Bart. Was involved in the Disruption and was one of the most influential people in the Free Church. He was minister of Free St Cuthbert's, Edinburgh. He was appointed Joint Principal Clerk of the General Assembly in 1855, and was its Moderator in 1869.

3. James Bowman Lindsay, born at Carmyllie, was a distinguished scientist who discovered the possible uses of electricity for heating and lighting as early as 1835. He pioneered wireless telegraphy and was a noted linguist.

4. On 7 September 1838 Grace Darling and her father, the lighthouse keeper on Longstone, in the Farne Islands, rescued survivors of the wrecked Dundee vessel, *SS Forfarshire,* bound from Hull to Dundee.

5. A factor of 50 gives an approximate modern value.

6. The Caledonian Hall, Castle Street, was in the upper floor of a building used until about 1980 by George Stephen's, ironmongers.

7.   The Thistle Hall, Union Street, was incorporated into the Royal Hotel as its diningroom.

G Jamieson, *Tay Square Church Dundee – A Centenary Retrospect,* Dundee, 1932

The Story of St Paul's nd. (In brochure of stewardship campaign, 1963)

Meadowside St Paul's Church of Scotland, A Guide for Visitors, Dundee, 1998

Meadowside St Paul's Church of Scotland, Five into One, A Historical Note, Dundee, 1998

D E Stimpson and AG Robertson, *A Historical Note* (Historical notes issued on the occasion of the union of Meadowside and St Paul's congregations)

Historical notes appearing in the congregational magazine

McKean and Walker, *Dundee, An Illustrated Architectural Guide,* Edinburgh, 1993

W Norrie, *Dundee Celebrities,* Dundee, 1873

Sara Stevenson (ed.) *David Octavius Hill and Robert Adamson,* Catalogue of their Calotypes taken between 1843 and 1847 in the Collection of the Scottish National Portrait Gallery, Edinburgh, 1981

C W J Withers, *Highland Communities in Dundee and Perth 1787-1891,* Abertay Historical Society Publication No 25, Dundee, 1986

Dundee *Year Book for 1911*

Northern Warder, 30 December, 1847, 6 January 1848

The Piper o'Dundee, 22 August 1888, 14 November 1888, 27 February 1889, 21 August 1889, 8 September 1889

Letters from D E Stimpson of 9 May and 14 June 1998

DPL Sp 2/158, 5/184

DPL Lamb 172(5), 172(6)

DCC Combined Statutory and Descriptive List

DCA CH2/1364, CH2/1218/71, CH3/92, CH3/94, CH3/322, CH3/323, CH3/324, CH3/333

DCA CH3/91/1 Minutes of United Associate Presbytery of Dundee

DNB Vols. VIII and XXXVIII

MENZIESHILL

Menzieshill church is in Charleston Drive. In harled brick, it stands slightly higher than the roadway. Established as a Church Extension charge in 1962 to serve the recently built Menzieshill housing estate and the surrounding area, it was granted full status in 1968.

In December 1978, the Rev. W Strang Money, recently retired minister of The Steeple congregation, was appointed part time associate minister, a post which he held until 1984. The Rev. Jack Mitchell was ordained in June 1987 and appointed auxiliary minister, until inducted into the charge in 1989.

A Silver Jubilee service was held on 29 November 1987.

The manse is in Charleston Drive.

Ministers

1962	John McKenzie KELLET MA	Ord. To Edinburgh South Leith 1969 (FES X 303)
1969	Robert Mair DONALD LTh	Ord. Dem. 1977 (FES X 303, DNC Vol.87)
1977	Stanley A BROOK BD	Ord. To Edinburgh Holy Trinity 1987 (PM, YB)
1989	Jack MITCHELL MA BD CTh	Ind. Dem. 1996 (PM)
1996	Harry James BROWN LTh	From Benholm and Johnshaven linked with Garvock St Cyrus (PM)

DPL   Lamb 373(26,27,28)

MID CRAIGIE

Mid Craigie church is situated in Longtown Terrace, near to and very visible from Kingsway East. It is a small harled brick building set in its own grounds. The charge began as a Church Extension to serve a housing development constructed in the late 1930s under pre-war slum clearance acts. The congregation was raised to full status in 1940. It is now classed as an Urban Priority Area Charge. Messrs J B Hay, builders, Dundee, built a Hall Church in 1938 at a cost of £4,090, slightly under budget. It was originally intended that in time a church would be built, but over sixty years later the hall continues to be used for worship.

On 21 March 1975 the charge was linked with Dundee Wallacetown, under the ministry of the Rev. T J L Blair, minister at Wallacetown. This linking was severed in 1981.

In 1996 Presbytery gave its approval to the congregation's ecumenical partnership with the neighbouring St Ninian's Episcopal Church. The two congregations agreed to co-operate in a wide range of activities. In 1998 Presbytery welcomed a further report on the partnership, setting out the possibility of the uniting of resources of congregations, buildings and ministry, on the basis of the sale of the St Ninian's property and the development of the Mid Craigie building as a sanctuary and other offices. While the General Assembly of 1999 approved the union of the two charges to form the congregation of Mid Craigie and Linlathen United Church, effective from 1 January 2000, the Scottish Episcopal Church has still to give its agreement.

A 60th Anniversary Service was held on Sunday, 25 October 1998. The manse is at 96 Forfar Road.

Ministers

1939	David Webster McMURTRIE	Ord. as asst. in charge. To Glasgow Summertown 1940 (FES IX 511)
1940	Quintin GOLDER MA	Ord. probationer. To Glasgow Shearer Memorial 1943 (FES IX 511)
1943	Daniel Moncrieff McAULEY	Ord. Dem. 1948. Intro. Comrie St Kessog's 1954 (FES IX 511)
1948	James Charles PHILIP	From Latheron. To Blackridge 1954 (FES IX 511)
1955	William BULLMAN	Ord. Dem. 1973 (Died 1977) (FES X 303, YB)
1975	James Bernard WALKER MA BD	Ord. and introduced as Associate to linked charge with Dundee Wallacetown. To Galashiels Old and St Paul's 1978 (FES X 304, YB)
1979	David M DOIG BA BD	Intro. Dem. 1986 (PM, YB)
1987	Douglas J PAGE BD CPS	Ord. Dem. 1991 (PM)
1992	Colin A STRONG BSc BD	Ind. on basis of Term. Tenure (PM)

Notes from Session Clerk, March 1998
PM   1996, 1998, 1999

St ANDREW'S

St Andrew's church stands on rising ground in the Cowgate, originally being on the outskirts of the Burgh. The foundation stone was ceremonially laid on 4 June 1772 and the building completed in 1774. It was designed by Samuel Bell, architect, and probably adapted from plans of 1769 by James Craig, designer of the New Town, Edinburgh. The church is rectangular, built in rubble, perhaps originally harled, with fine stone dressings, twin Venetian windows with Ionic pilasters and swags above. There are arched stone doorways on either side of the central windows and two tiers of smaller arched windows. There is a fine tower with a classical steeple, recessed at each higher level in the James Gibb manner. Above the first stage the tower becomes octagonal, and the corners were at one time decorated by stone vases, slightly smaller than those which remain in position at the corners below. In the past a vase was smashed accidentally by a slater and the others were removed to restore symmetry. Two similar carved vases are placed on the top of the entrance gate pillars. The spire rises to 139 feet. James Ivory, Dundee, made the clock. An oval stone on the south façade is inscribed, *D.O.M.A. Pastores Presbytri Artifices Populusque, Taodunensis. A. AE. C. 1772.* [Under the auspices of God, the best and the greatest, We, the Presbyterian Ministers, the Incorporations, and the Citizens of Dundee have erected this Church, in the Year of Christ, 1772] There is a memorial on the front of the building to the Reverend Harcourt Morton Davidson, minister from 1886 to 1926, and his wife, who are buried below the pulpit.

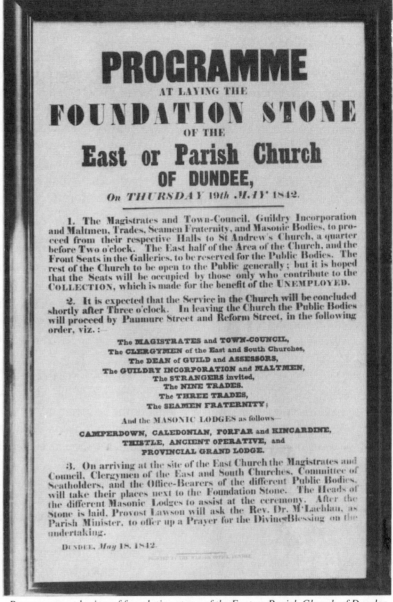

Programme at laying of foundation stone of the East or Parish Church of Dundee Thursday, 19th May 1842 following service held in St Andrew's Church

The rectangular interior has the pulpit in the middle of one of the long sides, with a semi octagonal gallery on six Doric columns round three sides facing it. The Taylor family gifted the imposing communion table in memory of Captain Norman Taylor, MC, killed in action in 1917. The brass font commemorates George Ormond, who served as beadle for over forty years until 1962.

The area near the church became the commercial heart of the Town. The historian, Charles Mackie, writing in 1836, stated, *The Cowgate is the most remarkable street for business in the town and may be with propriety termed the Exchange of Dundee.* The church and its steeple feature prominently in early paintings of the Town [James Methven's *Dundee from the River, circa* 1780, and E. Orme's *Dundee from the West* of 1803] There is a drawing of the church shown as an inset in Crawford's plan of 1777.

Thomas Pennant[1], who saw the church in the year it was completed, thought that it was *built in a style that does credit to the place, and which shews an enlargement of mind in the presbyterians, who now begin to think that the Lord may be praised in the beauty of holiness.* A modern suite of halls, connected to the church by a loggia, incorporates the former Glasite Church acquired in 1973. This octagonal building, known as the *Kail Kirk,* was completed in 1777 for the sect formed by the Rev. John Glas, formerly minister at Tealing.

In the late eighteenth century, despite pressure from the Presbytery and the Kirk Session of Dundee, the Burgh Council was unwilling to provide a fourth church to meet the needs of the expanding population. Tired of the civic procrastination, the Nine Incorporated Trades took the initiative and, with the support of the Three United Trades, a subscription list was opened. Members of the Kirk Session of Dundee and of the Trades gave some £1,400. A similar amount was raised locally, and from as far afield as London and Rotterdam. John Wesley was a contributor.

The church was thus built by the Kirk Session of Dundee, the Nine Incorporated Trades, the Three United Trades, to relieve overcrowding in the Burgh churches. The site, which had been owned by the Nine Trades, had been a builder's yard. Understandably, members of the Three United Trades carried out the building work. David Beath or Boath's estimate of £546 for the mason work was accepted; Thomas Baillie, the wright work at £745; William Law, the slater work at £115. The cost overran the estimates by £4/500. Samuel Bell, the architect, was entered as a master wright in 1762, being Boxmaster of the Wrights in 1779.

The first service was held on Sunday, 19 June 1774. The name *St Andrew's* was chosen, as in the pre Reformation church of St Mary altars supported by the ancient Crafts of Dundee stood in St Andrew's Aisle. However, for long it was popularly referred to as the *Cowgate Kirk*. For the first century of its existence the Kirk Session of Dundee and the Trades had oversight of the affairs of St Andrew's, each having the right in turn to present a minister. Originally the project had been divided into 24 shares, 9 to the Nine Incorporated Trades, 3 to the Three United Trades, and 12 to the Kirk Session. However, two of the Trades sold their shares to the Kirk Session and bickering began over the selection of a minister. Agreement was reached, with the Session and the Trades taking it in turn to nominate a minister. In 1872 the other Trades sold their rights in the church to the congregation, reserving in perpetuity their pews.

Seats were provided for the conveners of the Trades and other dignitaries in the front of the gallery, where they sat with their gold chains and other insignia of office. The coats of arms of the Crafts are emblazoned on the gallery front. The silver mace used by the Trades was the gift of the congregation, being ceremonially presented on Sunday, 2 May 1954.

William Scott, jeweller and silversmith, Dundee, who was trading in 1783, made silver communion cups.

The Trades presented stained glass windows in 1892 which were placed in the 3-light windows on either side of the pulpit. A bronze plaque below one of the windows, gifted by the trades, commemorates the service held on Sunday, 4 June 1972 to mark the bi-centenary of the founding of the Church.

The main centre panel of the east window depicts Ruth and Boaz in the cornfield, while the west window shows the Holy Family in the carpenter's shop at Nazareth. In the side lights are emblems of the different trades, as follows:

Bakers	– a sheaf of wheat on crossed peels
Shoemakers	– a cordiner's knife, half moon, ducal coronet
Glovers	– a gloved left hand back
Tailors	– a silken pavilion, striped red and white
Bonnetmakers	– an ancient bonnet
Fleshers	– implements of the trade
Hammermen	– hammer, crown imperial
Weavers	– panther with shuttle in its mouth
Dyers	– sack of wool

Above the main panel of the east window a smaller panel shows, within a circle as supporters, a woman holding a cornucopia and a griffin, while the central shield with the insignia of the Nine Trades is surmounted by the pot of lilies of Dundee.

The upper part of the main panel of the west window is also a circular device, divided into quarters, featuring the arms of Dundee and the arms of the Masons, Wrights and Slaters:

Masons	– three towers, bevel stock as chevron, pair of compasses
Wrights	– tools of the trade
Slaters	– tools of the trade

Surmounting the arms are the mottoes of Dundee, *Donum Die,* and of the Three United Trades, *Three joined in one.* The artists were Gordon and Watt, Woolmanhill, Aberdeen, and the work was carried out by Lindsay and Scott, glass merchants, Dundee.

In 1981 banners of the Nine Trades were placed on permanent display in the Church. On the west wall are those representing the Bonnetmakers, Tailors, Weavers; on the east wall the Bakers, Shoemakers, Nine Incorporated Trades.

A window on the north wall by Walter Pritchard, Edinburgh, represents *The Good Shepherd.* It was given in 1931 in memory of Joseph W and Janet A Simpson. In the west gallery a window depicts *St John the Evangelist.* Hope W Chalmers Neave placed it in memory of her husband, Bailie David Neave. The Scott window in the east gallery is the work of Mary Wood, Edinburgh, and shows Saint Andrew handling his net by the Sea of Galilee. The inscription reads, *Follow me and I will make you fishers of men.*

A window in the south west gallery was donated in 1967 by Mrs Jean Smith, wife of Robert A Smith. It is the work of Gordon Webster, Glasgow, and the theme is taken from *The Parable of the Sheep and the Goats.* Six small vignettes grouped round the central figure illustrate Christian loving kindness. Mr Webster also designed the window in memory of Nicol Skea, gifted by his mother in 1975. The central theme is *Christ's baptism,* while the upper section portrays the scene at the empty tomb. It bears the inscriptions, *He is not here: he is risen,* and *This is my beloved son.*

Mr Webster's work is furthered represented by three more windows in the gallery. A window on the south wall of the east gallery is on the theme of the Crucifixion, with a portrayal of the Last Supper in the upper semi circular part. It was gifted by Mr J Johnston Davidson in memory of his wife, Florence. It has the text, *If I be lifted up I will draw all men unto me.*

A window on the east wall of the same part of the gallery, on the theme of the Nativity, was donated by Mrs Stalker to commemorate her parents, James and Jane Gibb. The Wise Men are shown grouped round Mary and the Infant Jesus, with the angelic choir above. The superscription reads, *They saw the young Child with Mary His Mother.*

These windows were dedicated in May 1971, and a further Webster window was unveiled on 24 June 1973. This window on the north wall of the west gallery, based on the Ascension, was given by David Nicholson in memory of his wife, Jenny. It has the inscriptions, *Ascend, entreat me not* and *Unto My Father, to leave Thee.*

The window on the south wall of the west gallery was installed in 1957 by Mary Jane Davidson in memory of her mother, Georgina, and her sister, Anne. Andrew is shown introducing Simon Peter to Jesus, who calls him to be a fisher of men.

On Sunday, 30 November 1986 the congregation gifted a window in memory of the Reverend T R S Campbell, their former minister. This window, designed by Douglas Hogg, Edinburgh College of Art, takes as its theme, *The Word* centred on the Lamb of God. The Trades gave a window as a memorial to Mr Campbell on Sunday, 11 October 1987. This half moon window, designed by John Clark, shows St Andrew's Church, the old Trades Hall, and The Howff, where the Trades at one time met.

The Lesslie windows on the east and west gables were designed by James Ballantine, Edinburgh, and given by Lily Inglis Lesslie in 1929, in memory of her parents, Alexander Lesslie and Elizabeth Kermath. They bear the texts, *The Child grew and waxed strong in spirit* and *Fear not, for behold I bring you good tidings of great joy.*

The west front window, below the gallery, was erected in memory of the Carmichael family. Its inscription reads, *Suffer the little children to come unto me and forbid them not for of such is the Kingdom of Heaven.*

The east front window, below the gallery, was placed in memory of Thomas Walker, notary public, Dundee, who died in 1876. It is the work of Mayer and Company, Munich and London, and depicts the Good Shepherd finding the lost sheep.

The windows above the two south doors were gifted by Mrs Learmonth in memory of her mother, Mrs Sarah Turner, and dedicated on 22 September 1963. They were designed by A L Russell and bear the sacred monograms *IHC* and *XP.*

Bronze wall plaques commemorate those connected to the congregation who were killed in the two World Wars. There is also a bronze plaque in memory of members of the Boys Brigade who lost their lives in those wars.

St Andrew's Sessional School in William Street was organised following the settlement of the Rev. James Ewing as minister in 1837.

In 1927 the congregation acquired from the Glasites a rectangular building in close proximity to the church. This building cost £650 and was subsequently used for hall and Sunday School purposes, the upper floor being named the East Hall. Part of the property became the residence of the church officer. The Glasites had contracted in numbers and this building had been their church after they disposed of their larger octagonal property to a firm of house furnishers in 1904.

In 1975, a suite of halls was added, incorporating the former Glasite Chapel, linked to the rear of the church by a covered passageway, at a cost of £100,000. A service of dedication was held on Wednesday, 12 March 1975. The Glasite church was no longer used as a furniture store and it probably would have been demolished had this new use not been found for it. This two-storey building, erected in 1777, is octagonal in shape, white harled with a prismatic slate roof.

The steeple, which was damaged by lightning and restored in 1970, houses a carillon. This was the gift of Mr William Reid in memory of his sister, Miss Jane Spiller. Three bells dated 1773, removed from the steeple, stand on the pavement beside the entrance to the halls. The largest bell was presented by the Hon. Archibald Douglas of Douglas, and is inscribed, *Presented to the Kirk Session and Trades of Dundee for St Andrew's Church in that place, erected by them in 1773*. The second bell was presented by the Rev. Dr James Blinshall, minister of the Parish Church of Dundee. The third bell, the inscription on which is indistinct, appears to have been presented by Bailie John Jobson, Alex. Thoms, merchant, and Convener William Skirling.

In 1874 extensive alterations were undertaken, being supervised by Edward and Robertson, architects. The old sloping floor was levelled and the antiquated pews replaced. A new pulpit and platform were added and the gallery improved. The cost of the work was £2,000.

Some structural changes were made in 1892, the church reroofed, and the interior redecorated, following the installation of the stained glass windows gifted by the Trades. Major fabric repairs were carried out in 1939, when the building was repointed at a cost of £2,500, and in 1989 when the congregation required to raise £60,000 to cover the work.

In 1953 the grounds of the church were laid out as a memorial garden, funded largely by a legacy from Miss Miriam Brown. A plaque in the garden commemorates the Reverend Thomas R S Campbell, minister from 1950 to 1985.

The entrance to St Andrew's was the scene of one of the worst riots in Dundee's history. A meeting had been arranged in the church for 26 January 1841 in connection with the debate which led to the Disruption. Admission was by ticket only, but forgeries had caused the organisers to issue fresh tickets. The civil authorities anticipated trouble, and a large contingent of police, augmented by special constables, was on duty at the gates, which were locked once the church was full. A large crowd of around 5,000 remained at the entrance demanding entry. Stones were thrown, and an attempt was made to break down the gates with a battering ram. Threats were made to smash the church windows and set fire to the building. Several officers were injured. The magistrates were called, and the church meeting was terminated in the interests of public safety. The police dispersed the crowd with a baton charge. Five men were convicted of mobbing and rioting in connection with the incident, which occurred at a time of Chartist agitation and was an attempt to hi-jack the meeting.

At the Disruption of 1843 the minister, the Rev. James Ewing, and a substantial part of the congregation left to form St Andrew's Free. (See **Meadowside St Paul's**) Mr Ewing appears in the group photograph of Dundee Free Church ministers taken at Glasgow on 22 October 1843, reproduced in the catalogue of Hill and Adamson's calotypes. These photographs were used by David Octavius Hill RSA, for likenesses in his large painting entitled, *The First General Assembly of the Free Church of Scotland Signing the Act of Separation and Deed of Demission at Tanfield, Edinburgh, May, 1843*.

St Andrew's became a *quoad sacra* charge and the parish was disjoined from Dundee St Mary's on 3 March 1873.

A dinner to mark the Bicentenary was held in the Angus Hotel, Dundee, on Wednesday, 13 November 1974.

St Andrew's church is A-listed and the former Glasite Church is B-listed. The manse is at 77 Blackness Avenue.

Ministers

1775	Thomas RAITT	Ord. Elected by the Trades. To Lundie and Fowlis 1806 (FES V 337)
1807	William HAMILTON	Ord. Elected by Kirk Session of Dundee. To Strathblane 1809 (FES V 337)
1809	Alexander MACNEIL	From Braemar (Missionary). Elected by the Trades (Died 1853) (FES V 337)
1823	Gavin PARKER	Ord. (Asst.) To Union Terrace Chapel Aberdeen 1828 (Died 1845) (FES V 337)
1837	James EWING	Ord. (A&S) Elected by the Kirk Session of Dundee. Joined FC 1843 and became min. of St Andrew's Free. Father of Sir James Alfred Ewing, Principal of Edinburgh University (Died 1886)(FES V 337)
1845	James RANKEN	From Maxwelltown (A&S) To Kinnaird 1845 (FES V 337)

1846	Richard LOGAN	Formerly of Edinburgh Roxburgh Place Relief Church. Joined CofS 1845. Adm. (A&S) Died 1871 after prolonged illhealth (FES V 337, KofE 62)
1867	Robert Hope BROWN	Ord. (A&S) To Kilsyth 1871 (FES V 337)
1871	Alexander MILNE	From Hillside, Montrose. Adm. first min.of the parish in 1873. To Swinton 1878 (FES V 337)
1878	Alexander LEGGE	Ord. To Kilconquhar 1886 (FES V 337)
1886	Harcourt Morton DAVIDSON VD	Ord. Died 1926 (FES V 337)
1927	Robert Forrester Victor SCOTT	From Strathmiglo. To Glasgow Barony 1935. DD (Edinburgh 1944) (Mod. GA 1956) (FES VIII 489, IX 513)
1936	William Thomas SMELLIE OBE MA	From Rothesay High. To Pollockshields Titwood 1941 (FES IX 513)
1942	Thomas John BUNTING MA	From Glasgow St Gilbert's. Died 1950 (FES IX 513)
1950	Thomas Robertson Strathern CAMPBELL MA BD	From Aberdeen Gilcomston St Colm's. Died 1985 (FES X 305, PM)
1986	Ian Duncan PETRIE MA BD	From East Kilbride Westwood (Wyvern Feb. 1986)

Note

1. Pennant's 1772 engraving of the church, showing its harling, is reproduced in McKean and Walker's book listed in the bibliography below.

E Gauldie (ed.), *The Dundee Textile Industry 1790-1885*, Edinburgh, 1969

A C Lamb, *Dundee its Quaint and Historic Buildings,* Dundee, 1895

C McKean & D Walker, *Dundee, An Illustrated Introduction,* Edinburgh, 1984

Charles Mackie, *History of Dundee,* Dundee, 1836

A H Millar, *The First History of Dundee, 1776,*Dundee, 1923

Alison Scott, *St Andrew's Parish Church*, Dundee, n.d.

Annette M Smith, *The Nine Trades of Dundee,* (Abertay Historical Society Publication No 35) Dundee 1995

Sara Stevenson (ed.) *David Octavius Hill and Robert Adamson,* Catalogue of their Calotypes taken between 1843 and 1847 in the Collection of the Scottish National Portrait Gallery, Edinburgh, 1981

Life and Work, June 1968

The Piper O' Dundee, 14 September 1892

St Andrew's Parish Church Order of Service on Bi-Centenary of the Founding of the Church, Sunday, 4 June 1972

St Andrew's Parish Church 1774-1974, Order of Service on Bi-Centenary of the opening of the Church, Sunday, 16 June 1974

Wyvern The magazine of St Andrew's Parish Church, May 1970, July, 1974, August 1984, February 1986

DCA   CH2/1272

DCC   Combined Statutory and Descriptive List

DPL   Sp. 2/52, 9/11, 11/54, 14/205, 20/41

DPL   DNC Vol. 102

DPL   Lamb 408(33)

St DAVID'S NORTH

St David's North church stands at 273 Strathmore Avenue in the middle of the Lawton local authority housing estate developed in the 1920s.

The congregation has had a chequered existence, originating in the Disruption of 1843 when the Rev. George Lewis, minister of St David's, one of the Burgh Churches, and a large proportion of the congregation *came out.* They worshipped in an old mill, *in the lower flat of which we found refuge,* until 18 April 1844, when a church in Ward Road was ready for occupation. This church, which was seated for 1,000, cost £1,500, and was opened free of debt. On its front there was a stone medallion with the year *1843* and two blocks with carved *Burning Bushes.* When the church was sold it was decided these blocks should be preserved.

Mr Lewis[1], who was in the charge from 1843 until 1849, started a mission in Henderson's Wynd. The next minister was in poor health in 1864 and applied for assistance but an assistant and successor was not appointed until 1870. During this time the membership declined. In the 1860s St David's ran a mission in Brown Street School. Sunday School classes were conducted by young people of the congregation after the afternoon services. In 1873 a manse was erected in Dudhope Terrace, the cost of £1,400 being met by Mrs Curr, Rosebank, Stannergate.

The congregation was divided over the union of 1900, a small majority in 1905 electing to adhere to the remnant Free Church, *the Wee Frees,* which did not happen. In 1906 there was a proposal to sell the church which, under the Allocation Order, had become vested in the United Free Church. According to the Deacons' Court minutes, the Commission of General Assembly granted permission to sell the church on 28 November 1906. In 1907 it was indicated to Presbytery that the congregation wished to sell the church and manse and remove to *a more suitable locality,* the Blackness Road area being suggested. A Presbytery report of 28 March 1907 mentioned *a site in Rockfield Crescent or a site in the western part of Blackness Road.* The report was not in favour, the move being opposed by the kirk sessions of McCheyne, St Peter's and Martyrs, while Ryehill was against the Rockfield location. The church property was sold for £3,650 to Thomas Shaw, with conditional entry on 1 January 1908. The main condition seems to have been that the church would be restored to the congregation on two month's notice. The congregation now worshipped in the hall of the YMCA. There were prolonged difficulties with Presbytery and the case was referred to the Commission of Assembly who decided that St David's and School Wynd congregations should be united on 17 January 1909. This decision did not satisfy Presbytery, but having been instructed by the General Assembly to unite the charges, that court determined the union should be effective on 29 June 1909. The School Wynd Church was to be used, with the two ministers as colleagues. However, School Wynd congregation refused to hand over their property to the new board of management. It was reported to Presbytery on 15 November 1909, that the minister and Deacons' Court of St David's had leased a piece of ground in Blackness. The union was dissolved by Presbytery on 15 November 1910. St David's congregation accepted the offer of Willison congregation to worship with them temporarily in their Barrack Street church.

A new iron structure was erected in 1913 at the corner of Blackness Road and Seymour Street at a cost of £600. The congregation was renamed St David's in the West UF, this name first appearing in the minutes in April 1913. In February 1915, Presbytery approved plans for a new church to seat over 700 at Seymour Street. The estimated cost of the whole scheme was £6,500. However, wartime building difficulties resulted in the project being postponed in August of that year. The enterprise was revived in 1919 with a sketch of the proposed new church, designed by Todd and Miller, architects, appearing in the press on 11 April. On this occasion Presbytery refused approval.

In 1929 the United Free Church, in agreement with the Church of Scotland, was allocated a site in the new Lawton housing development. Following the decision to transport the congregation to the north of the city, the iron building was removed in 1929 to Wetherby Place, off Strathmore Avenue, and used for worship. It was nicknamed the *Tin Kirkie.* The foundation stone of a new stone church was laid on 14 September 1929 by the Very Reverend Dr J Harry Miller, former Moderator of the United Free Church General Assembly. The dedication service of the completed building was held on 10 September 1930, when the preacher was the Right Reverend Dr A N Bogle, Moderator of the General Assembly. The temporary church was used thereafter as a hall. The cost of this work was met from the sale of the properties of St David's in the West (£2,805) and School Wynd Church (£4,547), that congregation having been dissolved in 1926. The congregation was restored to full status in 1934.

In 1955 the former *Tin Kirkie* was purchased by Murroes Boy Scouts, and dismantled for removal to Murroes. It was later used as office premises by the haulage firm of Scott (Claverhouse) Ltd. A new church hall was opened on 6 May 1956. At this period the congregation had increased in membership to around 1,000. Substantial remedial work to the church was carried out in 1958 and 1966.

A carved wooden plaque commemorates those men of the congregation killed in the Second World War. In 1975 Wester Coates congregation, Edinburgh, recently dissolved, gifted a two manual organ to replace the Hammond electronic organ. This congregation also gave handsome chancel furniture. Three memorial stained glass windows were installed in the south windows of the chancel in September 1977. The central window has as its theme, *Christ, the Good Shepherd.* The side windows are in memory of John and Agnes McWalter and Martin and Mary McMillan. In 1979 communion silver and communion chairs were presented to the congregation on behalf of the recently dissolved congregation of Bonnethill. The gifts were rededicated at a service held on Sunday, 17 June 1979, when the Rev. Dennis Keillor, retired minister of Bonnethill, handed over the silver and chairs.

St David's Free became St David's UF in 1900, St David's in the West UF in 1915, St David's UF in 1929 on the removal to Strathmore Avenue, and St David's North on the union of 1929.

Following the move to the north of the City, the minister resided at 2 Foster Road, Downfield, until a manse was acquired at 38 Albany Terrace, *circa* 1934. This was disposed of around 1990 when the present manse was purchased at 2 Anstruther Road.

St David's North was linked with **Albany Butterburn** on 1 June 1986, under the ministry of the Rev. Gideon G Scott.

Ministers

1843	George LEWIS BA	Min. of St David's. Joined FC. To Ormiston Free 1849. Author of *Scotland, a half educated Nation* 1834, and a series of pamphlets dealing with the social conditions of his parish (Died 1879) (Ewing II 161, Lamb)
1849	Charles NAIRN	Ind. Ret.1869. Died 1873 (Ewing II 161, Lamb, PM)
1870	John DUNLOP DD	Ord. C&S. To Chair of Theology at Dunedin 1887 (Ewing II 161, Lamb, PM)
1887	Angus Cameron MACKENZIE	From Glasgow Bridgeton Free. Died 1923 (Ewing II 161, FUF 388)
1924	Albert Edward FIRTH	Adm. from Baptist Church as ord. missionary. To Colmonell 1927 (FUF 388)
1929	Hugh McKinven AGNEW MA	From Old Cumnock West. To East London St George's South Africa 1933 (FES IX 514)
1934	Robert Clephane MACANNA MA	From Innerleven. Dem. on appt. as Organising Secretary to Jewish Mission Committee 1937 (FES IX 514)
1937	Isaac Henry CLYDE BA	From Dalmuir Ross Mem. Died 1946 (FES IX 514)
1947	John TENNANT MA BD	From Finzean. To Foveran 1952 (FES IX 514)
1957	Francis Sinclair BANKS MA BD	From Kilmarnock Princes Street. To Strachur and Strachlachlan 1965 (Died 1978) (FES IX 514, X 305, YB)
1966	Thomas Mathieson McWILLIAM MA BD	Ind. To East Kilbride Greenhills 1972 (FES X 305)
1973	Gideon George SCOTT MA BD ThM	From Edinburgh Wester Coates (FES X 305)

Note

1. Mr Lewis's photograph is reproduced in the catalogue of Hill and Adamson's calotypes. Some of these photographs were used by Hill for likenesses in his large painting entitled, *The First General Assembly of the Free Church of Scotland Signing the Act of Separation and Deed of Demission at Tanfield, Edinburgh, May, 1843.*

C C Barnett, *The Seven Churches of the Hilltown,* n.d.

Thomas Brown, *Annals of the Disruption,* Edinburgh, 1893

Margaret Fraser, *St David's North Parish Church,* Dundee, 1980 (Booklet to mark the 50th anniversary of the church in 1980 in DCA GD/X100/5)

Sara Stevenson (ed.) *David Octavius Hill and Robert Adamson,* Catalogue of their Calotypes taken between 1843 and 1847 in the Collection of the Scottish National Portrait Gallery, Edinburgh, 1981

DPL Lamb 172(1)

DYB 1909

DCA CH3/91/18, CH3/580/9

THE STEEPLE

The Steeple church forms part of the City Churches complex in Nethergate, Dundee, being situated between St Mary's Tower (The Old Steeple) and The Slessor Centre, formerly Old St Paul's and St David's Church. On 3 July 1786 the Town Council minutes recorded their decision to study the feasibility of building a church *in the Kirk Yard and adjoining the present churches.*

The church was built in 1787 to the design of Samuel Bell, under the supervision of Bailie A Thoms, on the site of the nave of the medieval church of St Mary, ruinous since being destroyed by the English in 1548. The opening service was held on Sunday, 17 May 1789. It is a large rectangular plan Gothic building in ashlar. The south elevation has 4 unbuttressed bays of Y-traceried pointed arch windows. There is a continuous sill course. The north elevation has 5 bays and a central pointed arch door beneath a Y-traceried window. Originally, the pulpit was on the long south wall, but during alterations in 1963 it was relocated on the east wall. A description of the interior in 1888 stated, *The Steeple Kirk is at best but a big room with a pulpit and a gallery in it. The gallery runs in horseshoe fashion round the northern, eastern and western walls. The pulpit is placed between the southern windows and a platform for choir and harmonium is slightly raised from the floor in front of the pulpit.* [*Piper O'Dundee,* 4 July 1888]

Around 1890 an approach was made to the Council to provide a proper session house and vestry. The session met then in an inadequate room in the ground floor of St Mary's Tower. After some reluctance on the part of the civic authorities, this accommodation was provided a few years later in a free standing building to the north of the Tower, with a vestry being built on to the north wall of the church. In the 1950s external fabric repairs were carried out to the three churches then forming the City Churches. This work was completed in 1958. In the 1960s the Town Council authorised the redevelopment of the old Overgate and Nethergate area around the City Churches. The Steeple halls and session house, which were separate from the church, were demolished at this time. The high perimeter wall was also removed. Halls were constructed within the church building at the east end, the east and north galleries removed, and the pulpit relocated on the east wall. A new suspended ceiling was put in place.

Following the union of 1978, when the Steeple building was selected as the place of worship, the adjacent former Old St Paul's church was converted into the Mary Slessor Centre with its focus on Christian mission and service in the City Centre. This work was shared with the congregation of Meadowside St Paul's. After the withdrawal of that congregation, the project continued under the supervision of The Steeple. In 1997 this work included a daily café service aimed at befriending lonely and bereaved people. The sports centre provided a base for a range of community activities:- keep fit, line dancing, Scottish country dancing. Accommodation was provided for specialised services:- Prison Fellowship, Dundee Women and Children's Group (under the auspices of the Church of Scotland's Board of Social Responsibility). A Mary Slessor Exhibition was mounted in the Centre.

Substantial work was carried out in phases on The Steeple Church building and the Mary Slessor Centre, in connection with the Dundee City Churches Restoration Project. This was established after a report was prepared in 1989 by Simpson and Brown, architects, who had thoroughly surveyed the whole building, including St Mary's Tower and St Mary's Church. The third and final phase of the work was completed in 1996.

In 1911 a new communion table was presented by the Woman's Guild. In the 1920s gifts to the sanctuary included an oak baptismal font, carved lectern and communion chair. Around 1970 the Woman's Guild gifted two chancel chairs to match eight elders' chairs originally from St Enoch's.

For the first 133 years of the congregation ministers had lived in rented accommodation, but in 1922 Ava Lodge, 69 Magdalen Yard Road, was purchased for a manse at a cost of £1,425. This manse was sold in 1946.

A marble war memorial was erected in 1920. The members who lost their lives in the Second World War were commemorated by another marble plaque in 1946. A hearing aid system was also installed as a war memorial.

An organ was installed in 1912 at a cost of almost £1,000, met by congregational fund-raising, with a substantial donation by Andrew Carnegie, the philanthropist. This organ was replaced by a new instrument in the west gallery during the reconstruction completed in 1964.

A mission was conducted in the Greenmarket for some years in the nineteenth century, then moved to Gellatly Street, but discontinued due to financial problems in 1893.

A special service held in the church on Sunday, 4 November 1883 commemorated the 400th anniversary of the birth of the Reformer, Martin Luther. The service, conducted partly in English by the minister of

St Clement's (Steeple), and partly in German by the pastor of the German Mission in Dundee, was crowded, with hundreds failing to gain admission. To mark the bi-centenary of the building a number of special events were held over the period March to June 1989.

The Steeple building is A-listed. The manse is at 128 Arbroath Road.

The Steeple was formed by the union of *The Steeple* and *Old St Paul's and St David's and Wishart Memorial* on 12 October 1978.

The congregation of *The Steeple* in 1978 had been formed by the union of *St Clement's (Steeple)* and *St Enoch's* on 11 June 1963.

The Steeple Church was the name given to the new Fifth Charge of Dundee, worshipping in the building erected on the site of the nave of the medieval St Mary's Church and opened on 16 May 1789. As a collegiate church, The Steeple Church was under the administration of the General Kirk Session of Dundee. The parish of St Clement's was disjoined from St Mary's by the Court of Teinds on 3 December 1834 and **The Steeple Church** renamed **St Clement's (Steeple) Church.** The medieval church which was sited near the present City Square was dedicated to Saint Clement. The martyred Saint Clement appears on the reverse of the Burgh Seal, indicating the importance of this saint to medieval Dundee.

Ministers

1789 John ANDERSON	Adm. To Third Charge 1803 (FES V 322)
1805 Archibald McLACHLAN	From Greenock Chapel of Ease. To Third Charge 1806 (FES V 322)
1806 James THOMSON MA	From Newark Chapel Port Glasgow. Pres. by Town Council to joint charges of Steeple and The Cross. On death in 1836 of Dr Peters of The Cross appointed to The Steeple exclusively. Died 1857. Prominent in civic affairs, chiefly instrumental in procuring Royal Charter under which Infirmary and the Asylum were incorporated. He was for a period Editor of *Dundee Courier.* He appears in Harry Harwood's sketch, *The Executive.* (FES V 323)
1858 James DODDS	From Montrose Melville. To Glasgow St Stephen's 1860 (FES V 323)
1861 Robert SMITH	From Crail (Asst.) Dem. 1868 (Died 1886) (FES V 323)
1864 James MACKAY	Ord. Adm. to full charge 1868. To Brechin First Charge 1875 (FES V 323)
1876 Charles Richardson WHITE	From Glasgow Chalmers. Died 1880 (FES V 323)
1880 John TROUP	From Stoneywood. Dem. 1884 (Died 1886) (FES V 323)
1885 James Edward HOUSTON MA	Ord. To Cambuslang 1892 (FES V 323)
1894 James Muirhead BENSON MA BD	Ord. Dem. 1922 (Died 1925) (FES V 323, VIII 486)
1922 David Eastham AUTY BA BD	Ord. To Castle Douglas 1928 (FES V 323, VIII 486)
1928 John SHEDDEN	From Dalmellington. To Edinburgh Trinity 1932 (Died 1947) (FES VIII 486, IX 513)
1932 William Miln LOCKE MA	From Monifieth Panmure. To Edinkillie 1962 (Died 1962) (FES IX 513, X 305)

The Steeple

After the union of 1963 the St Clement's (Steeple) building was selected as the place of worship and was reconstructed to allow for halls and a vestry. St Enoch's church was used for a year for the services during the reconstruction work. In 1964 it was demolished and the site remained empty for many years until the Bank of Scotland built a new area office in 1996. The former manse of St Enoch's was sold and a new manse purchased at 342 Blackness Road, partly funded from the St Clement's (Steeple) manse fund.

Minister

1963 Walter Strang MONEY	From Saltcoats Landsborough. Dem. 1978 (Died 1989) (FES X 306, YB)

St Enoch's

St Enoch's had its origins in a station of the Free Church set up on 5 February 1865 under the ministry of William Angus Knight. The original adherents had formerly belonged to Free St John's, where Mr Knight had been assistant minister, but had left due to a disagreement. The group had unsuccessfully supported the appointment of Mr Knight as colleague and successor to the Rev. Alexander O Laird of St John's. A substantial number from Dudhope Free joined them. Initially, they worshipped in the Thistle Hall, Union Street, and Blackscroft Mission District was assigned to them. (The Thistle Hall was later incorporated in the Royal Hotel as the dining room.) The charge was sanctioned in 1866 and a temporary church built in Long Wynd at a cost of £656, being opened on 10 June of that year. The temporary building was erected on the north part of a large site fronting onto Nethergate. Although the site had been purchased, there was a lease with four years to run on part of it. Their permanent building was opened on Sunday, 4 January 1874, the foundation stone of the pulpit having been laid by Provost James Cox, Dundee, on 1 December 1873.

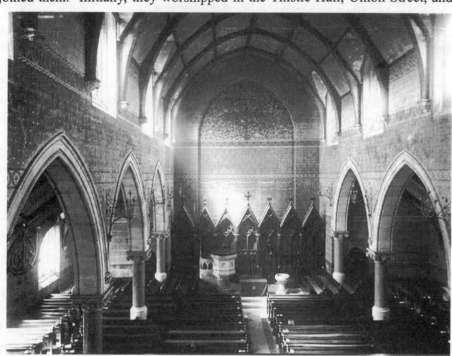

Interior of St Enoch's, Nethergate

The new church in the early decorated design was described as *good fifteenth century work* with a nave with two aisles, divided by arcades of three bays, with polished Peterhead granite shafts and carved capitals. On the south façade were two square towers with pinnacles 100 feet high and a central main door. The architects were Edward and Robertson, Dundee. The church cost £8,000 and was seated for 840. Shops flanked the front of the church.

Mr Knight was described as *academically gifted, independently minded and a very popular young minister.* He set up the St Enoch's Institute in order to *consider and discuss questions of Philosophy, Literature and Science.* The Institute met on Mondays from September until May. On the first Monday a lecture was given by the president, on the second an essay was read by a member, on the third a question was debated, and on the fourth a discussion was introduced by an appointed member.

Mr Knight preached in the Unitarian Chapel and published a paper on prayer which some of his co-presbyters deemed heretical. When the issue was brought before Presbytery Mr Knight left the Free Church and he and his congregation, who were very much attached to him, were admitted to the Church of Scotland by the General Assembly on 1 June 1874.

Ministers

1866	William Angus KNIGHT	Ord. min. of St Enoch's Free. Adm. to CofS 1874; first min. of par. 13 March 1876. Dem. 6 Dec. 1876 on appt. to Chair of Moral Philosophy, University of St Andrews. (LLD Glasgow 1879) Leading authority on and editor of the poet Wordsworth (Died 1916) (FES V 338, Ewing II 161)
1877	Hugh George WATT MA BD	Ord. DD (Glasgow 1897) Died 1922 (FES V 339)
1923	William Young COLQUHON MA	From Ellon. Died 1928 (FES V 339, VIII 489)
1928	John Henderson Seaforth BURLEIGH BD BLitt	From Fyvie. Dem. 1931 on appt. to Chair of Ecclesiastical History, Univ. of Edinburgh. Author of *A Church History of Scotland* (DD Aberdeen 1938) (Mod. GA 1960) (FES VIII 489)

1932	Andrew Neville DAVIDSON MA	From Aberdeen St Mary's. To Glasgow Cathedral 1935 (Mod. GA 1962) (Died 1976) (FES IX 514, YB)
1935	Ronald Miller Boyd SCOTT	From Auchterarder St Andrew's. To Kettins 1959 (FES IX 514, X 305)
1960	George HUDSON	From Sydney. To Tannadice with Oathlaw 1962 (DNC Vol. 63)

Old St Paul's and St David's and Wishart Memorial *was formed by the union on 15 October 1975 of* **Old St Paul's and St David's** *and* **Wishart Memorial.**
The congregation of **Old St Paul's and St David's,** *as it was in 1975, was formed by the union on 28 May 1947 of* **Old St Paul's** *and* **St David's.**

St Paul's, later Old St Paul's

The congregation of St Paul's had its origins in the Third Charge of Dundee which, from 1609, occupied part of St Mary's Church. St Paul's parish was disjoined from St Mary's on 3 December 1834. Following the union of 1929 the name was changed to Old St Paul's.

After the Reformation a collegiate ministry was established for the Parish of Dundee. St Mary's became the First Charge with the South Church the Second Charge from 1590. The south transept of the original pre-Reformation church of St Mary's was rebuilt in that year for its use. In 1609 the Third Charge was set up, also using the South Church. The two charges in the South Church were collegiate with that of St Mary's, known also as the East Church, until 1848 when they were separated and one suppressed.

The building called the South Church was destroyed by fire in 1645. In 1651 General Monck stabled his horses in the ruins, but eventually the South Church was restored. In 1836 the church was referred to as Greyfriars Church. The fire of 2 January 1841 again destroyed the South Church, along with the East and Cross Churches, and the Town Council as heritors paid for temporary accommodation for the South and Cross congregations until Martinmas 1843. The Kirk Session of Dundee petitioned Presbytery to take up the case with the Council. The churches had been insured for £1,000 each and the claim monies had been paid to the Council. A report on the state of the damaged buildings showed that reinstatement would be more expensive than rebuilding. A deliverance of Presbytery on 7 May 1845 stated it would be *more prudent to build new churches than repair the old walls.* It was decided that the Cross Church, which had occupied the north transept, should not be rebuilt, but that another site should be found. In 1847 the rebuilt South Church was opened under the name, St Paul's (South) Church.

Bailie John Fithie, father of the Rev. James Fithie, minister of Mains, gave a silver salver in 1665 which was used in the South Church. It measures 19" across and has a coat of arms and the inscription, *Johanes Fitheus in Amoris Tessaram Ecclesiae Taodunensi. Ad Sacrum Caenam Celebrandum Vas Hoc Argentum. Dono Dedit 1665.* It has the mark of Thomas Lyndsay, silversmith, Dundee. Three silver cups of the South Church bear the inscription, *Ex dono Jacobi Smith, Mercatoris* but no date. They have the mark of Robert Gairdyne, silversmith in Dundee in 1683. They were probably given by James Smith who was harbourmaster in 1696. Another cup is inscribed, *Gul. Guild S.S. Theol. Dr Ecclesiae Taodunensi Me Dono Dedit.* Dr William Guild, principal of King's College, Aberdeen, may have given it probably shortly after 1619.

The Second Charge – South Church

Ministers

1588	James ROBERTSON	Adm. Pres. to vicarage by James VI 21 May 1596. Signed Protestation for the Liberties of the Kirk 27 June 1617. Died *ca.* 1623 (FES V 319)
1624	John DUNCANSON MA	Elected by Town Council and Lord Commissioners of the Kirk. Died after 1 Sept. 1651 (FES V 319)
1658	George MARTIN MA	Adm. Son of Principal Martin of St Salvator's, St Andrews. Died 1660 (FES V 319)
1661	Alexander MYLNE	From Longforgan. Died 1665 (FES V 319)
1667	John GUTHRIE MA	From Arbirlot. Two of his sons were merchants in Stockholm. Grandfather of James Guthrie who returned from Sweden and acquired lands of Craigie in 1728. Died 1685 (FES V 319-20)

1686 Robert NORIE MA	From Dunfermline. Deprived by Privy Council 29 Aug. 1689 for not reading the Proclamation of the Estates. Dep. 26 Dec. 1716 for disloyalty. He was prosecuted before the Lords of Justiciary 29 July 1717 for intruding into parish churches, leasing making, and praying for the Chevalier, but the charge was deserted. Consecrated a Bishop of the Nonjurant Church at Edinburgh in 1724 and had district of Brechin assigned to him (Died 1727) (FES V 320)
1690 George ANDERSON MA	Adm. before 2 Nov. 1690. To Logie 29 Dec. 1690 (FES V 320)
1691 John SPALDING MA	From Kirkcudbright. Died before 29 March 1699 (FES V 320)
1700 John DALGLEISH MA	From Roxburgh. Died after 1 Nov. 1715 (FES V 320)
1716 John WILLISON[1]	From First Charge, Brechin. One of the most eminent evangelical clergymen of his day. Died 1750 (FES V 320-1)
1751 Gershom CARMICHAEL MA	From Monimail. Died 1761 (FES V 322)
1763 Alexander FERRIER MA	From Oxnam. Died 1764 (FES V 322)
1765 William BISSET MA	From Drumblade. Died 1773 (FES V 322)
1774 John SNODGRASS MA	From Norrieston Chapel. To Middle Church Paisley 1781 (FES V 322)
1782 David DAVIDSON	From Kippen. DD(Marischal 1810) He was reputedly the most popular preacher in Dundee of his time. *On sacramental occasions, he very often preached in the open air in the romantic Den of Mains, and at these time large numbers of persons flocked to hear him from Dundee.* Died 1825 (FES V 322, Norrie)
1826 Charles ADIE	From Tealing. Pres. by Town Council. DD (1833) To Dundee St Mary's 1848 (FES V 322)

The Third Charge – St Paul's

	Ministers
1611 William WEDDERBURN MA	From Pittenweem. Died 1616 (FES V 330)
1617 Colin CAMPBELL MA	From Kettins. Died 1638 (FES V 330)
1641 John ROBERTSON MA	From Auchterhouse. Was taken prisoner at the siege of Dundee, 1651, detained in London until 1653, and after returning to Dundee confined in prison. Died 1662 (FES V 331)
1662 William RAIT	From Principalship of King's College, Aberdeen. Died 1679 (FES V 331)
1682 Robert RAIT MA	Pres. by Town Council. Son of preceding. Deprived by Privy Council 1689 for not reading the Proclamation of the Estates. With Robert Norie, formerly of the Second Charge, formed their followers into an Episcopal congregation, worshipping from 1704 in Seagate Chapel (Died 1704) (FES V 331)
1691 William MITCHELL	From Leslie. Died 1712 (FES V 331)
1713 Robert KINLOCH MA	Ord. To Edinburgh High Kirk 1728 (Mod. GA 1747) (Died 1756) (FES I 67, V 331, KofE 50)
1729 James MONRO	From Kettle. Died 1744 (FES V 331)
1745 John GELLATLY	From Forgan. Died 1759 (FES V 331)
1759 James BALLINGALL	From Collessie. DD (Marischal Aberdeen 1762) (FES V 332)
1764 James BLINSHALL MA	From English Church Amsterdam. DD (Marischal Aberdeen 1762) Chaplain to George III 1795. Died 1803. In remembrance for his services to Thomas Guthrie's fund for orphans Blinshall Street was named for him (FES V 332)
1803 John ANDERSON	From Steeple Church. Died 1806 (FES V 332)

1806	Archibald McLACHLAN	From Steeple Church. To First Charge 1808. DD (Marischal Aberdeen 1808) (Died 1848) (FES V 332)
1808	Patrick MACVICAR	From Cross Church. DD (St Andrews 1827) Died 1842 (FES V 332)
1836	David ARNOT	Ord. A&S. To Edinburgh High 1843. Painter, sculptor and musician. DD 1843 (Died 1877) FES I 62, V 332, KofE 51)
1845	John TULLOCH	Ord. To Kettins 1849 (FES V 332)
1850	Andrew TAYLOR	Ord. DD(St Andrews 1868) Died 1873(FES V 332)
1874	Thomas MARTIN MA	From Rothesay New. To Lauder 1876 (FES V 333)
1877	James Edgar HILL MA BD	From Burntisland. To St Andrew's Montreal 1882 (DD Edinburgh 1899) (Died 1911) (FES V 333)
1883	William SMITH	From Collieston. Died 1897 (FES V 333)
1897	James Boath WOOD MA BD	From Buckie. Dem. 1947 (Died 1952) (FES V 333, IX 512)

St David's

Due to the expansion of the town, the parish of St David's was erected by the Commissioners of Teinds on 18 June 1823. The Town Council purchased a chapel in North Tay Street, which had been built in 1800 by the Haldaneites who called it the Tabernacle. About seventy subscribers agreed on 6 February 1822 to pay the Council the sum of £260 towards the cost of the purchase. According to the Burgh accounts, the sums received towards the purchase and fitting out of the building were £400 from the Kirk Session of Dundee and £305 from *Sundry inhabitants of Dundee*. Payments to tradesmen for the alterations amounted to £418. The overall cost to the Town of the new church seems to have been substantial for, at November 1841, the sum still outstanding was £1,325, a considerable amount at the time. The income which the Burgh received from St David's, mainly from seat rents, was significant, almost £1,000 in the seven years to Michaelmas, 1829.

It was a large rectangular building. Large-scale alterations were carried out with a gallery added, probably under the direction of David Neave, town architect in 1823. The church was completely renovated in 1883. The opportunity was taken then to replace the uncomfortable box pews, sitting in which had been likened to *being placed in a pillory*. [Lamb 408(23)] This reduced the capacity from 1,600 to 1,400. Additional windows to East Henderson's Wynd were inserted and a new platform was provided, with additional accommodation for the choir. The work cost £1,500, of which £1,000 was met by the Town Council. There is a record of boundaries and upset prices of burying places in the crypt being agreed in 1825, but whether these were ever sold is not known. An organ was installed in November 1898 at a cost of almost £500.

The minister and most of the congregation *came out* at the Disruption of 1843 with the collection on the following Sunday being recorded as six pence. Nevertheless, the congregation grew in the years after the secession and by 1859 it was stated to be the largest in the Town. The membership in 1898 was given as 1,750 and as 2,341 in 1913. Membership fell in the period after the First World War, due in part to the problems of being a city centre charge. However, in 1938 the membership was claimed as 1,368, with 83% communicating.

St David's ran a sessional school from the 1830s. In 1839 there were ten Sabbath schools throughout its parish. Adult education was also undertaken, there being a church subscription library in 1840 with a stock of 1,200 volumes. The Sessional school building was sold for £650 in 1892 to fund the construction of a hall in Blinshall Street to serve as a mission station.

A bazaar held in the Kinnaird Hall in 1881 raised most of the sum of £1,500 required to purchase a manse at Albany Terrace.

Ministers

1823	David MURRAY	From Dysart Second Charge. Pres. by Town Council. To Dysart First Charge 1829 (FES V 326)
1829	George TOD	From Tealing. Pres. by Town Council. Edited *Montrose Chronicle* from 1819 to 1822, and subsequently Editor of *Dundee Courier*. Died 1838 (FES V 326)
1839	George LEWIS	From Perth Middle. Pres. by Town Council. Joined FC in 1843. Min. of Free St David's. Author of pamphlets on social conditions in his parish. (Died 1879) (FES V 326-7)
1844	John Lindsay ADAMSON	From Thornton. Pres. by Presb. Died 1852 (FES V 327)
1852	Peter MYLES BA	Ord. To Monifieth 1853 (FES V 327)

1853	Robert Stevenson HORNE	Ord. To Slamannan 1856. His son, Sir Robert Horne, was Chancellor of the Exchequer 1921-2 (FES V 327)
1856	Adam Inch RITCHIE	Pres. by Magistrates of Dundee. To Fettercairn 1858 (FES V 327)
1859	John HART	Pres. by Magistrates of Dundee. Known as the *Dundee Spurgeon*. To Aberlady 1878 (FES V 327)
1878	Robert Sharp WARREN	From Stranraer. Died at Moffat 1919 (FES V 327)
1909	George Murdoch MACLEAN	From Duncansburgh A&S. Sen. Coll. 1938. Dem. 1947 (Died 1948) (FES V 328, VIII 487, IX 514)
1938	Karl Stewart Guthrie GREENLAW MA	From Kinloss and Findhorn C&S. Min of united charge 1947 (FES IX 512)

Old St Paul's and St David's

After the union of 1947 the Old St Paul's buildings were retained and renovated, a gallery erected, the church reseated, and the St David's organ rebuilt and installed. Stained glass windows from St David's were placed in the wall behind the new gallery. A window in memory of John Cuthbert, church officer of St David's, was placed in the vestry. St David's Church was sold in 1948 and was thereafter put to a number of uses. For many years it was the JM Ballroom and latterly a night-club called the Coconut Grove, but the building was destroyed by fire in 1995.

In 1950 memorial stained glass was fitted in the north window, gifted by a member in memory of his parents. This window has the figure of Christ, the source and fount of all life and power, as its central motif. He holds the chalice of suffering and sacrifice, while from His feet flow the four rivers of Paradise. He faces two angelic figures, one holding a burning lamp while the other releases a dove, symbolising spiritual illumination and the freedom of the soul. As a background to this group and extending behind the figure of Christ is the Cross of Redemption surmounted by the Crown of Thorns. Above the head of Christ is a Crown of Life, the reward of the faithful.

On either side of the central group are the figures of Saint Paul and Saint John bearing a celestial globe emblazoned with the Cross. Below the figure of Saint Paul is the text, *Stand fast in the faith, quit you like men.* At the feet of Saint John is the text, *The darkness is past, the true light now shineth.*

In the extreme left and right hand panels are angels representing the Christian virtues of Praise, Prayer, Humility and Justice guided by Truth. Entwined throughout the upper half of the design and reappearing in the tracery are the *True Vine* and the *Tree of Life.* Little cherubim in the tracery sing and rejoice, symbolising the freedom and happiness derived from a life of Christian inspiration. Above the cherubim are symbols of Faith (Cross), Hope (Anchor) and Love (Flaming Heart).

The base of the window has Moses bearing the rod and holding aloft the tablets of stone. The burning bush is also depicted. On the right Saint Columba represents the bringing of the Word to Scotland. A little ship symbolises the establishment of the Church. The Pelican and the Pascal Lamb are shown and are symbols of self-sacrifice, referring to the life and work of Christ.

Ministers

1947	Karl Stewart Guthrie GREENLAW MA	Min of St David's. CF1939-40. Dem. 1958 to take up appt. as Asst. Sec. and Deputy of the Church and Ministry Dept. (FES IX 512, X 304)
1959	Robert ARTHUR MA	From Glasgow Rutherford. Dem. 1975 (Died 1990) (FES X 304, YB)

Wishart Memorial

On 21 February 1837 Cupar Presbytery of the United Associate Secession Church was petitioned by a number of members of the three United Secession churches in Dundee (School Wynd, Bell Street and Tay Square) with a view to forming a fourth congregation to serve the east end of the town. A group of seceders had met for worship for the first time on the previous Sunday in the old Roman Catholic chapel in Baltic Street, let to them for £40 per annum. The congregation was formed by authority of the Synod on 30 August 1837. In November the managers reported a membership of between 70 and 80, four of whom were elders, and an average attendance of 250. Shortly after the first minister was inducted, the Roman Catholic chapel was given up in favour of the Caledonian Hall, Castle Street. The charge is referred to in the United Associate Presbytery of Dundee minutes as the *Fourth Congregation, Dundee.*

In June 1844 the first minister, Samuel Spence, advised his congregation that he was leaving the United Secession Church and applying for admission to the *Free Protesting Church of Scotland* (The Free Church). According to the Presbytery minutes the congregation *counted the step Mr Spence had taken as having a beneficial tendency rather than otherwise in reference to their prosperity.*

Wishart Church, Cowgate, with sittings for 736, was built in 1841. It was a U-plan galleried church with cast iron Corinthian columns and anthemion decoration. There were shops at street level, underneath the church. One of the shops was let as a public house and the building became known as *Heaven and Hell.*

The most celebrated member of the congregation was Mary Slessor, a Dundee mill worker, who was a missionary in Calabar, West Africa, from 1876 until her death in 1915. The family of the Rev. D P Thomson, Evangelist of the Church of Scotland from 1934, belonged to Wishart Church, his father being an elder.

In 1890 a daughter church was established when the minister and 76 members left to form Park Church.

As early as 1880 there had been moves to look for a site for a new church, but it was not until 1900 that the foundation stone was laid, the new church being opened in King Street on 12 September 1901, the site being the north side of an old quarry. At the time it was described as *a highly artistic creation, and a great ornament to the locality.* The church had a large nave, side aisle and transept. Below the church was a suite of three halls. The bible class gifted the pulpit and the Sunday school the baptismal font. The new place of worship was not far from the former church in Cowgate, which was later used by Messrs J B White, post card manufacturers, and then as a nursery.

Wishart UP became Wishart UF in 1900, Wishart Memorial UF in 1901, and Wishart Memorial in 1929.

Ministers

1838	Samuel SPENCE	From Liverpool Russell Street. Dem. 1844 and joined FC, becoming min. of Kilbirnie Free. (Small I 306-7)
1845	Robert Dick DUNCAN	Ord. Son of Professor Duncan and youngest of six brothers all ministers of United Secession Church. To Edinburgh Bread Street 1848. Bankrupt 1865, thereafter went to England and served churches there. (Died 1883) (Small I 308, KofE 304)
1849	John C BAXTER	Ord. To Stanley Street, Montreal 1875 (DD Queen's College, Kingston, 1877) (Small I 308)
1875	James GEORGE	From Gateshead. Disjoined 1890 to form new congregation of Park UP (Small I 308)
1890	William Anderson DUNBAR	From Aberdeen Woodside UP. Died 1922 (Small I 309, FUF 390)
1922	Thomas Fleming GILMORE BA	From Dornoch UF. To Abernyte 1933 (FUF 390, FES IX 518)
1933	Alexander McKenzie RUSSELL MM BD	Ind. Formerly in United Church of Canada. To Kirkmahoe 1939 (FES IX 518)
1940	James Hyslop TELFER MA	Ind. Ord. probationer. To Ayr Trinity 1952 (FES IX 518)
1953	Thomas Wright JARVIE	Ord. To Kilmarnock Riccarton 1968 (FES IX 518, X 307)
1970	John Raymond Horne CORBETT	Introd. Formerly Presb. Church of Canada, Two Mountains, Montreal. Appt. terminated 1973, thereafter to Montreal (FES X 307, TSC 36)

Old St Paul's and St David's and Wishart Memorial

After the union of 1975 the Old St Paul's and St David's buildings were chosen for the united congregation. The Wishart buildings were given to and adapted by the Dundee Cyrenians to become The Wishart Centre, a hostel for those with alcohol related problems. It was agreed at the union of 1975 that a deferred union with The Steeple Church would take place in 1978, on the retiral of the minister of The Steeple, the minister of Old St Paul's &c to be inducted to the united charge.

Minister

1976	John STEIN MA BD	Adm. Min of united charge 12 October 1978 (PM, TSC 55)

The Steeple

After the union of 1978 the Steeple building was selected as the place of worship and the Old St Paul's and St David's building was converted into the Mary Slessor Centre as a base for mission and service in the City.

Ministers

1978	John STEIN MA BD	Min. of Old St Paul's and St David's and Wishart Memorial. To Warden of Carberry Tower 1986 (PM)
1986	Graham Watson FOSTER MA BD ThM	From Invergordon. Died 1999 (PM)

Note

1. John Willison was one of the most prominent ministers of his day. He worked for the unity of the Church and opposed the tenets of John Glas. While sympathising with Ebenezer Erskine and the Seceders, he did all he could to prevent a schism. A strong opponent of Patronage, he was sent to London with two others in 1734 to petition Parliament for the repeal of the Act restoring Patronage. He visited Cambuslang in 1742 to witness the results of Whitefield's revival. During the '45 soldiers twice entered his church and threatened to shoot him if he prayed for King George, and for a time the church was closed and services were held in private houses. He was a very pious and devoted minister, evangelical, and noted for his diligence in catechising, and for his care of the sick. Willison Church, Dundee, was named for him. His grandson, George Willison, was a noted artist and painted James Boswell's portrait, now in the NPGS.

The Steeple Church 1789-1989, Dundee, 1989 (TSC)
W Norrie, *Dundee Celebrities,* Dundee, 1873
DPL   Lamb Collection 172(2), 172(4), 326(28), 408(23)
DCA   CH2/926, CH2/927, CH2/1218, CH3/650, CH3/906, GD/MUS/31/1
DCA   CH33/91/1 Minutes of the United Associate Presbytery of Dundee
DCA   State of Debts due to the Town, 1 November 1841; Report on Affairs of the Burgh 1829
DCC   Combined Statutory and Descriptive List
DYB   1892, 1901
Dundee Photographic Survey, 1916

STOBSWELL

Stobswell church is situated on a prominent site at the junction of Albert Street, Dura Street, Mains Loan and Forfar Road. It is a stone built L-plan church erected in 1876, designed by Charles Edward and Thomas S Robertson, who had built the mission school in Dura Street a year earlier. The style is rubble built gabled Gothic. The square slated tower with spire is asymmetrical, with the church entrance at the base of the tower. The gable on Eliza Street is buttressed with two 2-light traceried windows and a simple rose window. There are two 2-light traceried windows in Dura Street and a rose window in the north gable. The interior is L-plan with galleries to the north and east. There are fine stained glass windows by William Wilson, originally in Park Church.

The building was extensively refurbished over a ten year period. The completion of the work, which cost £400,000, was celebrated at a communion service on Sunday, 26 October 1997. The building was largely redesigned internally. A new hall was constructed in 1987 and a church office added. New furnishings were provided, including chairs for the side chapel, vestry fittings, oak encased organ speakers, and side chapel windows.

The church is B-listed. The manse is at 23 Shamrock Street.

Stobswell congregation was formed by the union of Ogilvie and Stobswell (formerly Park) on 1 January 1985 under the name Ogilvie and Stobswell, which was later changed to Stobswell.

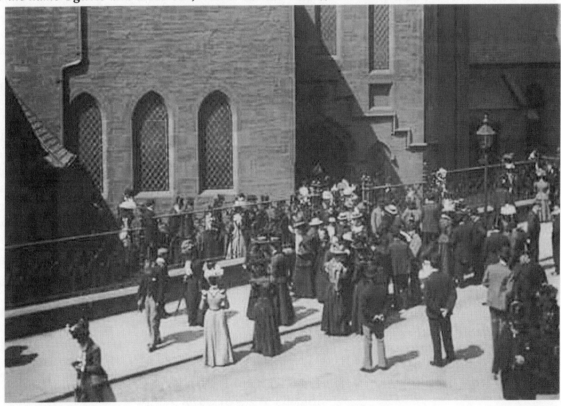

Ogilvie Church, Stobswell, early 20th century

Ogilvie

In the early 1860s Mr Henry Jack, an elder of Free St Andrew's conducted a prayer meeting in a house in James Park [now Langlands Street]. In the spring of 1868 Messrs George McCallum and J C Reid, also elders of Free St Andrew's, began prayer meetings in Gordon's Backlands, Dura Street, under the supervision of the Rev. James Ewing. A staff of lady visitors was set up, a Sunday school established, and meetings for adults held in the evenings. In 1871 the loft above a bakehouse in Eliza Street became the meeting place of what was known as Dura Street Mission. The Rev. Robert McLeod was the first missionary, and a hall was built for £800 in 1874 where afternoon and evening services were held. The Mission was formally constituted on 28 November 1875, by which time it appears plans for a church were well in hand. The church was opened on 18 May 1876 by Dr Alexander Whyte, Free St George's, Edinburgh[1]. The first minister of the charge was inducted on 27 July. The name of the congregation was changed to Ogilvie as a memorial to David Ogilvie of Messrs Malcolm, Ogilvie and Company, jute manufacturers, who was killed in an accident in the firm's works, which were located nearby.

The congregation opened a mission hall in Dundonald Street on 4 September 1890, at a cost of £600. The hall was sold in 1953 and the east gallery of the church converted into a hall. A pipe organ was installed in the church in 1899 at a cost of £700.

*In 1900 **Ogilvie Free** became **Ogilvie UF** and in 1929 **Ogilvie**.*

Ministers

1876	John F EWING MA	Ord. To Free West Glasgow 1879 (Died 1890) (Ewing II 161, PM)
1880	Archibald BLACK	From Armadale Free (W. Lothian) Died 1892 (Ewing II 161, PM)
1893	Henry Fotheringham HENDERSON MA	From Beith Free. DD (St Andrews 1914) Dem.1921 (Died 1939) Ewing II 161, FUF 387)
1921	John Alexander FLEMING MA	From Stepps UF. CF 1916-19.To Kilmadock West, Doune 1923 (FUF 387)
1923	Hugh ALEXANDER MA	From North Leith Coburg Street UF. Dem. 1952 (Died 1954) (FUF 386-7, FES IX 512)
1952	James Ekron LITTLE MA BD	From Pitsligo as C&S. CF 1942-7. Dem.1984 (Died 1993) (FES IX 512, PM)

***Stobswell** was formed by the union of **Park** and **Maryfield-Victoria Street** on 29 June 1976.*

Park

Park began as a UP church extension for the north east of Dundee in an area of the City where there was considerable housing development. A group of seventy-six members of Wishart UP church, along with their minister, the Rev. James George, were disjoined on 9 April 1890 at their own request and formed into a new congregation. By the close of the year the number of members had almost doubled and by the end of 1899 had risen to 235. However, there was difficulty in the early years in meeting the stipend. The congregation met at first in a small upper room of the old asylum in Park Avenue, removing to a hall of their own built in May 1891 at a cost of £1,200. A new church with sittings for 680 was constructed at a cost of £3,200, about half of which was borrowed, and opened on 23 December 1899. Built of snecked rubble, the church, with a square section tower on a canted angle, was designed by Leslie Ower, architect, Dundee. The elevation to Park Avenue has a large 2-bay gable and large 4-light windows. The Morgan Street elevation is similar, but narrower and taller. There is a gallery.

The building is B-listed.

***Park UP** became **Park UF** in 1900 and **Park** in 1929.*

Ministers

1890	James GEORGE	From Wishart UP. Dem. 1907 (Died 1914) (Small I 313, FUF 387)
1907	James Miller GRAHAM	Formerly of Union Church Tientsin. To Tealing UF 1926 (FUF 387)
1926	Daniel Harper GERRARD MA	From Leith St Ninian's UF. To Glasgow Anniesland Cross 1929 (Died 1958) (FUF 387)
1930	James George Dawson SCOTT MA	From Anstruther Chalmers Memorial. To Logiealmond 1935 (FES IX 512)
1936	James MACKAY MA	From Glasgow Hutchesontown and Caledonia Road. Dem. 1962 (Died 1973) (FES IX 512, X 304)
1963	John Hedley McINDOE	Ind. To Lanark St Nicholas 1972 (Mod. GA 1996) (FES X 304)
1972	Alan John ROY BSc MA BD	Formerly with Overseas Council. Min. of united charge 1976 (FES X 304, PM)

***Maryfield-Victoria Street** was formed by the union on 8 December 1965 of **Maryfield** and **Victoria Street**.*

Maryfield

Early in 1886 the established Church obtained the use of a chapel attached to the old Dundee Royal Lunatic Asylum. It was opened by the Rev. Dr Colin Campbell who called it **St Mary's in the Fields.** There were no definite arrangements for regular services, which were organised from week to week by one or two ministers. The small building had bare forms in place of pews, and a platform with a desk and chair served for a pulpit. Services were maintained until the summer when the building was closed. However, the kirk session of Dundee took matters in hand, resolving that a chapel of ease should be established. The General Assembly approved a deed of constitution and the building was fitted out with pews, pulpit and vestry. The name of the congregation was changed to **Maryfield.** Through the exertions of Dr Grant of St Mark's, the sum of over £500 was raised which, along with grants from the Baird Trust and the Home Mission Committee, was sufficient to buy and equip the building. The Rev. James Dowie started work on Sunday, 26 December 1886, and was ordained and inducted to the charge in the following February.

Originally, the church stood in the middle of a market garden with access by a rough cart track from Morgan Street. In the 1890s the surrounding area was developed with the building of blocks of tenements. The church was extended to hold 500, under the supervision of R Keith, architect. It was reopened on 18 May 1890 by the Rev. H G Watt, St Enoch's, when the sermon was preached by the Very Rev. John Cunningham DD. A bazaar held in September 1894 raised £1,300 to pay for the extension.

A set of communion vessels was donated anonymously in 1887. A font made of Dumfriesshire stone and carved to a design by J Murray Robertson was gifted by the builder of the church, Mr R Sheach. A two manual organ was added in 1891. Two extra communion cups were given by some officebearers in 1892. The Woman's Guild gave two silver communion cups in 1910. A memorial tablet for the Great War of 1914-18 was placed in the vestibule in 1921. Around 1922 a manse was acquired at 15 Duff Street and the debt incurred was cleared by 1928. A programme of restoration and redecoration was undertaken in 1923 and a hall erected in 1931.

The parish of Maryfield was disjoined from Dundee St Mary's on 5 February 1904.

Ministers

1887	James DOWIE	Ord. Adm. first min. of parish 12 February 1904. Dem. 1922 (Died 1932) (FES V 336, VIII 489)
1922	John McILWRAITH BA	Adm. Formerly asst. at St Mary's Dundee. To Aberdeen St Ninian's 1929 (FES V 336, VIII 489)
1929	William Cecil BIGWOOD MA BD	Ord. To Keith St Rufus 1935 (DD 1955) (FES IX 511)
1936	Robert Alexander ROBERTSON MA	From Liverpool Fairfield. To Dundurn Crieff 1952 (FES IX 511)
1952	Alastair Jack McTAVISH MA	From Lochgelly Churchmount. To Georgetown Grand Cayman 1959 (FES IX 511, X 303, Notes)
1960	William CAMPBELL	From Alvie and Insh. Min. of united charge 8 Dec. 1965 (FES X 303)

Victoria Street

This congregation began as a preaching station of the UP Church on Sunday, 1 June 1873. In 1871 the Elders' and Managers' Association had called for the establishment of a congregation in the east end of the town. A congregation was formed on 3 July and a session constituted on 15 September 1873. Initially, services were held in a schoolroom but by November a site for a church had been secured in Victoria Street. The church was opened on Sunday, 5 September 1875. It was seated for 860 and cost over £5,500. The design by Edward and Robertson, architects, Dundee, was to an Italianate rectangular plan with a square section tower. The construction was in squared rubble with ashlar dressings. Ten years later the building was free of debt, the communion roll stood at 734, and the stipend was £300. A mission hall in Grove Street, Springhill, was sold in 1953. The former church building is B-listed.

Victoria Street UP became Victoria Street UF in 1900 and Victoria Street in 1929.

Ministers

1875	William ROSE	From Airth. Ret. from active duty due to illhealth 1897. Died 1904 (Small I 310, FUF 389)
1897	Thomas Gillies CONOCHIE MA	Ord. C&S Dem. 1902 (FUF 389)

1903 John FORSYTH	From Jedburgh Boston UF. To Glasgow Burnbank 1910. (FUF 389)
1910 John Alexander GRAHAME	From Glasgow Lancefield UF. Died 1916 (FUF 389)
1916 William NICOLSON MA	Ord. To Elgin High UF 1920 (Died 1921) (FUF 390)
1920 George Alexander MILLS MA	From Stornoway English UF. To Greenock Middle 1928. (FUF 390)
1928 Hugh Gordon ROSS MA	From First Church Pittsfield Mass. Dem. 1940 (Died 1950) (FUF 390, FES IX 517)
1940 Joseph Blair GILLON MA	From Montrose South. To Edinburgh Lauriston 1947. (FES IX 517)
1948 James Eadie LYON	From Addiewell. To Kilconquhar and Colinsburgh 1965 (Died 1995) (FES IX 517, X 306)

Maryfield-Victoria Street

After the union of 1965 the Maryfield church was chosen as the place of worship of the united congregation. The Boys Brigade acquired Victoria Street church as their battalion centre for Dundee. The Maryfield manse was sold.

Ministers

1965 William CAMPBELL	Min. of Maryfield. To Nigg 1970 (FES X 303)
1971 Kenneth James MACKAY MA BD	Ord. His appt. was min. without charge, acting as min. of this charge. To Edinburgh Sighthill 1976. (FES X 303, PM)

Stobswell

After the union of 1976 the Park buildings were retained. The manse of Park congregation at 23 Shamrock Street became the manse of Stobswell. The manse of Maryfield-Victoria Street at 4 Clive Street was sold.

Minister

1976 Alan John ROY BSc MA BD	Min. of Park. Min. of united charge 1985 (PM)

Ogilvie and Stobswell

After the union of 1985 the Ogilvie building was retained as the place of worship of the united congregation. Stobswell church and halls were used while substantial renovations were being carried out to the Ogilvie property at a cost of around £400,000. The name of the congregation was changed to **Stobswell** around 1990.

Ministers

1985 Alan John ROY BSc MA BD	Min. of Stobswell. To Aberuthven with Dunning 1993 (PM)
1994 Gordon D IRVING BD	Ord. To Kilmacolm Old 1998 (PM)
1999 Jane Louise BARRON	Ord. (PM)

Note

1. Dr Alexander Whyte was a leading figure in the Free Church, and a voluminous writer. He was Moderator of the General Assembly in 1898 and Principal of New College, Edinburgh in 1909.

C McKean and D Walker, *Dundee, an Illustrated Introduction,* Edinburgh, 1984

DCA CH2/1214, CH3/1215

DCA CH2/1214/24 *Maryfield Parish Church Dundee 1886-1936*

DPL Sp. 2/98

DPL Lamb 401(3)

DCC Combined Statutory and Descriptive List

W Stewart, Notes entitled, *Stobswell Church A Look Back,* 1999

STRATHMARTINE

Strathmartine church stands at 513 Strathmartine Road on the northern outskirts of Dundee. A stone on the south wall bears the date *1843,* but the church dates from 1845 and originally was a very plain rectangular structure with low walls, the pulpit placed in the middle of one of the long walls and the pews ranged lengthways.

In 1892 the gift of £1,300 from the Carmichael family, original members of the congregation, whose house opposite the door of the church bears their monogram, allowed substantial alterations and remodelling in the Norman style to be carried out. The walls were heightened, and a new western gable to the street was built, providing a vestibule the breadth of the church. The west front incorporates a number of interesting architectural features crowned by a modest square belfry. The unusual door handle originally did duty in a convent in Venice. There is a St Cuthbert's Cross finial on the gable of the Norman doorway. The entrance with its nook-shafted, round headed arch has alternate billet, chevron, and nailhead mouldings, with *alpha* and *omega* and *Chi-Rho* symbols in the tympanum. The decoration on the capitals of the columns on each side of the doorway was copied from a fragment found in a heap of debris in Jedburgh churchyard. There are triple round-headed lights to each side of the door. David Baxter, architect, of Johnston and Baxter, Dundee, supervised the work.

A copy of the Rev. Robert Lorimer's book, *Mains and Strathmartine United Free Church,* which belonged to his son, Professor W L Lorimer, and is now in Dundee City Archives, has the annotation, *The reconstruction of the Church in 1892 and the extension of the Hall in 1896 were carried out in accordance with designs prepared by the author of this book. W.L.*

The communion table is of cypress wood ebonised, and is a reproduction of the altar in the cathedral of Ratisbon, Bavaria. The pulpit is also finished in ebony and presumably was placed on the east wall during the renovations. The baptismal font incorporates a capital stone retrieved from debris during the demolition of a medieval building in the centre of Dundee. It bears a carving of the lion rampant and the *fleur de lys* and is thought to have come from either the ancient church of St Clement or the Tolbooth. A gallery was added in 1955.

There are stained glass windows above the pulpit. The centre window, representing Christ the sower, was installed in 1926 in memory of the Rev. Robert Lorimer. The companion lights were dedicated to the memory of members of the congregation killed in the 1939-45 war. Those who died in the 1914-18 war are commemorated in a brass plaque.

The church hall was enlarged in 1896. One window is protected by an iron grille of the form invented by Michaelangelo, known as a *kneeling window.* A large new sports hall, incorporating new offices, designed by McCabe and MacDonald, was built on the site in 1993 at a cost of around £300,000, superseding the suite of halls into which the former Downfield North building at the foot of St Mary's Road was converted in 1952. This property was sold, with the proceeds being applied towards the cost of the new complex.

The church is B-listed. The manse is at 19 Americanmuir Road.

*Strathmartine congregation, formerly **Downfield Strathmartine,** was formed by the union of **Strathmartine** and **Downfield North** on 2 February 1941.*

Downfield (EC), Downfield North

In December 1884 a meeting of members of the Established Church was held in the village of Downfield, following which a deputation met Mains and Strathmartine kirk session and asked that services be arranged for the Downfield district. They wished to have fortnightly evening services initially, which they hoped would lead to the setting up of a church in the area. The Downfield Public School was to be used for their services. The kirk session gave its approval. The mission took root, and in 1889 the kirk session was approached again with a proposal that a church be erected, but the session did not agree. A further proposal that Mains and Strathmartine Church be re-sited by the heritors on a new site west of West March farmhouse (and thus be much nearer the growing village of Downfield) met with a resounding refusal from the heritors. A church was built at the corner of St Mary's Road and Cox Street, and opened for worship on Sunday, 24 September 1893. It was a mission station until full status was granted in 1912, when the parish of Downfield was disjoined from Mains and Strathmartine.

In 1929 Downfield (Established Church) became Downfield North.

Ministers

1891 David Duthie McLAREN MA BD	Ord. To Oldham Street Liverpool 1893 (FES V 326)
1896 David Harrower LOCHHEAD	Ord. Died 1907 (FES V 326)
1908 William SIMPSON MA BD	Adm. first min. of charge. To Maud 1919 (FES V 326)
1919 Henry DODD LRCP FP&S	From Shurrery. Dem. 1941 (Died 1942) (FES V 326, IX 507)

Mains and Strathmartine Free, UF, and Strathmartine

At the Disruption of 1843, the minister of the parish church remained with the establishment but Free Church services were held in the district in a barn at Westmill. In 1844 a feu for a church was granted and the charge sanctioned. The church was erected in 1845 and a manse provided on an adjacent site. The first communion roll on 1 October 1845 consisted of 160 names. The General Assembly of May 1845 sanctioned the charge.

Mains and Strathmartine Free became Mains and Strathmartine UF in 1900 and Strathmartine in 1929.

Ministers

1845 Alexander Gordon MACGILLIVRAY MA	Ind. To Edinburgh Roseburn Free 1866 (Died 1889) (Ewing II 163, KofE 475)
1866 Robert LORIMER BA MA	Ord. Sen. min. 1909. Died 1925. Father of W L Lorimer, translator of *The New Testament in Scots* (Ewing II 163, FUF 386)
1909 John DOUGLAS MA	Ord. C&S. Dem. 1915 (FUF 386)
1916 Andrew CUMMING MA	Ord. C&S. To Paisley Lylesland UF 1921 (FUF 386)
1921 David Bromfield SMITH MA	From Kilmun C&S. Sole min. 1925. To Glasgow Kelvinside North 1929 (FUF 386, FES IX 507)
1930 John William BURNSIDE MA	From Livingston Tulloch. To Paisley Abbey Close 1940 (FES IX 507)

Downfield Strathmartine

After the union of 1941 the Strathmartine church buildings were used by the united congregation. The Downfield North church buildings were transformed into parish halls by the National Church Extension Committee. Known as the North Halls, this property was sold in 1993, demolished shortly afterwards and flats erected on the site. The name of the congregation was changed to **Strathmartine** in 1960.

Ministers

1941 John ALEXANDER MA	From Fraserburgh St Andrew's. To Carsphairn 1961 (Died 1981) (FES IX 507, X 301, DNC)
1962 Robert Govan CLARKSON	From Fraserburgh West. Dem. 1989 (FES X 301, YB)
1990 Stewart McMILLAN BD	Adm. (PM)

R Lorimer, *Mains and Strathmartine United Free Church,* Dundee, 1909
DCC Combined Statutory and Descriptive List
DCA GD/X100/2, CH3/9/3

TRINITY

Trinity church is situated at 73 Crescent Street near the junction of Victoria Street, Albert Street, Arbroath Road and Princes Street. It has a prominent site on sloping ground facing towards the River Tay. The church is quite a large building, with a three stage square clock tower of 110 feet which is a major landmark to mariners. A clock by George Rattray was installed in 1891. The church was designed by George Mathewson, architect, Dundee in 1839-40, with the Norman Gothic tower being heightened under the supervision of C & L Ower, architects, Dundee in 1877. It is built of squared coursed rubble with pointed ashlar dressings and is rectangular in plan with Neo-Romanesque detailing. Two tall round-headed windows light the gallery stairs and flank the central doorway at the base of the tower. It is dated *1840*. On the south elevation are four tall round arched windows with Y-arched tracery. On the west gable two similarly detailed windows flank the 3-light sanctuary window. What was originally the schoolroom, but converted in 1888 to a hall, the plans again being prepared by the Owers, is at right angles to the north elevation.

The interior has five bays and a projecting organ chamber. There is a U-plan gallery on tall, clustered, cast iron columns. Alterations were carried out in 1877, including a cusped-panelled gallery behind the pulpit and fronting the organ chamber. At this time a good stained glass window was inserted. The interior renovations and the work on the tower were funded by the proceeds of a bazaar held in the Kinnaird Hall from 30 November to 2 December 1876[1]. The church was altered again in 1891, when the scheme of improvements included general renovations and the erection of a vestry, an organ chamber and an organ by Brindley and Foster, Sheffield, at a cost of £1,500. To raise funds for this project a function, called the *Grand Oriental Bazaar,* took place in the Victoria Art Galleries on 26, 27 and 28 March 1891. The organ replaced the harmonium in use since 1876. A stained glass window was inserted in the new chancel by James Hunter, Jun., solicitor, in memory of his father, factor for many years of the Wallace Craigie estate, upon which the church stands. Substantial repairs to the church were carried out in 1951. A new pipe organ by Rushworth and Dreaper was installed in 1955.

The former Savings Bank building, 146 Victoria Street, at the corner of Princes Street, was purchased in 1987 to provide additional hall accommodation. This building, built in 1914, has a domed clock tower and is B-listed.

Trinity church is B-listed. The manse is at 75 Clepington Road.

*Trinity congregation was formed on 29 September 1981 by the union of the charges of **Baxter Park**, **St Matthew's** and **Wallacetown**.*

Baxter Park

The minister and congregation of Wallacetown Church Extension *came out* at the Disruption of 1843. With the consent of the Trustees, as Wallacetown Free, they occupied the church (the building now used by Trinity) until 1853 when the Trustees sold it. Thereafter they worshipped for four years in a schoolroom lent by Baxter Brothers, linen manufacturers, until in 1857 they built a church. This church on the south side of Crescent Street was opened on Wednesday, 16 December 1857. A manse was bought in 1874. In 1892 the church was sold to the School Board, and a new church erected near Baxter Park. The architect was Alexander Johnston, Dundee. Dr J Hood Wilson of Barclay Church, Edinburgh, Moderator Designate of the Free Church General Assembly opened it for worship on 20 September 1894. The congregation took the name of Baxter Park from about the time of the laying of the foundation stone on 14 October 1893, although the change is not officially recorded in the Presbytery minutes.

*Wallacetown Free became **Baxter Park Free** in 1893, **Baxter Park UF** in 1900 and **Baxter Park** in 1929.*

Ministers

1843 Patrick Leslie MILLER	Min. of Wallacetown Church Extension. Joined FC. Member of a deputation sent to America to plead the cause of the FC. To Groat Market, Newcastle 1847 (Died 1866) (Ewing II 159, PM, Norrie)
1847 John SKENE MA	Ord. Ret. 1877. Died 1892(Ewing II 159,PM,AYB)
1877 James FENTON MA	Ord. C&S. Dem. 1914 (Died 1924) (Ewing II 159, FUF 381, PM)
1914 John Bruce WILSON MA	From Strathdon and Glenbuckat UF. To Balquhidder UF 1917 (FUF 381)

1917 John LINTON MA	From Coupar Angus North UF. Dem. 1928 (Died 1928) (FUF 381)
1928 David Cross MURRAY MA	From Keith North UF. To Edinburgh Haymarket 1933 (Died 1964) (FUF 381, FES IX 503)
1933 Frederick Mark MUSK BA	Intro. To Dunbar Abbey 1934 (FES IX 503)
1944 John Nelson HALL	Intro. To Edinburgh Nicolson Street 1949 (Died 1974) (FES IX 503)
1949 John Alexander Miller SCOTT MA BD	Ord. To Stevenston High 1954 (FES IX 503, X 299)
1955 Gilbert Cecil McCUTCHEON MA BD	From Drumblade. Dem. 1973 (Died 1984) (FES X 299, YB)
1975 Donald Baxter JOHNSTONE MA BD	From Burra Isles, Shetland. Dem. 1978 (FES X 299)

St Matthew's

This was a church extension of the Established Church created mainly through the efforts of the Rev. Dr Watson of St Mary's. A chapel of ease was constituted on 5 August 1875, but the Rev. John Mills had conducted services in Blackscroft School from 1874. Dr Watson opened the church on 3 October 1875, on a site which was part of the glebe of St Mary's. The parish of St Matthew's was erected on 12 January 1885.

The building in Ferry Road was designed by A Johnstone, architect, Dundee, the cost being about £3,800. The church when opened was described as *English Gothic with transepts, with a vestry and classroom. The main entrances are through the tower and porch placed on opposite sides of the church. The tower is 90 feet, finished by a plain corbelled parapet with roof. The sides of the church are broken up by four 3-light windows, with four 2-light windows above for lighting the gallery, and two large single light windows in the transepts, all the windows being separated by buttresses. A large 3-light window, with a smaller window on each side below, light the west end, and the east end is lighted by a circular window filled with trefoil plate tracery, also large side light windows having borders of stained glass. Accommodation is for 800. An open timber stair inside the church adds to the effect of the interior besides being less costly than outside stone stairs. The pulpit is placed on a raised platform at the east end.*

In February 1892 a peal of tubular bells was placed in the tower at a cost of £120. In 1911 two stained glass windows were placed in the church, the gift of the Misses Adie in memory of their parents and brother. A bazaar was held in 1899 to raise money for repairs to the building and to provide an organ. The building was restored in 1971, the work costing £9,500. A manse at 214 Ferry Road was bought in 1914 but sold in 1952 when a smaller building in East Haddon Road was purchased.

Ministers

1874 John MILLS MA	Ord. Adm. first min. of parish 4 February 1885. Dem 1913 (Died 1923) (FES V 340)
1913 Alexander MAUCHLINE MA BD	Adm. Formerly Professor of English, Scottish Churches College, Calcutta. Served as lieutenant RGA in First World War. Dem. 1920 on appt. as missionary at Blantyre, Nyasaland (FES V 340)
1920 Matthew Welsh NEILSON MA BD	Ord. To New Deer 1924 (FES V 340)
1924 Hugh Clark McCOLL MA	From Kilbirnie. Dem. 1928. Asst. St Mungo's Alloa (Died 1944) (FES V 340, VIII 490)
1928 Colin Ross MUNRO MA	From Hamilton West UF. Dem. 1931. To Old Church Alexandria 1932 (FES VIII 490)
1933 Robert KERR MA	From Ardclach South. To Kinkell 1946 (FES IX 516)
1947 John Frederick HART	Ind. To Glasgow Paisley Road 1952 (FES IX 516)
1953 James STEWART	Ord. Dem. 1980 (FES IX 516, DNC)

Wallacetown

On 1 May 1839 the Established Presbytery approved a site for a church to serve the Wallacetown area near Princes Street. A subscription list was opened and with help from the Young Men's Church Society a church was opened for worship on Sunday, 24 May 1840, bonds being granted on the security of the building. The construction cost and furnishing came to slightly over £3,000. In 1843 the minister and most of the congregation joined the Free Church, retaining the building although the title deeds declared that it was to be used in connection with the Church of Scotland. On 31 March 1853 it was sold by public roup by the bondholders and purchased for £1,585 by the Established Presbytery in competition with the seceding congregation. In the following year it was reopened as a chapel of ease of the Established Church. The Presbytery appointed the Rev. James Anderson as missionary for the church and district. In 1856 Mr Anderson was ordained and presented as minister by Presbytery *jus devolutum*. The debt incurred in buying the building was cleared in 1861. The parish of Wallacetown was disjoined from St Mary's on 9 March 1874.

To mark the 60th anniversary of the opening of the church the congregation held a conversazione in Victoria Art Galleries, Dundee, on 29 November 1900. In 1975 the congregation was temporarily linked with the charge of Mid Craigie. The linking was severed in 1981.

Ministers

1840 Patrick Leslie MILLER	Ord. Joined FC in 1843. Min. of Wallacetown FC until 1847 (Died 1866) (FES V 341)
1856 James ANDERSON	Ord. To Forteviot 1857 (FES V 341)
1857 Andrew GRAY MA	Ord. To New Parish Dumfries 1858 (FES V 341)
1859 Alexander McLEAN	Ord. To Strachan 1861 (FES V 341)
1862 John Lindsay ADAMSON	Ord. Adm. first min. of par. 1 April 1874. Res. 1883 (Died 1885) (FES V 341)
1883 James Montgomery CAMPBELL	Ord. To St Michael's Dumfries 1905 (FES V 341)
1906 John Morrison McLUCKIE	From Ruthrieston. To Lady Yester's Edinburgh 1910 (Died 1928) (FES V 341, KofE 91)
1911 John Stewart ROBERTSON MA BD	From High Kirk Kilmarnock. To First Charge Montrose 1918 (FES V 341)
1919 Stanley Buchanan CAREY MA	From Douglas Water. Dem. 1926. To St Andrew's Guelph, Canada 1927 (FES V 341, VIII 490)
1926 John Alexander MACKAY MA	From Cluny Kincardine O'Neill. To Chapelton 1930 (FES V 342, VIII 517)
1931 John FAIRLIE MA	From Glasgow St Peter's. Died 1950 (FES VIII 517)
1950 William Uist MACDONALD MA	From Cardonald St Nicholas. To Aberdalgie and Dupplin 1971 (FES VIII 517, X 306)
1971 Thomas James Loudon BLAIR MA BD	From Campsie Trinity. Min. of linked charge with Mid Craigie 21 March 1975. To Galston 1981 (FES X 306, YB)

Trinity

After the union of 1981 the Wallacetown buildings were retained. Baxter Park church was sold and used by another denomination for a number of years. It was demolished in 1997 for a housing development. St Matthew's was also demolished.

To mark the 150th anniversary of the church building a series of events were held from February to September 1990, with a service of Rededication on 2 September 1990.

In 1995 the Rev. James H Simpson BSc, was introduced to the charge as Auxiliary Minister. He resigned as Auxiliary in 1998.

Ministers

1981 Albert B REID BD BSc	From Perth Letham St Mark's. To Ardler, Kettins and Meigle 1993 (PM YB)
1993 James Lynch WILSON BD CPS	From Strichen (YB)

Note

1. A fuller account of the alterations and improvements carried out is given in the *Dundee Advertiser* for 29 June 1877.

J A Rollo, *Historical Sketch of Wallacetown Parish Church Dundee*, Dundee 1889
Trinity Parish Church, Dundee 1989 (Booklet in DCA GD/X100/14)
Aberdeen Year Book for 1892 (AYB)
DYB 1892
DCA CH2/958, 959DPL Lamb 173(3), 174(15), 401(2)
DCC Combined Statutory and Descriptive List

WEST

[Since the following two chapters were completed the West congregation has been formed by the union of Roseangle Ryehill and St Peter's McCheyne on 22 September 1999. Roseangle Ryehill church has been chosen as the place of worship. For the purposes of this volume the uniting congregations have been treated separately, the article on St Peter's McCheyne appearing after that on Roseangle Ryehill]

ROSEANGLE RYEHILL

Roseangle Ryehill church at the junction of Perth Road and Roseangle was built to accommodate the congregation of Free St John's, then located in Small's Wynd. It has a striking Gothic silhouette with high quality details. It was designed by James Hutton, architect, Dundee, and is cruciform in shape with a semi-octagonal apse to the south, the full width of the nave. The north elevation, with the tower to the left and square at the base, has gabled windows with the carved heads of Luther, Knox and Chalmers in the tympanum. The side elevation has three flowing traceried windows between buttresses. A renovation in 1969 removed the pulpit to the side from the centre, with the organ and choir being moved from the sanctuary and placed in the gallery to the rear of the church. The organ case of 1895 is by R & J Sibbald. Among the features of the church are the unbroken pointed arch of the roof, the intersection of the nave and transept roofs, and the 180 feet tall spire. The plaster rib vaulted ceiling is supported on tall clustered columns.

Three stained glass windows in the apse are of St Peter, St John and St Paul. The war memorial windows in the transepts are by Stephen Adam of Glasgow. In the vestibule, between two memorial windows, is a memorial by William Lyon Mackenzie-King, Prime Minister of Canada, to his grandfather, William Lyon Mackenzie, *reformer and patriot*, who was born nearby in Springfield and went to Canada from Dundee. This window by A L Russell was originally placed in the former St Mark's Church in 1952. There are six wooden plaques, memorials to those who died in the two World Wars, representing the three constituent congregations of Ryehill, St John's and St Mark's.

There are halls below the church and a hall adjacent to the church in Perth Road. The buildings, excluding the hall on Perth Road, are B-listed. The manse is at 7 Hillside Road.

*The congregation of **Roseangle Ryehill** was formed by the union of **Roseangle** and **Ryehill** on 3 September 1980. **Roseangle** was formed by the union of **St John's** and **St Mark's** on 12 September 1968.*

St John's

The Rev. John Roxburgh, minister, and the congregation of St John's, or the Cross Kirk, the Fourth Charge of Dundee, *came out,* with few exceptions, at the Disruption of 1843. A top flat machine loft in Brown and Allan's Seabraes Spinning Mill, Perth Road, was fitted out as a temporary place of worship. A church was built in Small's Wynd not long after the Disruption. Plans of this church, designed by Mr Smith, architect, were laid before the Kirk Session and approved on 21 June 1843, suggesting that he may have been engaged even before the schism. The church seems to have been finished by 7 March 1844, when the Session met for the first time in Free St John's vestry. The congregation was able to raise the total cost of the project of around £1,000, for in May 1844 reference was made in the Deacons' Court minutes to a surplus in the church building fund. This church was one of four Dundee Free Churches described in 1873 as *remarkably plain erections.* It was built in a style based on the arrangement of Tanfield Hall, Edinburgh, where the first Free Church General Assembly met. A school in Park Wynd (afterwards mission premises) was conveyed to the congregation by the former trustees in 1844. This may have been the building referred to as *St John's School of Industry.*

Mr Roxburgh appears in the group photograph of Dundee Free Church ministers taken at Glasgow on 22 October 1843, and in a single photograph, reproduced in the catalogue of Hill and Adamson's calotypes. These photographs were used by David Octavius Hill RSA for likenesses in his large painting entitled, *The First General Assembly of the Free Church of Scotland Signing the Act of Separation and deed of Demission at Tanfield, Edinburgh, May, 1843.*

In 1860 a manse at Nethergate was presented to the congregation. The church and manse were sold in 1881, the church being acquired by the University College authorities, and another manse was purchased in Windsor Street in 1883. A Farewell Service was held in the church on Sunday, 3 February 1884.

The splendid new church in Perth Road was opened on Thursday, 7 February 1884, when the preacher was the Rev. Dr Walter C Smith[1] who preached from the text, *How amiable are thy tabernacles, O Lord of hosts.* Special services in connection with the opening were held on the following Sunday when Dr Marcus Dods[2] preached in the morning and the Rev. D M Ross, the minister, in the afternoon. The new church was far removed aesthetically from that described in 1873. A writer of a magazine article in 1889 remarked that, *A Free Kirk with stained glass windows and instrumental service is as much a sign of the times as is the phonograph and electric light; and truly Free St John' with its glorious windows, Eiffel-tower-like pillars, and artistic decoration, is one of the most interesting of the Kirks of Dundee.* The reference to the Eiffel Tower was topical, it having been constructed in 1889. Presumably, the instrument was a harmonium for an organ was installed in 1896.

In the summer of 1903 fabric repairs were carried out, the interior redecorated, and electric lighting installed. The congregation worshipped temporarily in Hawkhill Church, by courtesy of the managers of Tay Square Church. In 1910 the purchase and removal of adjoining houses improved the amenity of the church. Improvements to the church were made in 1939.

In 1865 it was reported to Presbytery that the Park Wynd Mission held afternoon and evening services and a weekly prayer meeting. The Mission Halls were sold to University College, Dundee, in 1953. There was division in the congregation in 1864, following the decision to appoint a colleague and successor to the Rev. Alexander O Laird. Some members wished the Rev. William A. Knight[3] assistant to Mr Laird, appointed. As he was not chosen his supporters left with him in February 1865 to form what became Free St Enoch's. Later, Mr Knight and his St Enoch's congregation left the Free Church, being admitted to the Established Church in 1874.

St John's Free became *St John's UF* in 1900 and *St John's* in 1929.

Ministers

1843	John ROXBURGH DD	Min. of Fourth Charge of Dundee. Joined FC. To Glasgow Free St John's 1847 (Mod. Free GA 1867) (FES V 328, Ewing II 161, PM)
1848	Alexander O LAIRD	From Abbotshall. Ret.1867. Dem. 1883 (Died 1891) (Ewing II 161, PM)
1867	David SOMERVILLE DD	Ord.C&S.To Rothesay Free 1878 (Ewing II 161,PM)
1878	David Morrison ROSS DD	Ord. C&S. To Glasgow Westbourne 1898. DD (Edinburgh 1901) (Ewing II 161, PM)
1898	George Herbert MORRISON MA	From Thurso First Free. To Glasgow Wellington UF 1902. DD (Glasgow 1913) (Mod. UF GA 1926) (Ewing II 161, FUF 388)
1902	Alexander B MACAULAY MA	From Forfar East UF. To Stirling North UF 1911. DD (Glasgow 1914) (FUF 388)
1911	John McCONNACHIE MA	From Uddingston Chalmers UF. CF 1915. DD (St Andrews 1931) Sen. Min. 1946. Died 1948 (FUF 388, FES IX 515)
1946	George Gordon CAMERON MA	From Glasgow Kent Road St Vincent. To Paisley Glenburn 1958 (FES IX 515, X 305)
1959	James Grahame LEES MA	From Glasgow Victoria Tollcross. To Edinburgh Lothian Road 1965 (FES X 305)
1966	Thomas Alexander HAY	Ord. Dem. 1968 (FES X 305)

St Mark's

As part of the settlement of the Dundee Stipend Case the Town Council paid Presbytery the sum of £2,000 in discharge of their liability to erect and endow a sixth charge in the Town. This capital sum was increased to £6,000 by donations. A site in Perth Road at the top of Greenfield Place was purchased and the foundation stone laid on 12 March 1868. The church with sittings for 800, costing £6,000 including the site, was opened for worship on 7 June 1869.[4] The parish of St Mark was created by the Established Presbytery on 3 July 1871.

The building in two-tone ashlar with coloured bands and details was designed by Pilkington and Bell and described as *Venetian Gothic.* The principal entrance is by a porch in the centre of the wide north gable. Above is a traceried window with four lights. There is carving in the tympana. The octagonal tower with spire has decorated bands and finials. There is a large rose window in the south gable. The pulpit is built in the form of a gallery in front of the organ, forming the centre of a semi circle, the seats being curved. The main gallery is U-shaped on stout masonry columns and timber twisted barley sugar columns. The hammer beam roof is carried on cast iron columns. The church was enlarged and reopened on 18 January 1880, adding 260 sittings. The south gable was projected southwards and a large hall and two classrooms were added, with a vestry over one of the classrooms. A recess for the organ was formed behind the pulpit. The cost of this work, supervised by Ireland and Maclaren, architects, Dundee, was £1,900. An organ by J Stringer and Company, Hanley, was installed and inaugurated by William T Best[5] organist, on 24 March 1880. Robert Adamson, Hermon Hall, gifted a bell, in 1871. Four stained glass windows were inserted in 1897. A further four by Stephen Adam, Glasgow, were erected on the east side of the church in 1904 by Dr C M Grant as a memorial to his wife, with the themes, A*ffection, Industry, Charity and Bible Study.* A new hall was added in 1936. A mission hall was sold in 1948. St Mark's was regarded as the model *quoad sacra* charge of the Established Church.

The church building is A-listed

Galleried pulpit of St Mark's, Perth Road
Dr C M Grant was minister from 1877 until 1913

Ministers

1870 Donald MACLEOD	From First Charge Montrose 16 June 1870. Adm. first min. of parish 1871. To Jedburgh 1877 (FES V 339)
1877 Charles Martin GRANT MA BD	From Partick St Mary's. DD (Edinburgh 1900) Dem. 1913 (Died 1916) (FES V 339)
1913 Joseph Robert PRENTER BA MA	From Leith St Paul's. Dem. 1925 (Died 1946) (FES V 339, VIII 490)
1925 David Bruce NICOL MA BD MC	From St Margaret's Edinburgh. To Govan 1929 (Died 1930) (FES VIII 490)
1930 Vincent Cassels ALEXANDER	MA BD From Aberdeen Rubislaw. To Kilbarchan West 1940 (FES IX 516)
1941 James Victor LOGAN MA	From Stewarton Cairns. CF 1943-6. To Eckford 1955 (FES IX 516, X 306)
1956 Douglas Brian THOMPSON BA ThM	From Aberdeen Carden Place. To Edinburgh Corstorphine Old 1960 (Died 1976) (FES X 306, KofE 403)
1961 James Alexander BREMNER MA	From Edinburgh St Paul's Newington. Min.of united charge 1968 (FES X 306)

Roseangle

After the union of 1968 the minister of St Mark's was inducted to the united charge and the buildings of St John's were used. St Mark's buildings were acquired by the Gate Fellowship and the church continued to be used for worship.

Minister

1968 James Alexander BREMNER MA
Min. of St Mark's. Ind. 12 Sep.1968 Dem. 1979 (Died 1989) (FES X 306, DNC, YB)

Ryehill

In 1871 the UP Presbytery was approached by the recently formed Elders' and Managers' Association who desired an extension of the Church in Dundee and saw the need for at least two new congregations, one in the east end and one in the west end. The Rev. John Brand, minister of Bell Street Church, was Convener of a committee set up to look at Church Extension and in January 1876 his motion, that a conference of those interested in a new west end congregation be called, was approved by Presbytery. The opening services of Ryehill were held in Gray's Assembly Rooms, Nethergate, on Sunday, 5 March 1876, being conducted by Mr Brand. A hall in Mid Wynd was built at a cost of £930 and opened for worship in September. Presbytery recognised the new congregation on 31 October 1876.

The foundation stone of a new church at 79 Perth Road was laid by ex Provost James Cox on 19 May 1878. The church was built at a cost of £9,000 and opened for worship on Friday, 20 February 1880 when the distinguished Principal John Cairns preached.[6] The collections that evening and on the following Sunday amounted to over £1,500. Designed by G S Aitken, architect, Dundee, the building was noted for its grand, gabled facade to the street, with its richly ornamental traceried window. With a semi circular auditorium, created within a rectangular exterior on a difficult site, it was a notable example of a tradition within the United Presbyterian Church; a preaching place with the congregation in gallery and ground floor gathered round the pulpit like a family around the fireside.

There was dissension in the congregation in its early years, apparently resolved when the first minister, Mr Drummond, demitted.

Ryehill UP became Ryehill UF in 1900 and Ryehill in 1929.

Ministers

1877 James DRUMMOND MA	From Alexandria UP. Dem. 1888. Ind. To Burnhead UP 1893 (Small I 312-3)
1890 James AITKEN MA	From Edinburgh Lothian Road UP. DD (St Andrews 1900) Dem. 1920 (Died 1927) (Small I 313, FUF 387)
1920 George BLAIR MA BD	From Uddingston Park UF. DD (St Andrews 1930) Sen.Min. 1946. Died 1970 (FUF 387, FES IX 513, X 304)
1946 Adam JACK MA BD	From Glasgow Ibrox. To Kirkcudbright St Cuthbert's 1964 (FES IX 513, X 304)
1965 James Murdoch ROGERS BA BD DCult	From Second Saintfield N.I. Min. of united charge 1980 (FES X 304)

Roseangle Ryehill

After the union of 1980 the Roseangle buildings were chosen for use by the united congregation. Ryehill church was converted into flats by a housing association, while retaining the distinctive outside appearance.

Ministers

1980 James Murdoch ROGERS BA BD DCult	Min. of Ryehill. Dem. on appt. to Gibraltar 1993 (PM)
1995 Joyce LYNN MIPM BD	Ord. To Orkney Shapinsay 1998 (PM)

Notes

1. Dr Walter C Smith, born in Aberdeen, was Moderator of the Free General Assembly in the Jubilee year of 1893. He lectured in evangelistic theology and published religious works. He also wrote a number of novels and poems.

2. Dr Marcus Dods was a leading theologian. He was minister of Renfield Street Church, Glasgow, before being appointed to the chair of New Testament Exegesis in New College, Edinburgh.

3. The Rev. William A Knight left St Enoch's Church to become Professor of Moral Philosophy at St Andrews University. He left the Church of Scotland later for the Anglican Church. He was biographer of the poet Wordsworth and editor of his works.

4. There was a debate in Dundee in 1865, in Presbytery and in the Press, over the style of church to be erected in the West End. There was a strongly held view that, as the times were prosperous and the more affluent people chose to live in spacious and elegant houses, the new church should be *elegant* and a credit to the area and the town, rather than a *square stone box* with the object of providing the maximum accommodation for the minimum outlay. The recently erected East Free Church in Broughty Ferry was held up as an example of what could be achieved.

5. William T Best held a number of important posts as an organist in England. He played an important part in familiarising the public with the organ works of Bach. He published works on organ playing.

6. Principal John Cairns personified the life and faith of the United Presbyterian Church. He held a charge at Berwick from 1845, being appointed to the chair of Apologetics in the United Presbyterian Theological College, Edinburgh in 1867, becoming Principal in 1879. He was Moderator of the UP Synod in 1872.

John T G Baxter, *Ryehill Church 1876-1976,* Dundee, n.d.

C McKean and D Walker, *Dundee, An Illustrated Introduction,* Edinburgh, 1984

J M Smith, *Jubilee of St John's Church (present building) 1884-1934,* (booklet issued in 1934)

Roseangle Ryehill Church, A Visitor's Guide n.d.

E S Towill, *People and Places in the Story of the Scottish Church,* Edinburgh, 1981

Dundee Advertiser, 8 December and 12 December 1865

Piper O' Dundee 22 May 1889

DCC Combined Statutory and Descriptive List

DYB 1904

DCA CH2/1267, CH2/1228, CH3/1225, CH3/34, CH3/1348

DPL Lamb 173(2)

St PETER'S McCHEYNE

St Peter's McCheyne church is situated at 328 Perth Road at the road junction known as The Sinderins. The church was designed by Pilkington and Bell and built in 1870 as a memorial to the Rev. Robert Murray McCheyne, the first minister of the nearby St Peter's Church. The building is Gothic in style, being in ashlar with lighter stone and details. It was extended to the south around 1899

The tower and spire is in the north east corner. There is a pointed arched door with carved tympana in the twin gabled north elevation. A memorial to McCheyne is set in a gabletted niche. The Shepherds Loan doorway has a carved tympanum. The south gable has a large trefoiled rose window over two lancets and a Celtic cross finial. The interior is galleried with high quality woodwork. A visitor in 1888 described the interior as *the beau ideal of a large audience chamber. The semi circular form and the sloping floors of area and gallery bring everybody within easy range of the pulpit. The pulpit is really half pulpit, half platform, and rich in carving and upholstery.*

A pipe organ gifted by ex-Provost A H Moncur was installed in 1899 and inaugurated on 11 October. It was renewed and electrified in 1937. A partial renovation of the organ was carried out in 1996 at a cost in excess of £12,000. A bronze plaque and memorial windows commemorate members killed in the 1914-18 War. There is a bronze plaque honouring those who died in the war of 1939-45.

The building is B-listed. The manse is at 22 Hyndford Street.

St Peter's McCheyne congregation was formed by the union of St Peter's and McCheyne Memorial on 24 August 1982.

St Peter's

When the Rev. John Roxburgh came to St John's or the Cross Kirk, the Fourth Charge of Dundee, in 1834, he found that the parish had a population of 6,000, in addition to his own congregation, showing the need for church extension in the west end of his parish. In 1835 the Kirk Session of St John's appealed for subscriptions for the purpose of *erecting a chapel in the north west end of the Hawkhill.* The building was to be *plain and substantial, so as to secure at once both quantity and cheapness of accommodation.* When Mr Roxburgh opened the church on 15 May 1836, the area that it served was disjoined from St John's parish. The district assigned to the congregation was described as *all to the west of a line commencing at the River Tay, immediately to the west of Mr David Brown's house, and then along McDonald's Lane* (now Westfield Lane), *crossing diagonally the Perth Road, and then along East Wynd* (now Millar's Wynd) *to Hawkhill Road.*

The church was designed and built by the brothers Hean, Dundee builders. The plain simplicity of the building is offset by the clock tower and stone spire, completed in 1839 against the east gable. The tower contained a peal of bells moved by waterpower. The clock by Alexander Kelt was installed in 1872. The church was reseated in 1886. A pipe organ was introduced in 1912. In 1919 two stained glass windows were gifted in memory of Captain Alexander Guthrie and installed on either side of the organ, with the themes, *Christ and the Little Children* and *Christ the Good Shepherd.*

In 1836 it was decided to ask three prominent ministers from the evangelical wing of the Church of Scotland, Dr Chalmers, Dr Welsh and Mr (later Dr) Candlish, to draw up a list of suitable young men for the new charge. They proposed Mr White, Edinburgh, Mr Dymock, Liberton, Mr Bonar, Jedburgh, Mr Somerville, Jedburgh, Mr McCheyne, Larbert and Mr Gibson, Glasgow. All six candidates preached before the congregation with McCheyne being unanimously called. On the occasion of the congregation's jubilee in 1886 ex Bailie Macdonald wrote in a pamphlet, *With what discernment these men were recommended is proved by the eminent position to which they all afterwards rose in the Church.*

At the Disruption of 1843 the charge was vacant through the death from typhus of the Rev. Robert Murray McCheyne, contracted during his pastoral visitations. The procedure for placing a successor, the Rev. Islay Burns, was well in hand. Inducted on 7 June 1843, Mr Burns was the first minister ordained by the Free Church. With a considerable outstanding debt, the Free Church retained the church building.

In 1846 St Peter's Kirk Session petitioned Presbytery unsuccessfully over the very contentious issue of the monies which the recently formed Free Church had received from American churches which accepted slave owners as members, calling for these funds to be repaid. The matter had been brought to public attention by the lecture tour in Scotland, including Dundee, of Frederick Douglass[1], an escaped American slave.

In 1857 St Peter's opened a mission in Mission House, Taylor's Lane, off Perth Road. There was a weekly prayer meeting in Shepherd's Loan schoolroom. The first meeting of Dundee Free Presbytery was held in St Peter's vestry.

On 18 May 1913, the centenary of his birth, a service was held in memory of Robert Murray McCheyne. In his address the minister, the Rev. Alexander White, stated that *men made pilgrimage to* [St Peter's] *from all lands, as if it were a shrine.*

*The Established Church charge of **St Peter's** ceased at the Disruption of 1843.* ***St Peter's Free** became **St Peter's UF** in 1900 and **St Peter's** in 1929.*

Ministers

1836 Robert Murray McCHEYNE	Ord. Perhaps no minister in the Church of Scotland is better remembered for his saintliness of character, and his success in a short ministry as a preacher of the Gospel. In 1839 he accompanied Andrew Bonar and others to Palestine to consider the expediency of establishing a Jewish Mission[2]. Died 25 March 1843 and is buried beside his church. An imposing monument marks his grave. (FES V 340)
1843 Islay BURNS DD	Ord. To Chair of Church History FC College Glasgow 1864; later held Chair of Apologetical Theology. DD (Aberdeen 1864) (Died 1872) (Ewing II 162, DPL Lamb, Norrie)
1864 Duncan MACGREGOR MA	From Glasgow Hope Street Free Gaelic. To Glasgow Augustine Free 1876 (EWING II 162, DPL Lamb)
1876 John JENKINS MA	From Culross Free. Dem. 1905 (Died 1906) (Ewing II 162, FUF 389)
1905 Alexander WHITE	From Troon Portland UF. War Service with YMCA. Died 1934 (FUF 389, FES IX 516)
1934 Thomas MACKIE MA	From Glengarnock. Died 1940 (FES IX 516)
1940 David Good GRAY MA BD	From Dunfermline Townhill. War Service with CofS Huts and Canteens 1944-5. Dem. 1972 (Died 1990) (FES IX 517, X 306, YB)
1973 George FAIRLIE BVMS MRCVS BD	From Lairg with Rogart. To Glasgow Cathcart 1982 (FES X 306, PM)

McCheyne Memorial

The mission which St Peter's Free congregation began in Taylor's Lane in 1857 prospered and it was decided to build a new church to be called *The McCheyne Church.* It was erected at The Sinderins and opened on 12 May 1870 by the Rev. C H Spurgeon[3] of the Metropolitan Tabernacle, London. St Peter's organised a bazaar, which raised £1,600 towards the building costs. The charge was sanctioned in 1871. The original buildings consisted of church and church officer's house, with halls underneath. Ampler hall and classroom accommodation was provided in 1899 when the building was enlarged.

*****McCheyne Memorial Free** became **McCheyne Memorial UF** in 1900 and **McCheyne Memorial** in 1929.*

Ministers

1872 Alexander H REID	From Gartly (until 1887) (Ewing II 160, PM)
1887 Alexander ALEXANDER MA	Formerly held Chair of Church History in Madras Christian College. To St Andrew's Presb. Church, Waterloo, Liverpool 1901. DD (1913) Mod. Presb. Church of England 1917 (FUF 385)
1902 Andrew Neil SUTHERLAND MA	From Rothesay UF. CF 1915-6. Died 1918 (FUF 385)
1919 Kenneth Ian McIVER MA	From Kilcreggan. To Trinity, Claughton, Birkenhead 1924 (Died 1929) (FUF 385)
1925 Andrew James FORREST MA BD	From Shettleston Eastbank. Dem. 1951 (Died 1962) (FUF 385, FES IX 510, X 302)
1952 Duncan Gunn DARROCH MA BD	From Kilmorack. Dem. 1976 (Died 1978) (FES IX 510, PM, YB)

1977 James Harrison HUDSON DipTh BA BD	From Hamilton Trinity. Min of united charge 2 Aug. 1982. (DNC, PM)

St Peter's McCheyne

      After the union of 1982 the McCheyne buildings were retained for worship. St Peter's church was sold to a congregation of the Free Church.

Minister

1982 James Harrison HUDSON DipTh BA BD	Min. of McCheyne Memorial. Dem. 1999 (DNC, PM)

Notes

1. Frederick Douglass, originally called Frederick Augustus Washington Bailey, was born in 1817 on a Maryland plantation and educated surreptitiously, the teaching of slaves to read being illegal. He became a leader of the anti slavery movement and came to Britain and Ireland in the 1840s on a two year speaking tour. He addressed a packed meeting in School Wynd UP church, chaired by the Rev. George Gilfillan.
2. In February 1838 the possibility of a mission to the Jews was discussed in Glasgow Presbytery and in the Glasgow Missionary Society. The General Assembly of that year appointed a Committee for *the conversion of God's ancient people* and instructed its members to collect funds and information. Next year Dr Black of Aberdeen, Dr Keith of St Cyrus, Robert Murray McCheyne, and Andrew Bonar of Collace were sent to Palestine on a mission of enquiry. Following an accident in the Holy Land, Dr Black and Dr Keith returned home by way of the Danube. They fell ill in Pest, where they were visited and ministered to personally by the Archduchess Marie Dorothea, wife of the Viceroy of Hungary. The Archduchess, a Protestant, on hearing of their mission, encouraged them to consider the large number of Jews at Pest, assuring them that should the Church of Scotland wish to establish a mission there she would assist them. As a result, the Church decided to start the first Jewish Mission in Hungary.
3. Charles H Spurgeon was a great religious orator, and at the age of 22 the most popular preacher of his day. He was strictly Calvinistic. The Tabernacle built for him in Newington Causeway, London, held 6,000.

Thomas Brown, *Annals of the Disruption,* Edinburgh, 1893
DCA CH3/338, CH2/103/49
DNB Vol. LIII
DPL Sp. 1/66, 2.47
DPL DNC Vol. 106
DPL Lamb 174(1,3,4)
DCC Combined Statutory and Descriptive List
DYB 1899, 1904, 1913

WHITFIELD

Whitfield began as a Church Extension charge in 1969 to serve a large new local authority housing development, over 5,500 new houses being constructed in the area between 1967 and 1975. A church was erected in Haddington Crescent. The church complex is an L-shaped building, consisting of a church and hall and other offices.

During the 1980s the area changed significantly with the upgrading of many of the dwellinghouses, the demolition of some property, and new building.

The Rev. A D C Greer MA LLB was appointed Associate Minister in 1981, an appointment which he held until 1985. The Rev. Hector G McMillan was appointed Associate Minister in 1985, a post which he held until 1990.

Ministers

1969	Hugh Charles ORMISTON BSc BD	Ord. To Associate at Kilninian and Kilmore linked with Tobermory linked with Salen and Ulva linked with Torosay and Kinlochspelvie 1978 (YB)
1978	J Ronald DICK BD	From Kilwinning Mansefield. To Corsock linked with Kirkpatrick Durham 1982 (PM, YB)
1983	David DONALDSON MA BD	From Bathgate St David's. To Duddingston 1990 (YB)
1991	George GAMMACK BD	From Associate Aberdeen Mastrick. Dem. 1999 (PM, YB)

C A Whatley (ed.) *The remaking of Juteopolis, Dundee circa 1891-1991,* Dundee, 1992
(Abertay Historical Society Publication No 32*)*

ABERNYTE

Abernyte church is situated on rising ground, with a beautiful view of the Carse of Gowrie and the River Tay. The church, which is cruciform in shape, has been described as unquestionably *one of the most beautiful of the rural churches of Scotland…The rafters of the church are an architect's delight.* There is no record of when the church was built, but it was rebuilt in 1736 and reconstructed in 1837, with the porch being added in 1870.

*In 1929 **Abernyte** became **Abernyte North**. The congregation of **Abernyte** as it now is was formed by the union of **Abernyte North** and **Abernyte South** on 15 January 1933.*

Abernyte (Abernyte North from 1929)

Abernyte was a pre Reformation church and a prebend of Dunkeld. Among those recorded as having held the living were Richard de Creych, canon of Dunkeld in 1413, and Alexander Barber, archdeacon of Caithness in 1415. Emoluments from the church of Abernyte were assigned for the maintenance of four of the vicar's choral in Dunkeld Cathedral.

There was a vicar's residence, which may form part of the subsequent manse. The matter of the repair of the manse was discussed in Presbytery in 1665, and a stone in the west wall of the manse bears the date *1666* suggesting that the repairs may have been carried out then. The upper rooms of the manse are on four different levels, indicating that there may have been a number of alterations and additions. The semi circular portion of the front of the manse was added around 1820.

During the latter years of the ministry of the Reverend James Wilson assistance was required, and the Reverend James Hamilton was appointed assistant. Mr Hamilton was a friend of Robert Murray McCheyne of St Peter's, Dundee, and of Andrew Bonar of Collace. McCheyne and Bonar preached frequently at Abernyte. Hamilton was very active in the Revival movement and crowds flocked to his services.

Ministers

1567	William HAITLIE	Min. in 1567. To Benvie 1576, returned between 1580 and 1585 with Lundie also in his charge. Still min. in 1591. (FES V 307)
1574	Michael GREIG	Reader in 1574 (FES V 307)
1593	George HAITLIE	Reader. Pres. To the fourth part of the fruits of Abernyte with both parsonage and vicarage by James VI, 1577. Adm. to Kinnaird about 1590, trans. and adm. before 1593, trans.to Rossie before 1599, probably holding both in conjunction as he was still min. here in 1614 and 1623. Died 1628. (FES V 307)
1620	James HAITLIE MA	Adm. before 1620 (probably colleague) FES V 307)
1628	Thomas WHITEHEAD MA	Adm. before 1628 (probably colleague) (FES V 307)
1651	John MINIMAN MA	Ord. Dep. 1662. Denounced and put to the horn 1674, for holding conventicles. (Died before 16 Oct. 1684)(FES V 307-8)
1664	Andrew SHIPPERT	Adm. and installed. Died 1703 (FES V 308)
1704	Thomas MITCHELL	Ord. Dep. by Commission of Assembly 1729 (Died 1732) (FES V 308)
1733	George BLAIR	Ord. Dem. on app. as Master of Grammar School, Dundee 1738 (FES V 308)
1739	Alexander CORSE	Ord. 1739. Died 1754 (FES V 308)
1755	James JOBSON	Ord. 1755. To Errol 1759 (FES V 308)
1760	James ADAMSON MA	Ord. Pres. by George II 1759. Died 1807 (FES V 308)
1808	James WILSON	Ord. Pres. by George III 1807. Died 1850 (FES V 308)
1844	John SMEATON	Ord. (A&S) To Tulliallan 1848 (FES V 308)
1848	Robert GRAHAM	Ord. (A&S) To Errol 1858 (FES V 308)
1858	Robert Mackay LEITCH BA MA	Ord. Pres. by Victoria. Dem.1872; took orders in Church of England (Died 1904)(FES V 309)
1873	Allan MENZIES MA BD	Ord. Pres. by Victoria. Dem. 1890 on app. to Chair of Biblical Criticism, St Andrews University (FES V 309)
1890	William Liston MILROY MA	Ord. Died 1925 (FES V 309, VIII 485)

1926 Henry Reid CHALMERS From Duffus. Dem. 1933 (Died 1955)
(FES VIII 485, X 297)

*In 1900 **Abernyte Free** became **Abernyte UF** and in 1929 **Abernyte South**.*
Abernyte South

In June 1843 evening services were provided for adherents of the Free Church in the parish. In December 1844 it was reported to Presbytery that Mr Dickson, who had been supplying the station, wished to give up. It was decided that the station should be closed unless the Home Mission Committee provided supply. In the following month James Logan, probationer, was appointed. The charge was sanctioned by the General Assembly in May 1845, on condition that the preaching station at Rait, in the Presbytery of Perth, should be combined with it under the name Abernyte and Rait Free Church.

The group is believed to have worshipped initially in Southfield granary. Sites on the Ballindean Estate were offered but the Presbytery committee did not consider them suitable for a church. On Presbytery's advice they moved to the church which had been built by the Haldane Brothers, known as Haldanes' Tabernacle (See **Balfour Burgher** ceased 1845) which they purchased in 1847. This was suggested as a temporary home until a site at the village of Ballindean became available. In 1850 Presbytery confirmed its opposition to a church, other than at Ballindean. The minister was recommended to *preach at Rait as often as he shall find practicable.* There were continuing difficulties in obtaining a site for a church and a minister was not settled until 1850. Sadly, the first minister called, Mr McCosh, died before the date of the induction. In July 1850, the Reverend Joseph Wilson, formerly minister of the Reformed Presbyterian Church, Meadowside, Dundee (See **Balgay**) was received by Presbytery as a minister of the Free Church. He served at Abernyte before being inducted as its minister in October. The church was not erected until 1854, stones being used from the Tabernacle which was demolished. A manse was provided in 1855. The church was enlarged in 1884 with seating capacity for 200.

Ministers

1850 Joseph WILSON Adm. Formerly min. of Reformed Presbyterian Church, received into FC. Died 1873 (Ewing II 158, PM)

1873 John WILSON DD Ord. Dem. 1886 (Ewing II 158, PM)

1886 George Innes SMITH MA Dem. 1933 (Died 1941)
(Ewing II 158, FUF 379, FES IX 502)

Abernyte

Following the union of **Abernyte North** and **Abernyte South** of 1933 both churches were used on alternate Sundays until 1950 when the South church and manse were sold.

The congregation was linked with Inchture and Kinnaird linked with Longforgan on 28 February 1983.

The Rev. Iain T Adamson MA BSc MSc PhD was appointed Auxiliary Minister of the linked charge in 1986, a post which he held until he retired in 1993.

The Rev. R M Donald BA was appointed Associate Minister in 1994, a post which he held until 1998 when he was inducted to the pastoral charge of Kilmodan and Colintraive.

Ministers

1933 Thomas Fleming GILMORE BA From Dundee Wishart Memorial. Dem. 1950 (Died 1972)
(FES IX 502,X 297)

1950 James Eaglesham DOTT BA Ord. To Glasgow Macgregor Memorial 1955
(FES IX 502, X 297)

1956 Alan Pirrie KINNEAR MA From Sandsting and Aithsting. Dem. 1971 (Died 1973)
(FES X 297)

1974 George Gordon CAMPBELL MA From Moffat with Wamphray. Dem. 1978 due to failing health (Died 1980) (FES X 297, YB, Cong.)

1980 Stewart LAMONT BSc BD nd. Formerly with BBC. Dem 1982 (PM, YB)

1983 Robert DALY MA JP Min. of Inchture & Kinnaird linked with Longforgan Died 1988 (PM)

1989 James Alexander Penrice JACK Ord. (PM)
BSc BArch BD

L Melville, *The Fair Land of Gowrie*, Coupar Angus, 1939
F McGurk, *Papal Letters to Scotland of Benedict XIII of Avignon 1394-1419*, Edinburgh 1976
DCA CH2/748, CH3/688, CH3/9/3

AUCHTERHOUSE

The church of **Auchterhouse** has ancient origins but the present building, standing on rising ground, dates mainly from a rebuilding in 1774/5, incorporating work of 1630. The building erected in 1630 consisted of a chancel, nave and square tower at the west end. An old doorway is built up in the south front, there is a bell tower at the western end, and there are fragments of early window tracery set in the walling and gateways. An old burial aisle to the east was included in the church last century. The church was inscribed to the Virgin Mary, indicated by the invocation, *Ave Maria*, together with the fleur de lis carved on an old skewput stone. The inside of the church is attractive with good stained glass, and an arch in the chancel forms an interesting feature. An ancient stone font is still used. The interior of the church was 'modernised' in 1881. There is a very old parliament clock.

Auchterhouse Church

A pre-Reformation prebend of Dunkeld, Auchterhouse is mentioned in 1238 as a vicarage in the Diocese of Dunkeld and, according to Bagimont's Roll of 1275, was valued at £8 Scots. There is a reference in a charter of Robert III (1390-1406) of the foundation of *ane chaplene in the kirk of Uchterhouse*. It is noticed in 1426-7 when it was endowed with chaplainries for the safety of souls of knights who fell at Red Harlaw in 1411. It may have been the chapel recorded to have been attached to the church of Lundie, three miles distant. In 1460 Papal Indulgence was granted for those who contributed to the building and repair of the Church of the Most Glorious Virgin of Auchterhouse.

An account for £100 7s 6d Scots, dated 26 July 1717, is for the purchase of two communion cups, less an allowance for one old cup. The cups bear the inscriptions, *This communion cup. For the Kirk of Auchterhouse. Gifted Be Wr Hay of Dronlaw and Reneud Anno 1717* and *This communion cup. Belonging to the Parish of Auchterhouse. Bought with the Box Monie, Anno 1717.* A further pair of communion cups was purchased in 1795. A manse was built in 1789.

On 19 December 1797 a thanksgiving service was held for the naval victory at Camperdown of Admiral Adam Duncan, who lived at nearby Lundie.

*Auchterhouse was linked with **Murroes and Tealing** on 27 February 1983. The manse of the linked charge is at Balgray, Tealing.*

Ministers

1563 Sir Duncan GRAY	Vicar and reader in 1563, 1565 and 1579. His protocol book is preserved. (FES V 309, VIII 485)
1563 Alexander TYRIE	Min. in 1563 and 1568. To Meigle 1572, readmitted before 1582, with Strathmartine, Tealing and Mains also in his charge till 1590. Pres. to parsonage and vicarage 3 July 1564. Dem. 1603 (FES V 309, VIII 485)
1568 James MELVILLE MA	Pres. to parsonage and vicarage July 1568 (FES VIII 485)
1604 David KINNEAR	Adm. about 1604. Member of Assemblies of 1610 and 1616. Died 1633 (FES V 309)
1633 John ROBERTSON MA	Adm. To Third Charge Dundee 1641. (FES V 309)
1642 William WEMYSS	Adm. about 1642. Died 1655. (FES V 309)

1656	James AUCHENLECK MA	Adm. (FES V 309)
1665	James CAMPBELL	Ord. Suspended on his own confession of fornication, 13 Dec. 1665. He was involved in scandal with Marjorie Ramsay, Countess of Buchan. They were subsequently married. He was brother of laird of Lundie. Afterwards min. of Lundie and Fowlis, having exchanged charges with John Robertson in 1667. (FES V 310)
1667	John ROBERTSON MA	From Lundie and Fowlis. Died between 1692 and 1700 (FES V 310)
1688	Andrew ROBERTSON	Presb. Min. in 1688 (FES V 310)
1702	Patrick JOHNSTONE MA	Ord. Died 1740 (FES V 310)
1740	David SCOTT MA	Ord. Pres. by Earl of Airlie. Died 1773 (FES V 310)
1774	James SCOTT	Ord. Pres. by Hon. Walter Ogilvy of Clova 1773. Died 1804 (FES V 310)
1804	George ADDISON MA	From Glenisla. Pres. by Trustees of David Ogilvy of Airlie. To Liff and Benvie 1817 (DD St Andrews 1830) (FES V 310)
1818	George WINEHOUSE MA	From Clova (Missionary). Pres. by Walter Earl of Airlie. Died in London 1851 (FES V 310-1)
1844	Hugh Arbuthnott LYELL	Ord. (A&S) Died 1878 (FES V 311)
1878	William Mason INGLIS MA FSA(Scot)	Ord. Author of *Annals of An Angus Parish* and *An Angus Parish in the Eighteenth Century*. Died 1912 (FES V 311)
1912	John Kirkland CAMERON	From New Parish Ardrossan. CF during First World War. Dem. 1942 (Died 1947) (FES V 311, VIII 485)
1942	John WELSH MA	From Polmadie St Margaret's as C&S. To Wemyss St Mary's by the Sea 1950 (FES IX 502)
1950	Allan Douglas GALLOWAY MA BD PhD	Ind. Dem. On appt. to Chair of Religious Studies, Univ. of Abadan, Nigeria, 1954 (FES IX 502)
1956	Victor Charles BENNIE	Formerly at Oathlaw (term. app.) Dem. 1960 (Died 1962) (FES X 297)
1960	Robert Forrester Victor SCOTT DD	From London St Columba's. DD (Edinburgh 1944) (Mod. GA 1956) Dem.1968 (Died 1975) (YB 1960, FES X 297)
1968	James HAMILTON BA BD	From Loanhead. Dem. 1982 (FES X 297, YB)
1983	Helen JOHNSTONE MA BD HdipRE	Ord. To Kitwe Zambia 1989. (PM, YB) (Died 1999)
1989	William M MACMILLAN LTh	From Whithorn St Ninian's Priory. To Kilmory with Lamlash 1993 (PM, YB)
1995	Sydney GRAHAM DipYL Mphil	Ind. (PM)

A Jervise, *Memorials of Angus and Mearns*, Edinburgh, 1861

W M Inglis, *Annals of an Angus Parish,* Dundee, 1888

W M Inglis, *An Angus Parish in the Eighteenth Century,* Dundee, 1904

N Tranter, *The Queen's Scotland, The Eastern Counties,* London, 1972

A Warden, *Angus or Forfarshire,* Dundee, 1885

FOWLIS AND LIFF

Fowlis and Liff congregation was formed by the union of Fowlis with Liff and Benvie on 7 June 1953.

Fowlis

The church of **Fowlis** or **Fowlis Easter** was dedicated to Saint Marnoch. It belonged to the Priory of St Andrews. In 1446 Andrew, Lord Gray, granted to the parish a collegiate endowment. The church was restored in 1889 at a cost of £2,500. There has probably been a church here at least from the twelfth century. The present building dates from the time the charge became collegiate, *circa* 1450. There is an aumbry or sacrament house in the north wall, to the right of where the altar stood. This is one of the finest sacrament houses in the country. On it is depicted Christ holding the globe and cross. To the right an angel bears the cross, while to the left another angel is seen with the pillar of scourging. Above is the angel of the Annunciation, with scroll opening out towards the Virgin, behind whom is a closed book. Her insignia, the pot of lilies, the symbol of purity, can be observed. Part of a fine rood screen with its fifteenth century oak doors survives.

Fowlis Easter Church
This building dates to around 1450

The building has good plain Gothic windows. There are many masons' marks visible on the stonework of polished ashlar with occasional snecking. The church has jougs, which until relatively recently were still chained to the wall to the left of the elaborate doorway on the southern wall. The doorway has an ogival hood, and the moulding over the door shows a helmet with swan and lions, the arms of the families of Gray and Wemyss.

Corbels that surmounted the gallery, or rood loft, which accommodated the musicians, can be seen opposite one another on the north and south walls. A door on the north wall has a holy water stoup ornamented with *fleur de lis*

and quatrefoils. There is a similar piscina at the right hand side of the south door, without ornamentation. The fine timber open roof was put up in 1889, during the improvements previously mentioned, and replaced a flat ceiling, the work being supervised by T S Robertson, architect, Dundee. The opening of the roof brought into relief the large west window. At the same time the old box pews were removed and replaced, the seating arrangements being changed to face the east. The pulpit which, formerly, had been in a central position at the west end of the nave, was offset at the chancel. A central aisle replaced the two side aisles. The former burial aisle was converted into a chancel to hold the pulpit, communion table, organ, font and reading desk. The round window in the gable, with stained glass, shows the arms of the Grays, with their motto *Anchor Fast*. The stained glass window was erected in 1867 in memory of John, 16th Lord Gray. Under the floor of the chancel is the burial vault of the Gray family.

The baptismal font is octagonal in shape, with sculptured panels depicting, 1. The Baptism of Christ, 2. The Arrest in the Garden, 3. *Ecce Homo*, 4. The Scourging, 5. Christ bearing the Cross, 6. The Crucifixion, 7. The Resurrection, 8. Christ calling the souls of the Fathers out of Limbo. A bronze alms dish of German origin, dated 1487, is embossed with a Garden of Eden scene. There are emblematic flowers in the foreground, and at the back a turret with a pathway leading to the Earth. The German inscription is translated, *I bide the time in quietness.*

The church possesses painted panels, dated to 1480, considered the finest in Scotland. The panel painting of the Crucifixion shows over twenty figures, including St John, Mary Cleophas, The Virgin Mary, Salome, and Mary Magdalene with hands clasped. The centurion is seen pointing upwards to the scroll, which bears the words, *Truly this was the Son of God.* Near him is the High Priest, and to his left a figure dressed in ermine, wearing a crown and holding a sceptre, is probably intended for King Herod. On the right of the cross, blind Longinus is thrusting his spear, guided by two soldiers, into the Saviour's side. Above, the souls of the two thieves are seen issuing from their mouths. This painting was shown at an exhibition of medieval art in London in 1923. The inscription on a spar below has no reference to the picture. It reads, *They built this church to St Marnock; if you ask in what year* (then) *in 1453, because he* (Lord Gray) *had been at Rome on a pilgrimage as one who was under a vow. "But Thou...Amen"* [Psalm xli, 10]

Another panel shows a figure of the Godhead, with St Catherine on the right, and, on the left, John the Baptist pointing to the Lamb in his hand, with the Virgin holding the Child in her arms. The centre of the picture has been obliterated, while below can be seen the lowering into the tomb, with Mary, Mary Magdalene, and the Apostles looking on. Five panels below are probably part of the Crucifixion picture. The central figure may represent the donor, Lord Gray.

A third panel depicts a number of Saints and Apostles; 1. St Catherine with sword and wheel, 2. St Matthias with spear and book, 3. St Thomas with carpenter's square and book, 4. St Simon with book and saw, 5. St John the Evangelist with poisoned chalice and dragon emerging from it, 6. Christ with hand raised in benediction and open book, his foot resting on an orb, 7. St Peter with book and key, 8. St Anthony as a hermit with staff and book, and a collared pig at his feet, 10. St Paul (uncertain), 11. St Ninian as a bishop with pastoral staff, right hand raised in benediction, with manacles from his right wrist. A flag shows the Gray arms.

The paintings were probably carried out during the lifetime of Patrick, 4th Lord Gray. There is an exact copy of the Crucifixion panel on glass in the church of St Peter's, Cologne. It seems to have been a stock picture of the Van Eyck School. The wall paintings were restored in 1974.

The church is A-listed. The former hearse house, dated 1841, is in snecked rubble with stugged ashlar dressings. The renovation of the hearse house, at a cost of £34,000, was approved in 1997. This building is B-listed.

A roughly hewn stone, which stands in the middle of the churchyard, was the gathering point for meetings and processions connected to the church. It was also a market stance.

*The parishes of **Fowlis Easter** and **Lundie** were united on 31 January 1618. The parishes were disjoined on 7 June 1953 when **Fowlis** united with **Liff and Benvie** under the name **Fowlis and Liff** and **Lundie** united with **Muirhead of Liff** under the name **Lundie and Muirhead of Liff**. (q.v.)*

Fowlis Easter or Fowlis in Gowrie

Ministers

1563	Nicolas SPITTAL	Min. in 1563, with Longforgan and Benvie also in his charge in 1567. To Benvie before 1574 (FES V 357)
1574	Patrick MORTIMER	Reader in 1574 (FES V 357)
1576	Patrick GALLOWAY	Min. in 1576, with Longforgan also in his charge. To Perth 1581 (FES V 357)
1581	Robert RYND	From Mertoun. Pres. to the vicarage by James VI. To Longforgan 1590 (FES V 357)
1594	Andrew MORTON MA	Min. in 1594. To Lundie 1595 (FES V 357)
1595	Gilbert RAMSAY MA	Min. in 1595 and in 1607 (FES V 357)
1608	Andrew MORTON MA	Above mentioned. From Lundie. Re-trans. To Lundie after 21 Sept. 1610 (FES V 357)
1614	Henry FITHIE MA	From Kinnell. Union of parish with Lundie during his ministry. Died 1620 (FES V 355)

Lundie and Fowlis Easter (after union of 1618)

[The early history and succession of ministers appears under **Lundie and Muirhead of Liff**]

Liff

The church is situated in the village of that name. The medieval church was dedicated to St Mary and given to the Cistercian Abbey of Scone by Alexander I. It was in the Diocese of St Andrews and the Deanery of Angus. According to the Rev. Thomas Constable, minister of the charge and author of the OSA *circa* 1790, the church was built in 1774, except for the aisle. The manse was built around 1759/60.

The present building was erected in 1839 by William MacKenzie, Perth. It is Gothic and rectangular, with a tower and spire centrally placed at the east end which has the main entrance. The construction is in stugged pink and cream sandstone courses with ashlar dressings. The vestibule has two stone geometric stairs to the gallery. It contains a carved memorial stone to James Cock of Locheye and family. [Cox of Lochee] There is a plaster cast of a ninth century stone depicting horsemen, found at Bullion Farm, Invergowrie, and now in the Royal Scottish Museum. There are original pitchpine pews, some convertible to communion tables. The horseshoe gallery, the front of which is panelled, is supported on timber columns. An alms dish is dated 1751.

During the early years of his ministry, the Rev. John Wilson gathered about £500 for *beautifying the church and procuring an organ*. The church was improved and an organ installed. J & W Guthrie, Glasgow erected stained glass windows in memory of Mr Wilson in 1893. The figures of St John and St Paul appear on the north side of the pulpit and of Moses and Christ on the south side.

A single storey rectangular hearse house, dated 1876, is built in stugged rubble with ashlar dressings.

Liff church is B-listed.

*The parishes of **Liff, Invergowrie,** and **Logie** were united on 3 September 1613. On 8 August 1753 **Benvie** was also joined with them. **Logie** was disjoined again in 1877. **Invergowrie** was also disjoined in 1917.*

Liff

Ministers

1563	John BUCHAN	Min. in 1563 (FES VIII 492)
1566	Nicolas SPITTALL	Min. of Fowlis Easter and Longforgan in charge here also (FES VIII 492)
1567	Ninian HALL	Min. in 1567 with Invergowrie and Logie also in his charge. To Invergowrie in 1571 (FES V 347)
1574	Andrew HANY	Reader here and at Logie (FES V 347)
1601	John CHRISTISON	Min. of Logie, had charge here also. (FES V 347)
1608	John DUNCAN	From Lundie between 1608 and 1613 when he also had charge of Logie and Invergowrie (Died 1650) (FES V 347)

Liff, Invergowrie, and Logie

Ministers

1613	John DUNCAN	Min. of Liff. Dem. before March 1637 (Died 1650) (FES V 347)
1637	James DUNCAN MA	Pres. by Charles I. Still min. 15 July 1643 (FES V 347)
1649	Patrick BALLINGALL MA	Adm. Still min. 5 June 1650 (FES V 347)
1650	Andrew WEDDERBURN MA	Adm. Dep. 11 June 1664. Restored by Act of Parliament 1690, but did not return here on account of his health, and because the people adhered to John Christison. (FES V 347)
1664	William SKINNER MA	Adm. Pres. by Charles II. Died 1673. (FES V 348)
1673	John CHRISTISON MA	From Kemback. App. By James, Archbishop of St Andrews. Pres. by Charles II. Deprived by Act of Parliament restoring Presbyterian mins. Received into communion 1694. Died 1703 (FES V 348)
1704	Alexander SCOTT MA	Ord. Died 1724. (FES V 348)
1726	Thomas DONALDSON	Ord. During his ministry Benvie united with Liff, Invergowrie and Logie. Died 1758 (FES V 348)

Liff, Invergowrie, Logie and Benvie

Ministers

1753	Thomas DONALDSON	Min. of Liff, Invergowrie and Logie. Died 1758 (FES V 348)
1758	James PLAYFAIR MA	Ord. To Benvie 23 March 1743. To this charge in terms of Decreet of Annexation 19 Nov. 1758. Grandfather of W H Playfair, distinguished Edinburgh architect. Died 1772 (FES V 348)

1773	John PLAYFAIR MA FRS	Ord. Pres. by John, Lord Gray. Son of preceding. Dem. 1783;subsequently Professor of Mathematics, jointly with Dr Adam Ferguson, in University of Edinburgh. He later held chair of Natural Philosophy (Died 1819)(FES V 348-9)
1785	Thomas CONSTABLE MA	Ord. Pres. by George III and Charles, Lord Gray. DD (St Andrews 1809) (FES V 349)
1817	George ADDISON MA	From Auchterhouse. Pres. by Francis, Lord Gray He was described as a man of high intellectual powers and an admirable preacher. He was proposed for Mod. of GA but declined. DD (St Andrews 1830) Died 1852 (FES V 349)
1852	Lachlan McLEAN	From Kinfauns. Pres. by John, Lord Gray and Victoria. Died 1868 (FES V 349)
1869	John WILSON MA	Ord. Pres. by Lady Gray. During his ministry Logie was disjoined. Died 1892 (FES V 349-50)

*The early history of **Logie** and **Invergowrie** churches and the succession of ministers appear under **Logie and St John's (Cross)** and **Invergowrie** respectively.*

Liff, Invergowrie and Benvie

Ministers

| 1877 | John WILSON MA | Min. of Liff, Invergowrie, Logie and Benvie. Died 1892. (FES V 349-50) |
| 1892 | George DINGWALL MA BD | From Craigiebuckler, Aberdeen. During his ministry Invergowrie was disjoined. Died 1918 (FES V 350) |

Liff and Benvie

Ministers

1916	George DINGWALL MA BD	Min. of Liff, Invergowrie and Benvie. Died 1918 (FES V 350)
1919	William Sutherland BUCHAN MA BD	From Galashiels West. To Portobello St James 1924.App. editor of CofS YB 1921 (Died 1955) (FES V 350, KofE 238)
1925	John MACLEAN BD	From Renton. Dem. 1953. (Died 1958) (FES VIII 492, 519, X 307)

Benvie

The parish of Benvie belonged to the Diocese of St Andrews and was in the Gowrie Deanery. David, Bishop de Bernham dedicated the church, on 9 September 1243. About 1350-60 there are mentioned at Benvie the land of St Martin and the Vennel of St Mary, the latter probably being the parish church. John Scremonig was provided to the parish church of *Banvi* in 1400, vacant by the resignation of John Carpentarii. There are the ruined remains of a medieval church north west of the village of Invergowrie. A stone in the churchyard bears the arms of James Scrymgeour, second Viscount Dudhope, whose family held the lands of Benvie until 1654. The name is also recorded as *Banevyn* or *Banevill*. An old bell which belonged to the church of Benvie was stated by Warden in 1885 to be kept at the manse of Liff. Its inscription was *Michael Bvrgerhvys 1631 M Hendrie Fithie.*

Ministers

1560	William LUDE	Pres. by David Lude, factor of Benvie (FES V 350)
1574	John BLAIR	Reader in 1574 (FES V 350)
1574	Nicolas SPITTALL	From Fowlis, with that parish and Longforgan also In his charge. To Longforgan 1576 (FES V 350)
1576	William HAITLIE	From Logie, with Abernyte and Lundie also in his charge. To Abernyte before 1585 (FES V 350)
1585	Robert SCRIMGEOUR	Min. in 1585 (FES V 350)
1590	Patrick WATTERSTON MA	Min. in 1590. To St Andrews and Deerness Orkney 1591 (FES V 350)

1591 Alexander SCRYMGEOUR	Adm. To Inchture in 1599, but seems to have attempted to retain this charge. On 14 March 1601 he claimed possession as successor to Thomas Ramsay. In 1613 the Synod ordered him to demit, which he did in 1614, into the hands of Scrymgeour, Constable of Dundee . (FES V 350, VIII 492)
1599 John OGILVIE MA	Adm. about 1599, having Kinnaird also in his charge. Pres. to the vicarages of Inchture and Kinnaird by James VI in 1601. To Kingoldrum 1606 (FES V 350)
1619 John RAMSAY MA	Adm. (FES V 350)
1627 Henry FITHIE MA	Pres. by Sir John Scrymgeour of Dudhope. To Mains 1633 (FES V 350)
1633 Andrew SHIPPERT MA	Adm. Pres. by Sir John Scrymgeour. Still min. 21 July 1650 (FES V 350)
1655 William GRAY	Min. in 1655, with Fowlis also in his charge. Dem. before 9 June 1664 (FES V 350)
1665 Alexander SCRYMGEOUR MA	Pres. by John, Earl of Dundee and coll. by Archbishop of St Andrews. Pres to the vicarage by the Archbishop 1669. Died 1686 (FES V 350-1)
1687 George THOMSON MA	Ord. Because he prayed for James VII at a meeting of the Presb. his gown was pulled off by the populace. He was imprisoned about the time of the Revolution. Dem. 1692 (Died 1692) (FES 351)
[Alexander RANKIN MA]	Adm. a deacon under Episcopacy. Intruded 1692 to 1706 (Died 1729) (FES V 351)
1707 George OGILVY MA	Ord. To Kirriemuir 1713 (FES V 351)
1716 Thomas BEVERIDGE MA	Ord. Pres. by John, Lord Gray. Died 1731 (FES V 351)
1731 Thomas LAWRIE MA	From Bathgate. Died 1741 (FES V 351)
1743 James PLAYFAIR	Ord. To Liff in terms of Decreet of Annexation in 1758 (FES V 351)

Fowlis and Liff *was formed on 7 June 1953 by the union of* **Liff and Benvie** *with* **Fowlis** *which was disjoined from* **Lundie**. *Both churches continued in use.*

The parishes of **Lundie and Muirhead of Liff** *and* **Fowlis and Liff** *were linked on 17 May 1995 under the ministry of the Rev. Martyn R H Thomas, minister of Lundie and Muirhead. The Rev. Kenneth Ian Malcolm BD, was appointed Auxiliary Minister to the linked charge for a five year term in the first instance.*

Ministers

1954 William Osler NICOLL MA	From Riccarton. Dem. 1979 (FES IX 518, YB)
1980 Charles W MILLER MA	From Anstruther. Dem. 1994 (YB)
1995 Martyn R H THOMAS CEng MIStructE	Min. of Lundie and Muirhead (PM)

A Dalgety,*The Church and Parish of Liff,* 1940
Church of Foulis Easter, booklet outlining history and describing building and contents, n.d.
A Warden, *Angus or Forfarshire,* Vol. IV, Dundee, 1885
F McGurk (ed.) *Calendar of Papal Letters to Scotland of Benedict XIII of Avignon 1394-1419,* Edinburgh, 1976
Aberdeen Year Book for 1892
DCC   Combined Statutory and Descriptive List
DCA   CH2/254
DPL   Lamb 190(16)

INCHTURE AND KINNAIRD

Inchture church is situated in Main Street, Inchture. There is little record of the church building prior to the nineteenth century. A meeting of heritors in 1799 considered extensive repairs and alterations, which were claimed to be urgently required. In 1834 the fabric was in such a state of disrepair that the heritors decided to build an entirely new church to the plan of William MacKenzie, Dundee, at a cost of £1,114. No plan of this building is now available, but it is believed to have been Gothic in style. The material used was the old red sandstone from a local quarry. On Sunday, 14 December 1890, fire broke out and the whole church was gutted, leaving only the walls and the steeple standing. A new church was erected in 1891 on the site of the former one, at a cost of £1,129. The architect was Duncan Stewart, factor of Rossie Estates.

The kirk session possess two very old silver communion cups inscribed *Gifted by P L K to the Kirk of Insture 1692*. In 1835 Lord Kinnaird presented two silver cups inscribed, *Presented by the Right Honble. George William Fox, Lord Kinnaird, Baron Rossie, etc., to the Kirk of Inchture when rebuilt A..D. 1834.*

*The congregation of **Inchture and Kinnaird** was formed on 12 January 1941 with the union of **Inchture** and **Kinnaird**, both churches being retained as places of worship.*
*Inchture as it was in 1941 was formed by the union of **Inchture** and **Rossie** by Act of Parliament of 22 August 1670.*

Rossie

The church of **Rossie** or **Rossinclerach** was dedicated to St Coman of Tyrconell, but there was a later dedication or rededication to St Laurence and St Coman by Bishop David de Bernham on 13 August 1243. It is mentioned in the reign of Malcolm IV (1153-1165) when the gift *in the abbacy of Rossie* which David I made to Matthew, Archdeacon of St Andrews was confirmed. The chapel of Fowlis was at first a chapel in the parish of Rossie. Rossie and Fowlis are included among the possessions of the Priory of St Andrews in a bull of Pope Alexander II of 31 December 1163. The Priory of St Andrews raised an action in the early thirteenth century in a dispute over an appointment to Rossie of Master William de Grenlaw by the Bishop of St Andrews. Following the Reformation, the church became a Presbyterian place of worship, until the parish was united with Inchture in 1670. The building became ruinous, but was restored by the ninth Lord Kinnaird as an Episcopalian chapel in 1866. Later, it was set apart as a memorial chapel of the Kinnaird family.

Ministers

1565	David ROBERTSON	Min. in 1565. Pres. to vicarage by James VI 1570; had Inchture and Kinnaird also in his charge in 1574. To Inchture before 1585 (FES V 344)
1574	David COOK	Reader in 1574 (FES V 344)
1591	Thomas RAMSAY	From Inchture. Died 1597 (FES V 344)
1599	George HAITLIE	From Abernyte. Pres. to vicarage by James VI 1607. To Abernyte before 1614 (FES V 344)
1628	James BLAIR	Pres. by Charles I. Died 1647 (FES V 344)
1650	Andrew OLIPHANT MA	Adm. Removed before 26 March 1682, probably for refusing the Test. In 1690 the Synod of Fife proposed he should return to his charge he having expressed his repentance for his compliance with Prelacy (FES V 344)

Inchture

The first ecclesiastical building in the parish of Inchture may have been a chapel mentioned in the charters of William the Lion and Richard, Bishop of St Andrews. This chapel was given the status of a parish church during that king's reign, being granted to the Priory of St Andrews, along with the chapel of Kinnaird, which later also became a parish church. David de Bernham, Bishop of St Andrews, dedicated, or rededicated, Inchture on 13 August 1243. Reconfirmation of the *union of the mensal church and lands of Inchechure, St Andrews diocese, and the annexed chapel of Kymard [Kinnaird] same diocese* is recorded in 1381.

John Millar, minister, wrote in his article on the parish for the OSA, *Church and manse are both old. The cure was served before [1710] by a Mr Carstairs [who] continued for some years after to have a place of worship in the parish for the benefit of the Episcopals in it who still adhered to him.*

Ministers

1563 Nicolas SPITTAL MA	Min. at Fowlis, also in charge here till 1572 (FES VIII 490)
1565 Alexander JARDEN	Canon of St Andrews Priory. Min. in 1565 (FES V 342)
1567 John SMYTH	Reader in 1567, exhorter at Longforgan and Canon of St Andrews Priory (FES V 342)
1574 James WICHTAND	Reader in 1567 and at Kinnaird. Pres. to vicarage Aug. 1573 on death of Arthur Tailyour. Died 1579 (FES V 342, VIII 490)
1579 Archibald SIBBALD	Pres. to the vicarage by James VI (FES V 342)
1585 David ROBERTSON	Canon of St Andrews Priory. Min. of Rossie in 1565;trans. and adm. before 1585, with Kinnaird and Rossie also in his charge; still min. in 1588 (FES V 342)
1589 Thomas RAMSAY	Adm. in 1589. To Rossie about 1591 (FES V 342)
1599 Alexander SCRYMGEOUR MA	Adm. before 1599 with Benvie also in his charge. Pres. by James VI to vicarage in 1606 on dem. of John Ogilvy, min. at Kingoldrum. To Kinghorn 1620 (FES V 342, VIII 490)
1626 Alexander ROBERTSON MA	Adm. Probably one of eighteen ministers in Synod dep. by Committee of Visitation in 1649. In 1662 was recommended by Synod for charity being aged and in distress (Died 1667) (FES V 342)
1653 John AUCHENLECK MA	Adm. To Newburn 1663 (FES V 342)
1664 Robert WHITE	Ord. To Ferryport on Craig 1666 (FES V 342)
1682 James CARSTAIRS MA	From Tannadice. Pres. by Alexander, Archbishop of St Andrews. Died 1709 (FES V 342)
1710 George BLAIKIE	From Redgorton. Died 1725 (FES V 343)
1715 Thomas CARSTAIRS	Episcopal min. intruded here Oct. 1715 to Jan. 1716 (FES VIII 491)
1726 James OGILVIE MA	From Footdee. To First Charge, Aberdeen, 1729. (FES V 343)
1729 John RANKINE MA	From Clunie. Pres. by George II. Died 1737 (FES V 343)
1739 Thomas RANDALL MA	Ord. To First Charge, Stirling, 1770 (FES V 343)
1771 Thomas RANDALL	Ord. Pres. by George III. Son of preceding. To Outer High Church, Glasgow, 1773. He assumed surname of DAVIDSON when he inherited estate of his maternal uncle. Much loved evangelical minister.DD (Harvard 1793) (Died 1828) (FES V 343, KofE 98)
1774 John MILLAR MA	From Newburgh . Pres. by George III. Died 1799 (FES V 343)
1799 Alexander DAVIE	Ord. Pres. by George III. Died 1840 (FES V 343)
1836 John Adamson HONEY	Ord. A&S. Pres. by William IV. DD (St Andrews 1868) Described as a *tall, handsome, courtly gentleman of the olden time, and a keen sportsman.* Died 1898 (FES V 343)
1884 John Adamson HONEY MA	From Clova A&S. Son of preceding. Died 1924 (FES V 344)
1920 Thomas Downie MEREDITH MA	From Lochee A&S. To Edinburgh St Luke's 1927 (Died 1944) (FES V 344, VIII 491, KofE 484)
1928 Peter John McIVER	From Craigneuk. Dem. 1939 (Died 1949) (FES IX 518)

Kinnaird

Kinnaird church is located in the small village of that name on the Braes of Carse. The present church, plain in appearance and with Gothic windows, was built in 1815, according to a stone inset. The interior was renovated in 1890. To distinguish the parish from several others of the same name it was sometimes styled Kinnaird in Gowrie. There is a watch house in the churchyard, presumably used to frustrate the activities of the *Resurrectionists.* Kinnaird in medieval times was a dependant chapel of Inchture and was given by William the Lion and Richard, Bishop of St Andrews, to the Priory of St Andrews.

On several occasions in 1675 it is recorded that there was no preaching *because the barn doors, wherein the minister did formerly preach, were closed, all the seats removed, and the kirk not in a condition to preach in.* The writer of the essay on Kinnaird in the OSA, the Rev. David Spence, stated that the church had been built in 1674 and the manse in 1786. He was inducted in 1784. Two silver communion cups are dated to 1723. Two handsome silver boat shaped patens for holding bread were presented by the Ladies' Work Party to mark the minister's semi jubilee in 1924.

Ministers

1574	James WICHTAND	Reader here and at Inchture (FES V 345)
1590	George HAITLIE	Adm. about 1590. To Abernyte before 1593 (FES V 345)
1601	John OGILVIE	Min. of Benvie, had charge here also in 1601 (FES V 345)
1607	Robert SEYMOUR MA	Pres. to the vicarage by James VI. To Abbey Church of Holyrood (Canongate) 1621 (Died 1623) (FES V 345, KofE 56)
1622	Robert MONTGOMERIE MA	Adm. To St Quivox 1623 (FES V 345)
1633	John BARCLAY MA	Adm. Pres. to the vicarage by Charles I. App. By the Presb. in 1644 to proceed to England to preach to Lord Couper's regiment at York. To Monifieth 1649 (Died 1675) (FES V 345, 362)
1649	Thomas KINNARES MA	Adm. There were a number of occasions in July and August 1651 when there was no service the minister *being with the army* and *the enemy being at Perth.* Died 1677 (FES V 345)
1659	William PIERSON MA	Ord. A&S. To Paisley 1663 (FES V 345)
1678	John SHAW MA	From Carnock. Conformed at the Revolution but suspended by the Privy Council 1700 (FES V 345)
1707	James ADAMS MA	Ord. Pres. by Sir David Threipland of Fingask. Died 1734 (FES V 345-6)
[George BLAIKIE		Pres. by George II 1734 but the GA found, 1736, that he could not be adm. min. of parish, and that parish must be settled according to the rules of the Church (FES V 346)]
1736	James MYLN	Ord. Died 1783 (FES V 346)
1784	David SPENCE MA	Ord. Pres. by George III. Died 1830 (FES V 346)
1825	John SPENCE	Ord. A&S. Son of preceding. Pres. by George IV. Died 1866 (FES V 346)
1845	John RANKEN	From Dundee St Andrews A&S. Pres. by Victoria. Died 1868 (FES V 347)
1869	William SINCLAIR	Ord. Pres. by Victoria. Died 1879 (FES V 347)
1879	James Rose MACPHERSON MA BD	Ord. To Dingwall 1899 (FES V 347)
1899	John Milne ANDERSON MA BSc BD	Ord. Dem. 1941 (FES V 347, VIII 491)

Inchture and Kinnaird

After the union of 1941 both churches were used for worship. On 4 April 1963 the charge was linked with **Longforgan** under the minister of Inchture and Kinnaird and on 28 February 1983 to **Abernyte**.

The Rev. Dr Iain T Adamson MA BSc MSc PhD was appointed Auxiliary Minister of the linked charge in 1986, a post which he held until he retired in 1993.

Ministers

1941	Henry Taylor Ferguson BD	From Dundee Hilltown. To Edinburgh Craigmillar Park 1953 (Died 1977) (FES IX 518, KofE 273)
1954	Robert DALY MA	From Blantyre Stonefield. Died 1988 (FES IX 518, X 307)
1989	James Alexander Penrice JACK BSc BArch BD	Ord. (PM)

C Burns (ed.) *Calendar of Papal Letters to Scotland of Clement VII of Avignon 1378-1394*, Edinburgh, 1976
P C Ferguson (ed.) *Medieval Papal Representatives in Scotland 1125-1286*, The Stair Society, Edinburgh, 1997
L Melville, *The Fair Land of Gowrie*, Coupar Angus, 1939
DCA   CH2/188, CH2/418
DPL   Sp. 5/190

INVERGOWRIE

Invergowrie church stands on a corner site in Errol Road in the village. The building, which cost around £5,000, was designed by John Robertson, architect, and is similar to his St Laurence's church in Forres opened in 1906. Invergowrie is a rectangular plan Gothic church with a 3-stage tower to the northwest angle. A hall at the northeast angle forms an L plan complex. The masonry is snecked pink and cream rubble with ashlar dressings. The exterior walls are in freestone from Newton Quarry, near Elgin.

The interior has walls rendered and lined in snecked rubble, with droved ashlar dressings. There are four pointed arches with clustered piers to an aisle on the north elevation. There is a prominent timber roof. The hexagonal oak pulpit has balustraded stairs and carved panels depicting a vine, flowers, wheat etc. There is a Caen stone font. The two-manual organ is by Joseph Brook & Company, Glasgow. The stained glass panel to the choir room depicts the Rev. Robert S Walker conducting an open-air communion service. He was the first minister of Longforgan Free Church. This window was one of a pair in the former Free Church, the other having been lost. There are memorials on the south wall to Donald Davidson, minister 1901-29, and to Adam Philip, Free Church minister from 1881 and Moderator of the United Free Church General Assembly in 1921.

In 1900 Mrs Armitstead of Castle Huntly gifted communion plate. She also gave the baptismal font. Mrs Armitstead, who became Lady Armitstead on the elevation of her husband to the peerage, was a noted benefactress of the church in its early years[1]. A bronze plaque honours those who died in the war of 1914-18, with the church bell being dedicated to their memory. A plaque from the former East Church recognises the sacrifice of the men of that congregation in the same war.

For long music had been provided by a harmonium, but in 1934 an organ was acquired from Erskine Church, Carnoustie. In 1959 alterations were carried out to the church hall, creating an upper and a lower hall.

The manse in Main Street was sold in 1989 for £108,000 and a new manse built in 1991 in Boniface Place at a cost of £105,000. In the following year the church was fitted with a new carpet, through the generosity of Mrs Sheila Thomson. The Woman's Guild gave a chancel decoration depicting a wooden cross on a blue background. This was dedicated on Sunday, 3 September 1995 by the Rev. Iain Craig, the former minister, at a service marking the jubilee of the union of the two Invergowrie churches.

The church building is B-listed. The manse is at 2 Boniface Place, Invergowrie.

Invergowrie, as it now is, was formed by the union of **Invergowrie St Columba's** *and* **Invergowrie East** *on 2 September 1945.*

The ancient church of **Invergowrie**, known also as Dargie Church, now roofless, was dedicated to St Peter, which may not have been the original dedication. It is said to have been the earliest Christian church built north of the Tay. According to legend there was a church, probably wooden, on the site in AD 431. Archbishop Spottiswoode gives the date of erection as AD 697. The founder is sometimes given as St Curitan, *circa* 710, St Boniface being his Roman name. There is also a tradition that St Ninian, or his followers, came here about 400, preaching the gospel on the hillock at Dargie. The name Ninewells may be connected to that saint. The church of Mains was dedicated to Ninian, suggesting that there might have been a Ninianic influence in the area. Dargie church belonged to the Abbey of Scone, having been given by Malcolm IV. It was at Invergowrie that the Reformer George Wishart prayed, *that this realm be illuminated with the light of Christ's apostles.* The parish of **Invergowrie** was united to **Liff, Benvie and Logie** on 3 September 1613.

A mission station in Invergowrie village, under Longforgan Parish Church, was begun in October 1886 in a small corrugated iron church, known affectionately as the *Tin Temple*, to serve the large proportion of the population of the village and of Kingoodie who adhered to the Established Church. Indeed, some members of the Auld Kirk had sittings in Longforgan Free Church, situated in Invergowrie. The Rev. Robert Logan, assistant to the parish minister, was given charge of the mission in 1890 and remained there until 1896. The Rev. Alexander M Thomson succeeded Mr Logan and in turn was followed by the Rev. Alexander Waddell, a probationer who was ordained in 1899. Sadly, Mr Thomson had served only a short period, dying in 1897. The iron church stood on the site of the present church garden and car park, and was opened on Sunday, 14 November 1886 by the Rev. Henry Cowan.

The Mission Station was created a Chapel of Ease in 1899 and the fine stone church built in 1909. The church was dedicated on 30 April of that year when the Right Rev. Dr Theodore Marshall, Moderator of the General Assembly, officiated. A hall was later added, being dedicated on 29 April 1911. The next stage in the attainment of full status for the congregation was reached a few years later. A petition by Lord Kinnaird and others for the *disjunction and erection into a parish of St Columba's Church, Invergowrie* was presented to Presbytery on 3 November 1915. The proposed parish boundaries were detailed. On 2 February 1916 Presbytery was advised that, by a Decree of the Court of Teinds, Invergowrie was now disjoined, and, with the addition of an adjoining district taken from Longforgan, a new parish *quoad sacra* was erected. Interestingly, the congregation seems to have been known locally as *St Columba's*, probably from the opening of the new church in 1909, but as *Invergowrie* in Presbytery records. On the national union of 1929 the congregation became known officially as Invergowrie St Columba's. An attempt at this time to unite the two charges in Invergowrie was unsuccessful.

Ministers

1571	Ninian HALL	From Liff. To Biggar 1573 (FES V 344)
1574	Alexander FORBES	Reader in 1574 (FES V 344)

-o-o-o-o-o-o-o-o-o-o-o-

1899	Alexander WADDELL	Ord. To Eassie and Nevay 1901 (Died 1944) (FES V 345, FCofI)
1901	Donald DAVIDSON	From Robertson Mission Church (Missionary)Grassmarket, Edinburgh. Adm. first min. of parish 1916. Died 1929 (FES V 345, VIII 491)
1930	Allan BELL	Ord. To Aberuthven 1945 (Died 1974) (FES IX 518, FCofI)

Longforgan Free, UF and Invergowrie East

At the Disruption of 1843 the minister of Longforgan *came out.* No site could be obtained for a church in the village of Longforgan and a church was built at the east end of the parish at Balbunnoch, now the village of Invergowrie. The cost of the church was £412, much of the labour being voluntary. Until a site for a manse was secured in 1849 the minister had to live in Dundee. Mr David M Watson, papermaker, Bullionfield, was a noted benefactor of the Free Church at Invergowrie, including a library of over 1,400 books gifted in 1875. The library was transferred to New College, Edinburgh in 1962.

A tower was added to the church in 1906, when the pulpit was replaced and an organ installed. The new pulpit was designed by P H Thoms, architect, Dundee, and was built of stone and oak. A centre panel bore the carved letters, *Alpha* and *Omega*. Windows on either side of the pulpit recalled an incident in the life of the martyr, George Wishart, which occurred at Invergowrie, and an open air communion scene conducted by the first minister of the Free Church, the Rev. Robert S Walker. There were texts on the cornices in brilliant lettering, *Come unto Me, all ye that labour and are heavy laden, and I will give you rest,* and *Lord, to Whom shall we go but unto Thee. Thou hast the words of eternal life.* The communion table, gifted by Mr Thoms, was inscribed, *They shall hunger no more.* The baptismal font gifted by Mr and Mrs Islay Burns Murray, bore the text, *The promise is unto you and to your children.* The church bell was replaced, the old bell being given to a church on Loch Tay side. The new bell was inscribed:

What time I toll
Bethink thee of thy soul;
Whenso I ring
Lift up thy heart and sing;
What hour I call
Praise God for Christ, for all.

Longforgan Free set up a school within its premises and the present day Invergowrie Primary School can trace its origins to that school. The congregation ran a Sunday school at Kingoodie, where there was also a service and a prayer meeting. A monthly prayer meeting was held at Longforgan village, and members had at one time schools or classes at Millhill, Benvie and Denhead of Liff.

Longforgan Free *was sometimes referred to as* *Invergowrie Free.* *In 1900 it became* *Longforgan UF* *and in 1929* *Invergowrie East.*

Ministers

1843	Robert Skene WALKER	Min. of Longforgan. Died 1854 (Ewing II 163)
1855	John HUNTER	Ord. Dem. 1881. Died 1900 (PM)
1881	Adam PHILIP MA	Ord. C&S. Mod.UF GA 1921. DD (1921) Died 1945 (FUF 391)
1932	Harold Bruce SMART MA	Ord. C&S. To Caldercruix 1940 (Died 1988) (FES IX 518, FCofI)
1941	James Douglas DUFF BD	Ord. Min. of united charge 2 Sept. 1945 (FES IX 518)

Invergowrie

After the union of 1945 the East church and hall, and the St Columba's manse at 80 Errol Road were sold, and improvements were carried out to St Columba's church which became the place of worship of the united congregation. The East church building was bought by the Bullionfield Paper Mill for £650 to be used as a community centre for the employees. Following the closure of the paper mill in 1965 it became the village hall. The font from the East church was given to Aberluthnott church in 1966.

Ministers

1945	James Douglas DUFF BD	Min. of Invergowrie East. To Colven and Southwick 1950. Died 1994 (FES IX 519, FCoI)
1951	James Stevenson McEWEN MA BD	From Hawick St Margaret's and Wilton South. Dem. on app. as Lecturer in Church History,New College, Edinburgh 1953 (Died 1993) (FES IX 519, FCoI)
1954	James Bruce TORRANCE MA	Ord. Dem.on app. as Lecturer in Christian Dogmatics, Edinburgh University 1961 (FES IX 519, X 307)
1961	Iain Robeson CRAIG MA	From Glasgow Pollockshields West. Dem. 1988 (FES X 307. FCofI)
1989	Alastair Mackenzie HORNE BSc BD	Ord.To Falkirk St Andrew's West 1997 (PM)
1997	Robert J RAMSAY LLB NP BD	From Airlie, Kingoldrum and Ruthven linked with Glenisla linked with Kilry linked with Lintrathen (PM)

Note

1.   Lord Armitstead , who was Russian born, was a very successful Dundee business man. He represented the Burgh in Parliament for about ten years and was a friend of W E Gladstone.

D M Gauld, *Four Churches of Invergowrie*, Dundee, 1997 (FCoI)
St Columba's Church Invergowrie 1909-1934, Dundee, 1934 (semi jubilee booklet)
A Philip, *After Fifty Years 1881-1931*, Dundee, 1931
L Melville, *The Fair Land of Gowrie,* Coupar Angus, 1939
E S Towill, *The Saints of Scotland*, Edinburgh, 1978
W J Smith, *A History of Dundee,* Dundee, 1975
DCC Combined Statutory and Descriptive List
DCA CH2/192, CH2/193, CH3/220

LONGFORGAN

Longforgan church stands in the village of the same name as the parish. The building is Gothic in style being rubble built. There are three large pointed windows with Y-tracery in the south elevation. The church was rebuilt in 1794 upon the original fifteenth century building, with the 1690 tower and small spire being retained. Alexander Hutcheson refurbished the interior in 1899. On either side of the chancel are handsome carved oak screens in memory of the Paterson family of Castle Huntly, designed by Sir Robert Lorimer. In the chancel is a beautiful stained glass window illustrating the Ascension. The ground floor of the tower was at one time used as the village gaol. There are a number of carved stones preserved in the church. The round tablet bearing the 1690 inscription set into the tower has been replaced and the weathered original is inscribed, *Founded in the year 1690, and finished at the charge of Patrick Earle of Strathmore and Kinghorn, Viscount Lyon, Lord Glammiss, etc. the bells wer givn by the Session and the clock by the frank Contribution of the peple.* The tombstone of Sir John Galychtly of Ebrokis and his wife Mariota is dated 1450. Fragments of the pre-Reformation baptismal font show it to have been an octagonal basin mounted on a shaft, with eight panels round the sides bearing sculptured representations of incidents in the life of Christ. The remaining fragments show Christ bearing the Cross, the Scourging, the Entombment, The Return from Hades, and the Resurrection.

In June 1980 the church was struck by lightning and the tower and the main building damaged. Repair work costing £69,000 was carried out in 1981.

The building is B-listed.

It is claimed that **Longforgan** church was founded in the sixth century by St Modwenna, disciple of St Patrick, and a friend of St Brigida. She is reported to have died here on the same day as St Columba was born in AD 521. St Modwenna is commemorated in a stained glass window on the south wall. While it is not certain that the present church occupies the site of the church ascribed by tradition to Modwenna, it is likely that it does and that various alterations and extensions have been carried out on the same location over the centuries. During the renovation in 1899-1900, the remains of the west window of the earlier church were uncovered. The tower had been built against the west gable, thus obscuring this window. Much of the fifteenth century work was taken down in 1794, only the west gable and portions of the foundations of the side walls being left.

In pre-Reformation times Longforgan church belonged to the Priory of St Andrews. Forgan or Longforgan is listed in the Gowrie deanery of the Diocese of St Andrews in the thirteenth century (Not to be confused with the parish of Forgan in the Fife Deanery). Laurence Kant or Kanth is recorded as perpetual vicar of Longforgan in 1379 and in 1394. After his death David de Camera was confirmed as vicar in 1402.

It is worth quoting the description of the older church given in the OSA, written around the time of the reconstruction by *a proprietor in the parish, a Friend to Statistical Inquiries.* The author described the old church as *long and narrow and inconvenient, consisting of two parts and evidently built at very different periods. The eastmost, which belonged entirely to the estate of Castle Huntly, was a substantial building, all of ashlar Kingoody stone, and, from a very handsome cross on the east gavel, and several recesses of hewn stone within, probably for altars or shrines of some favourite saint, it had every appearance of having been the original church when the Roman Catholic religion prevailed, and from uniformity of building with the church of Fowlis Easter it is probable that both were built sometime in the twelfth century by the same Lady Gray, to whom both estates then belonged. The west end of the church, although apparently older, must have been of a much later date. It was a very insufficient building, of bad materials, and had every appearance of that ill judged parsimonious simplicity, so much affected by the enthusiastic first reformers. This, therefore, would appear to have been added to it at the Reformation.*

The remodelling of 1794/5 resulted in the north, south and east walls being taken down, the building widened and shortened, re-seated and re-roofed. Galleries were introduced on three sides, the pulpit was set in the centre of the south wall, and box pews were installed. The renovation of 1899 removed the galleries, a new west end gallery being erected, a chancel was built at the east end, and the building re-seated with modern pews. In 1995-6 substantial upgrading work was carried out to the church and church hall at a cost of £100,000, with substantial financial support from the Kirk's central Fabric Fund.

In 1886 the kirk session of Longforgan decided to open a mission station at Invergowrie to serve the substantial number of Established Church members resident in that village and in Kingoodie. An iron church was erected and opened on 14 November 1886. This church was served initially by the minister of Longforgan with the aid of an assistant or probationer. It was raised to the status of a chapel of ease in 1899 with an ordained minister. A stone church was built in 1909 and **Invergowrie** (qv) was disjoined from Longforgan as a parish *quoad sacra* in 1916.

***Longforgan** was linked with **Inchture and Kinnaird** on 4 April 1963 and with **Abernyte** on 28 February 1983. The Rev. Dr Iain T Adamson MA BSc MSc PhD was appointed Auxiliary Minister of the linked charge in 1986, a post which he held until he retired in 1993.*

Ministers

1565	John SMYTH	Exhorter (FES VIII 492)
1566	Nicolas SPITTALL	Canon of Priory of St Andrews. Min. of Fowlis Easter and Benvie, had charge here also. Removed in 1576. Died 1576 (FES V 351)
1571	John GOODFELLOW	Member of Chapter of St Andrews before Reformation (FES V 351)
1574	John SMITH	Reader in 1574 (FES V 351)
1577	Patrick GALLOWAY	Min. of Fowlis Easter, had charge here in 1577 (FES V 351)
1590	Robert RYND	From Fowlis Easter. Pres. to vicarage by James VI before 12 Apl. 1595. Died suddenly together with James Row, min. of Kilspindie, in a house in Dundee, 29 Dec. 1614 (FES V 351)
1615	James JARDEN MA	From Ferryport on Craig. Pres. by James VI. Died 1630 (FES V 352)
1630	Joseph LAURIE MA	From Stirling. Pres. by Charles I. To Second Charge Perth 1635 (FES V 352)
1635	David BROUNE MA	From Eassie. Pres. by Charles I. Died 1646 (FES V 352)
1649	Alexander MYLNE MA	Adm. App. by Commission of Assembly to *attend Lord Brechin's regiment for performing ministerial duties to them*, Nov. 1650 and March 1651. To Second Charge Dundee 1661 (Died 1665) (FES V 352)
1661	James MIDDLETON	From Second Charge Montrose. Died 1672 (FES V 352)
1673	Alexander SYMMER MA	Ord. Died 1683 (FES V 352)
1684	David FORRESTER MA	From Lauder. He was a partner in the Darien Scheme. Described as *a man most highly distinguished by integrity of life, erudition and orthodoxy.* Died 1697 (FES V 352)
[The parish was vacant for five years]		
1702	Thomas MITCHELL	From Coupar Angus. Dem. 1708 (Died 1713) (FES V 352)
1709	James HODGE	From Mains. In 1715 he was obliged to leave the parish for a time when William Elphinston intruded. Died 1737 (FES V 352-3)
[William ELPHINSTON		During the period Sept. 1715 to Feb. 1716 he intruded, with the connivance of the Strathmore family of Castle Huntly. *He waited on the Pretender at Glamis.* (FES V 353, VIII 492)]
1738	George LYON MA	Ord. Pres. by George II. Described as a man of *unimpeachable character. His charity, benevolence and attention to the poor made him extremely useful and much beloved.* Died 1793 (FES V 353)
1793	Adam CAIRNS	Ord. Pres. by George III. Died 1821 (FES V 353)
1822	Robert Skene WALKER	From Kinclaven. Pres. by George IV. Joined FC in 1843. Min. of Longforgan FC 1843-54 (Died 1854) (FES V 353)
1843	William RITCHIE	From St Martins. Pres. by Victoria. DD (St Andrews 1850) During the difficult time following the Disruption of 1843 he rendered valuable services by ministering to congregations in Dundee left without a minister. His overture resulted in the appointment of the first Sunday School Committee in 1850. Died 1895 (FES V 353)

1885	Neil Kennedy MACKENZIE MA	From Alves A&S. Died 1924 (FES V 353)
1925	William MACNICOL MA BD	From Chapel of Garioch. Depute Clerk of GA 1949-53, Principal Clerk 1953-5. DD (Glasgow 1953) (OBE 1964) Dem. 1963 (Died 1972) (FES VIII 492, IX 519, X 307)
1963	Robert DALY MA	Min. of Inchture and Kinnaird. Died 1988 (FES X 307, YB)
1989	James Alexander Penrice JACK BSc BArch BD	Ord. (PM)

C Burns (ed.) *Papal Letters to Scotland of Clement VII of Avignon 1378-1394*, Edinburgh, 1976

D M Gauld, Four *Churches of Invergowrie*, Dundee, 1997

L Melville, *The Fair Land of Gowrie*, Coupar Angus, 1939

F McGurk (ed.) *Papal Letters to Scotland of Benedict XIII of Avignon 1394-1419*, Edinburgh 1976

C McKean & D Walker, *Dundee an Illustrated Architectural Guide*, Edinburgh 1993

D B Taylor, *Longforgan Church, Castle and Village*, 1986

DCA   CH2/249

DCC   Combined Statutory and Descriptive List

DPL   DNC Vol. 100

DPL   Sp 5/190

LUNDIE and MUIRHEAD OF LIFF

*The charge of **Lundie and Muirhead of Liff** was formed on 7 June 1953 by the union of **Lundie** and **Muirhead** of Liff. Both churches continued to be used for worship. The manse is adjacent to the church at Muirhead.*

The medieval church of **Lundie** was dedicated to St Laurence and belonged to the Priory of St Andrews. It was rebuilt in 1846. In 1892 T S Robertson, architect, Dundee, restored the church at a cost of £1,200. A porch and a new bellcote were added, the apse removed and the neo-classical Duncan mausoleum erected. The building is in coursed squared rubble, with random rubble at the west gable, and the mausoleum in ashlar. There are pointed windows and a door to the south elevation of the 6-bay nave.

The interior has boarded walls and embrasures. There is a fragment of a sacrament house inset in the north wall. A narrow round-headed window in the north wall reveals a wrought iron memorial to the Rev. John Robert Lester, minister 1953-77. There is a stained glass memorial window from 1897 to the Hunter family of Easter Keith. There is a war memorial on the north wall. In 1892 framed texts from Psalms and the Lord's Prayer on plaques were affixed by Stalker and Boyd, Dundee.

The Duncan burial enclosure has the tombs of the Duncan family and others. The inscription over the mausoleum door, now converted to the vestry, reads COEMETERIUM GULIELMI DUNCAN EQ AURAT ET BARONETTI MEDICI REGII MDCCLXXXIV. It pertains to Sir William Duncan, physician to George II and uncle of Adam, Viscount Duncan of Camperdown.

When the reformer, Paul Methven, was in the Dundee area in the summer of 1558, he preached *in sindrie gentlemens places in Angus and also in Fyfe.* He administered the sacrament in the parish church of Lundie.

*The parishes of **Lundie** and **Fowlis Easter** were united on 31 January 1618. Andrew Hally, writer of the OSA essay, stated that the manse was situated at Lundie.*

*The union of **Lundie and Fowlis Easter** was dissolved on 7 June 1953 when **Fowlis** united with **Liff and Benvie** under the name **Fowlis and Liff** (The record of Fowlis is to be found under **Fowlis and Liff**)*

*The parishes of **Lundie and Muirhead** and **Fowlis and Liff** were linked **on 17 May 1995** under the ministry of the Rev. Martyn R H Thomas, minister of Lundie and Muirhead. The Rev. Kenneth Ian Malcolm BD was at the same time appointed Auxiliary Minister to the linked charge for a five-year term in the first instance.*

Lundie

Ministers

1566 Alexander CRICHTON	Parson. (FES VIII 692)
1567 Archibald KEITH	Adm. before 1567. Formerly of Logie Murdoch. To Longley (St Fergus) after Nov. 1567 (FES V 354)
1574 George COCHRANE	Reader in 1574 (FES V 354)
1577 John KNOX MA	Min. 1 Dec. 1577 (FES VIII 492)
1593 William RAIT	From Mains with that parish also in his charge. To Strathmartine about 1594 (FES V 354)
1594 Alexander SCRYMGEOUR	From Benvie, returned there in 1595 (FES V 354)
1595 Andrew MORTON MA	From Fowlis Easter, returned there after 19 Dec. 1608. To Lundie after 21 Sept. 1610 (Died 1613) (FES V 354)
1607 John DUNCAN	Min. in 1607. To Liff before 1613 (FES V 355)
1613 Andrew MORTON MA	Above mentioned (FES V 355)

Lundie and Fowlis Easter [After union of 1618]

Ministers

1614 Henry FITHIE MA	From Kinkell and adm. at Fowlis. Died 1620. Gave directions for the purchase of a bell for church of Lundie. (FES V 355)
[1620 Alexander FOTHERINGHAM	Pres. by Andrew, Lord Gray, and letters of charge issued to Archbishop of St Andrews 30 June 1620, but he was not settled (FES V 355)]
1620 James BLAIR DD	Ord. To another charge before 31 March 1636 (FES V 355)

1636	Donald BLAIR MA	Pres. by Charles I. Dep. in 1649 by Commission of the Kirk for supporting the royal cause and favouring the expedition of 1648 (FES V 355)
1660	William RIGG MA	Adm. Died before 26 April 1665 (FES V 355)
1665	John ROBERTSON MA	Adm. To Auchterhouse 1667 having exchanged livings with James Campbell (FES V 355)
1667	James CAMPBELL	From Auchterhouse having been suspended from that charge. The parish was vacant 9 May 1683 Mr Campbell having been *a great burden for three years by reason of his sickness.* Died 1682 (FES V 355)
1685	James BROWN MA	Adm. Pres. by Archbishop of St Andrews 1684 but settlement was delayed due to a dispute about the patronage. Dep. 1698 (Died between 1699 and 1707) (FES V 355)
1701	Walter AINSLIE MA	From Minto. Dep. for neglect of duty, 1710, but sentence annulled, 1714 (Died 1728) (FES V 355-6)
1711	George FLEMING MA	Ord. Died 1734 (FES V 356)
1736	James ANDERSON	From Guthrie. Died 1756 (FES V 356)
1758	George SWAN MA	Ord. Died 1763 (FES V 356)
1764	Andrew HALLY	Ord. Died 1795 (FES V 356)
1795	Walter TAIT	Ord. Pres. by his uncle, Alexander Duncan of Lundie. To Tealing 1797 (FES V 356)
1798	Charles CUNNINGHAM	Ord. Pres. by Adam, Viscount Duncan. To Dailly 1806 (FES V 356)
1806	Thomas RAITT	From St Andrew's Dundee. Pres. by Robert, Viscount Duncan. Died 1828 (FES V 366)
1821	Thomas IRVINE	Ord. A&S. Pres. by Robert, Viscount Duncan. Having lost his sight, he used his time in knitting for charitable purposes. Died 1874 (FES V 356-7)
1866	Peter Lorimer BURR	Ord. A&S. Pres. by Adam, Earl of Camperdown. Clerk of Presb. 1871-1904. DD (St Andrews 1895) Died 1909 (FES V 357)
1910	Charles Scott BURDON	From Blackhill. To Govan Dean Park 1919 (FES V 357)
1919	John SINCLAIR MA	From Fauldhouse. To Mains and Strathmartine 1926 (FES V 357, VIII 493)
1926	Robert Lamond MACNIE	From Loth. Died 1929 (FES VIII 493)
1929	John ROGAN	From Burntisland. Died 1929 (FES VIII 493)
1930	Alexander MONRO MA	From Menmuir. Dem. 1938 (Died 1949) (FES IX 519)
1938	William Lamb FORDYCE MA	From Glasgow St David's Knightswood. Dem. 1949 (FES IX 519)
1950	John CORDINER	Ord. To Mains of Fintry 1953 (FES IX 519)

Muirhead of Liff

At the Disruption of 1843, a congregation of those people in the parish of Liff adhering to the Free Church was formed, worshipping initially in a tent. A church was built in 1843 on a site at the Muirhead of Liff, and a manse added in 1844.

The church is a plain building with the date *1843* on the end wall. Local farmers gave and transported the stones for its construction. The manse was altered and enlarged in 1890. A Ladies' Room was built onto the church at the expense of Mrs Kennedy, the minister's wife. Plans were approved in 1997 for the addition of a new vestry and entrance hall at a cost of £60,000. In 1900 Mrs Kennedy gifted a small pipe organ.

Liff Free became *Liff UF* in 1900 and *Muirhead of Liff* in 1929.

Ministers

1843	William R MONCUR	Ind. Ret. 1876 (Ewing II 162, PM)
1877	John GALL MA	Ord. C&S. To Rutherglen Free 1879 (Ewing II 162, PM)

1880	John KENNEDY MA	Ord. Died 1915 (Ewing II 162, FUF 390-1)
1915	Alexander Anderson STRATHEARN MA	From Cargill UF. To Blair Atholl UF 1920 (FUF 391)
1921	Peter LOCKHART MA	Ord. To Broxburn West UF 1923 (FUF 391)
1923	Thomas TULLY MA	From Glasgow Whiteinch UF. Dem. 1936 (Died 1955) (FUF 391. FES IX 521, X 308)
1937	Thomas Edward NICHOL MA	From Darvel Easton Memorial. To West Calder 1950 (FES IX 521)
1950	Matthew John Robert LESTER	Ord. Min of united charge 6 June 1953 (FES IX 521)

Lundie and Muirhead of Liff

After the union of 1953 the minister of Muirhead of Liff became minister of the united charge. Both churches continued to be used for worship.

Ministers

1953	Matthew John Robert LESTER	Min. of Muirhead of Liff. Died 1977 (FES IX 519-20)
1978	William M M CAMPBELL BD CPS	From Braes of Rannoch with Kinloch Rannoch. To Hospital Chaplain Aberdeen 1986 (YB)
1987	Martyn R H THOMAS CEng MIStructE	Ord. (PM)

OSA Lundie and Fowlis
A Warden, *Angus or Forfarshire,* Vol. IV, Dundee, 1885
Dundee Warder, 13 June 1843:

> *Sermon has been supplied the two last Sabbaths by adherents of the Free Church. The schoolhouse in which the service took place was not only crowded but multitudes clustered around the doors and windows. There is to be a congregation formed and a place of worship erected. A site has been presented, stones for building to be supplied free by farmers and feuars.*

DCC Combined Statutory and Descriptive List

MONIFIETH PANMURE

Monifieth Panmure church is situated at 15 Panmure Street on the main road through Monifieth. The present church was opened in 1937, replacing the building now used as a hall. It is cruciform, built in brick and harled, and has an arched roof. The pulpit is offset at the crossing. The furnishings are light coloured. In 1979 a three-light stained glass window, designed by John Blyth, with the theme *Faith and Service to God,* was installed in the east transept in memory of the Fleming family.

The United Presbyterian Church opened a preaching station at Monifieth on Sunday, 4 July 1897. The meetings may have been held originally in a house in Brook Street. The station was under the supervision of Dundee UP Presbytery, the officiating ministers at the opening ceremonies being the Rev. George Smart of School Wynd, Dundee and the Rev. G W Howie, Newbigging. Newbigging UP congregation was supportive of the Monifieth project, to which some of its members were to transfer. In the following year some 90 members and adherents petitioned Presbytery to be congregated, but it was decided to place the station under the care of the minister and kirk session of Newbigging meantime.

On 17 May 1899, a hall seated for 300 and built at a cost of £850 was opened free of debt. The opening services were held on 11 June with the Rev. J L Munro of Selkirk officiating, and on the following Sunday the first communion was celebrated. The station was formed into a congregation with a membership of 106 on 5 July 1899, with Mr Alexander B Connon, probationer, in charge. The first elders were ordained on 27 August of the same year. Mr Connon was ordained and inducted as first minister of the charge on 3 July 1901. A manse at 8a Albert Street was purchased in 1937.

The centenary year of the origins of the congregation was marked by a service held on Sunday, 29 June 1997, at which the Very Reverend Professor James Whyte, St Andrews, preached the sermon.

*In 1900 **Monifieth UP** became **Monifieth Panmure UF** and in 1929 **Monifieth Panmure**.*

Ministers

1901	Alexander Bain CONNON BD	Ord. To Glasgow Parkhead UF 1908(FUF 391)
1908	Walter William Aitken BELL BD	Ord. To Glasgow Kinning Park UF 1915 (FUF 392)
1916	Harry LAW MA	Ord. To Lochgelly Macainsh 1922 (FUF 392)
1922	James GILFILLAN MA	From Bermuda. Died 1928 (FUF 392)
1928	William Miln LOCKE MA	Ord. To Dundee St Clement's 1932 (FUF 392, FES IX 520)
1933	James Kenneth CASSELLS MA	Ord. To Leith Kirkgate 1937 (FES IX 520)
1938	James BEGG MA BD	From Skelmorlie and Wemyss Bay Nth. Dem.1948 (Died 1964) (FES IX 520, KofE 125)
1949	Harry Valentine GIBBONS	From Polmont South. Dem.1965 (FES IX 520, X 307)
1967	Alexander Mackenzie JACK BA BD	From Goodmayes St Andrew's (PCE) Dem 1973 (FES X 307-8)
1974	David Blair JAMIESON MA BD STM	Ord. (FES X 308)

W D Chisholm, *Precious Stones – The 200 years story of an Angus Church and its people,* n.d.
J Malcolm, *The Parish of Monifieth in Ancient and Modern Times,* Edinburgh, 1910
R Small, *History of the Congregations of the United Presbyterian Church Vol. I,* Edinburgh, 1904
DPL   DNC Vol. 93

MONIFIETH ST RULE'S

Monifieth St Rule's church is situated in Church Street, Monifieth. The church is plain, with a galleried interior, and was built in 1813 to replace an older building. Designed by Samuel Bell, architect, Dundee, it was built under the supervision of David Neave, architect, Dundee, by Alexander Thomson, mason, Dundee. It is to a Gothic rectangular plan in coursed rubble with long and short dressed quoins. There is a stucco extension at the east end. It has a square 3-stage bell tower instead of its proposed spire. Originally the 36 feet high tower was boxed in the middle for pigeons belonging to the minister of the time.

The interior has a semi-octagonal gallery with timber clad cast iron Doric columns and a plain plaster ceiling. There are a number of stained glass windows, including the 1939-45 memorial by John M Aitken. Large memorial windows to Thomas Erskine of Linlathen, 1871, and the Rev. James Gerard Young, 1902, are by William Morris and Co. Smaller windows are in memory of James Guthrie Orchar, *circa* 1898, and Charles and Grace Low, *circa* 1897. The 1914-18 war memorial is in marble. There is a plaque to Patrick, Lord Ruthven, a general of Charles I and a companion in arms of Montrose.[1] The Dempsters have a family memorial. George Dempster was a merchant and burgess of Dundee and son of the Rev. John Dempster, last episcopal minister of Monifieth.[2] There are old heraldic stones in the east gable, taken from the former mausoleum of the Durhams of Grange.

The church was re-modelled and re-seated in 1873, at a cost of £1,000, by Edward and Robertson, architects, Dundee, a porch and vestry (since altered) being added. It was re-pointed and re-dressed in 1913. In 1914, Mr Alexander B Gilroy gifted a clock for the tower by George Rattray, Dundee and the old bell was replaced by chimes. The bell, cast in 1565, is reputed to have come from either a French frigate wrecked on the coast or a ship of the Spanish Armada. On it are several medallion portraits, including Charles V and Isabella his queen, the parents of Philip II of Spain who launched the Armada. The bell is inscribed *Henricus Je suis tout pour vrai. Jacob Ser. M.F. MDLXV*

St Regulus or St Rule is reputed to have come here with the relics of St Andrew. It is claimed that he founded a cell at Balmossie, a mile inland, which was later succeeded by the Culdee church nearer the sea, on which stands the present church. The Culdees were not ousted until 1242. There was a ninth century monastic foundation close to Balmossie Mill. There were several subsidiary chapels, one to the north on the banks of the Dighty known as Ecclesmonichty, dedicated to Saint Andrew. Another chapel dedicated to the Blessed Virgin Mary stood on a small island in the Tay, which is now only a sandbank, the Lady Bank. This is the reputed shipwreck site of David, Earl of Huntingdon. Monifieth was in the Diocese of St Andrews. According to the Rev. James Roger, author of the OSA, by tradition the four chapels in the parish were at East Ferry, which had a burial place, a second at Balmossie, a third at Ethiebealin, which was also called Chapel Dokit, and a fourth at Monifieth.

Following the Reformation the court of Monifieth kirk was known as the *assembly,* the term *session* not appearing in the records until 1581. The kirk assembly seems to have included deacons as well as elders. The pre-Reformation parish of Ballumbie was associated with Monifieth during the 1560s, linked with Dundee in the 1570s, and thereafter with Murroes. It is dealt with under **Murroes and Tealing**. The church possesses two beautiful silver chalices dated 1638 and 1642, presented by Jean Auchterlonie, Lady Grange. They were lost for a century but recovered by Mr Quig who became minister in 1921.

The Gerard Hall is a church-like building being a Sunday School Hall; the first built in Scotland in 1882 after the American model, and the gift of the Rev. Dr Gerard Young. Edward and Robertson designed it to a single storey Gothic rectangular plan with a north aisle and an additional wing to the east. It is in stugged snecked ashlar with polished dressings. Inside, the north aisle is formed by an arcade of four pointed arches on octagonal piers with robustly cut capitals of differing foliate pattern.

The church and the Gerard Hall are both B-listed.

The Rev. Samuel Miller, who left in 1843 to become minister of Monifieth Free, appears in the group photograph of Dundee Free Church ministers taken at Glasgow on 22 October 1843, reproduced in the catalogue of Hill and Adamson's calotypes. These photographs were used by David Octavius Hill RSA for likenesses in his large painting entitled, *The First General Assembly of the Free Church of Scotland Signing the Act of Separation and Deed of Demission at Tanfield, Edinburgh, May, 1843.*

Barnhill Chapel, later **Barnhill, St Margaret's**, was originally under the jurisdiction of Monifieth Kirk Session, the congregation having been formed in 1884 despite the reservations of Monifieth Parish Church.

Monifieth Parish Church *became* **Monifieth St Rule's** *in 1929.*

The manse is at Church Street. It is a modern building, replacing the previous manse of 1829 with a Doric portico, designed by David MacKenzie.

Ministers

1563	James LOVELL	Reader (FES VIII 494)
1565	Gilbert GARDEN or GARDYNE	Min. in 1565. Monikie was also in his charge in 1567. To Fordyce 1569 (Died 1623)(FES V 361, SR 94)
1569	Andrew CLAYHILLS	Adm. To Jedburgh about 1574. Returned to this charge 1598 (Died 1617) (FES V 361)
1574	James LOVELL or LYALL	Reader (FES V 362)
1574	Andrew AUCHINLECK	Min. of Barry, had charge of this parish 1574-98 (FES V 362)
1616	Patrick DURHAM	Adm. C&S to Andrew Clayhills. Died 1624 (FES V 362)
1624	George WISHART MA	Pres. by James VI. To Second Charge, St Andrews before 18 April 1626 (FES V 362)
1626	John RUTHERFORD MA	Pres. by Charles I. Died 1632 (FES V 362)
1632	Andrew WOOD MA	Pres. by Charles I. Died 1648 (FES V 362)
1649	John BARCLAY MA	From Kinnaird. Died 1675. Bequeathed £200 to poor of parish (FES V 362)
1676	John DEMPSTER MA	Pres. by Earl of Panmure. Conformed to the Government at the Revolution but was dep. for irregularity; reponed 1702 by Commission of Assembly. Died 1708. Great-grandfather of George Dempster MP *Honest George* (FES V 363)
1710	John BALLANTYNE MA	Ord. Was removed from his charge by the Jacobites in 1715 because he *would not read Marr's Declaration against His Majesty King George and desist from praying for him as King of Britain; also the keys of the church were violently taken from him by Panmure's orders, and the church possest by Mr Thomas Auchenleck, Episcopal preacher, till 4th Feb. 1716, at which time the minister came home again, the keys being at the church.* Died 1738 (FES V 363)
1739	William DALL	Ord. Died 1762 (FES V 363)
1763	James HENDERSON	From Dunnichen. Pres. by Earl of Panmure. Died 1787 (FES V 363)
1787	William JOHNSTONE	Ord. Pres. by Earl of Dalhousie (Died 1829) (FES V 363)
1816	John BISSET MA	Ord. Asst. 1808. Pres. by William Maule of Panmure and Adm. 1816. Died 1839 (FES V 363)
1835	Samuel MILLER	Ord. A&S. Pres. by William Maule of Panmure. Joined FC, min. of Monifieth Free 1843-4. DD (Princeton 1848) (Died 1881) (FES V 363)
1843	Alexander TODD MA	From Lochlee. Pres. by Lord Panmure. Dep. by GA 1853 (FES V 364)
1853	Peter MYLES BA	From Dundee St David's. Died 1855(FES V 364)
1855	James Gerard YOUNG	From Fintray. DD (St Andrews 1879) Died 1899 (FES V 364)
1900	David Duthie McLAREN MA BD	From Oldham Street Church, Liverpool. Dem. 1921 on appt. by Colonial Committee to Belize (Died 1939) (FES V 364, VIII 494)
1921	Gordon QUIG MA BD	From Glasgow St Paul's. Died 1946 (FES V 364, VIII 494)
1943	John HOWAT MA BD	From Glenmuick. Dem. on appt. as Secretary and Director of Religious Education, Youth and Education Department 1948 (FES IX 520)
1949	Francis Stewart Gordon FRASER MBE TD BD	From Nairn Old. MBE 1946. TD 1949. Died 1962 (FES IX 520-1, X 308)

1963	Duncan FINLAYSON	From Musselburgh St Ninian's. Dem. on appt. as Principal of St Colm's Edinburgh 1969 (FES X 308)
1970	Thomas MILROY	From Bathgate Boghall. Dem. 1992 (FES X 308, PM)
1993	Stephen J SMITH BSc BD	Ord. To Largs Clark Memorial 1998 (PM)

Notes

1. General Patrick Ruthven, earl of Forth and Brentford, was described by Montrose's biographer, Ronald Williams, as *an officer of world wide renown.* Elisabeth of Bohemia, *The Winter Queen,* referred to him in a letter to Montrose as *old Brainford.*
2. George Dempster was a merchant and burgess of Dundee and son of the Rev. John Dempster, last episcopal minister of Monifieth.

J Malcolm, *Parish of Monifieth in Ancient and Modern Times,* Edinburgh, 1910

Charles McKean and David Walker, *Dundee, An Illustrated Architectural Guide,* Dundee, 1993

A Warden, *Angus or Forfarshire,* Vol. 1, Dundee, 1884

Sara Stevenson (ed.), *David Octavius Hill and Robert Adamson,* Catalogue of their Calotypes taken between 1843 and 1847 in the Scottish National Portrait Gallery, Edinburgh, 1981

J Buchan, *Montrose,* Edinburgh, 1931

R Willams, *Montrose, Cavalier in Mourning,* nd

DCA CH2/270

DCC Combined Statutory and Descriptive List

DPL Sp. 2.41

MONIFIETH SOUTH

Monifieth South church stands in Hill Street, Monifieth. It is a stone built Gothic building, designed by James Maclaren, architect, Dundee, with the main entrance on the south gable. Above the door is a three-light tracery window, with a bellcote at the apex. There is a small round tower at the south east corner.

At the Disruption of 1843 the Free Church party had difficulty in obtaining a site for a church in the village and Monifieth Free Church, known also as Hillock, was built some three miles from the village of Monifieth. (See **Monikie and Newbigging**) In response to a request from 116 Free Church adherents, a preaching station was established in the village, being approved by Presbytery on 10 November 1869. An interim kirk session was appointed under Dr William Wilson of Free St Paul's as moderator.[1] The charge was sanctioned in 1870. Plans for a church were approved by Presbytery on 14 June 1871, the congregation to be called Monifieth South. The church was erected on a site given by the Earl of Dalhousie and opened in 1872. A manse was built in 1876. In 1884 a tower and a gallery were added to the church, and in 1904 transepts were built on at a cost of £1,000. A small hall was purchased in 1891. This hall had been built by the Deacons' Court of Monifieth Free (Hillock) *for the religious and educational benefit of members of the Free Church in the village of Monifieth.* Hillock Church was, as previously stated, three miles distant from the village. Services had been held in this hall on Sunday evenings by the Reverend Edward Cross and others. A large hall, seated for 400, was erected in 1909 beside the smaller hall. Along with other improvements the cost was £1,100.

In 1925 stained glass windows were installed in memory of the Reverend Crawford Smith. A service to mark the 125th anniversary of the opening of the church was held on Sunday, 28 September 1997.

Monifieth South Free became *Monifieth South UF* in 1900 and *Monifieth South* in 1929. The manse is situated at Queen Street, Monifieth.

Ministers

1871	Robert MACGREGOR MA	Ord. To Glasgow Augustine Free 1877 (Ewing II 163, PM)
1878	Crawford SMITH	Ord. Dem. 1923. (Died 1924) (Ewing II 163, FUF 392)
1923	Neil CAMERON MA	From Croy UF. Dem. 1958 (Died 1976)
		(FUF 392, FES X 308, YB)
1959	Donald William FRASER MA	Ind. Previously Asst. at Dunfermline Abbey (FES X 308)

Note

1. Dr William Wilson was very involved in Church Extension in Presbytery and in the Free Church as a whole, being Convener of the Assembly Home Mission Committee for ten years. He became Principal Clerk of the General Assembly and Moderator in 1866

J Malcolm, *The Parish of Monifieth in Ancient and Modern Times,* Edinburgh, 1910
C McKean & D Walker, *Dundee, An Illustrated Architectural Guide,* Edinburgh, 1993

MONIKIE and NEWBIGGING

Monikie and Newbigging was formed by the union of Monikie and Monifieth North and Newbigging on 6 June 1984. They had been linked charges since 6 September 1967. The manse of the charge is at 59b Broomwell Gardens, Monikie.

Monikie, as it was in 1984, was formed by the union of Monikie and Monikie Craigton on 8 January 1939.

Monikie

The medieval church of Monikie belonged to the Tironensian Abbey of Arbroath, being dedicated to St Andrew. The foundation dated from around 1190 when it was gifted to the Abbey by William the Lion. It was in the Diocese of Brechin. According to the Rev. William Maule, minister of the charge and author of the OSA, the church of *circa* 1790 was built or renewed about 1678. He described the manse as, *at present somewhat ruinous.* A new manse was built in 1794.

The present church is probably located on the site of the original chapel. In 1812 considerable alterations were carried out to the church under the supervision of Andrew Millar, architect. The kirk bell was set up in 1719 and is inscribed *Albertus Cely Fecit Aberdoniae 1718.* The interior of the church was reconstructed in 1903. At this time a memorial window to the Rev. John Reid was put in at the east end above the pulpit. Two silver communion cups were made in 1848 to match two older cups. In 1849 two pewter plates were bought. Thomas Kinnear gifted the communion table and chair in 1913.

Ministers

1561 Matthew GRIEVE	Vicar pensioner in 1561, Reader in 1567. Pres. to vicarage 1568 on death of Thomas Scrymgeour (FES V 365, VIII 495)
1563 Gilbert GARDEN or GARDYNE	Min. 1563-8, Monifieth also in his charge. To Fordyce 1569 (FES V 365, VIII 495)
1574 Henry GRIEVE	Pres. to vicarage 1571 on death of Matthew Grieve. Reader from 1574 to 1585 (FES V 365, VIII 495)
Charles MITCHELSON	(listed in Chisholm, *The Monikie Story.*)
Andrew CLAYHILLS	Monifieth also in his charge in 1569. To Jedburgh about 1574 and to Eckford about 1593. Burgess of Dundee 1602 (Died 1617) (FES V 361-2, Chisholm, *The Monikie Story*, A H Miller, *Roll of Eminent Burgesses of Dundee*)
1585 John DURHAM	From Flisk. Pres. by James VI 1612. Died Father of the Church 1639 *an auld agit man* (FES V 365)
1634 William AUCHINLECK MA	Adm. (probably as helper) before 16 Aug. 1634. To Barry 1642 (FES V 365)
1642 Patrick MAKGILL MA	From Barry. Pres. by Charles I. Died 1680 (FES V 365)
1680 William RAIT MA	Adm. Pres. by Lord Panmure. Took the oaths to William and Mary at the Revolution, but ceased exercising ministerial functions and dep. 1716 for joining the Jacobites (FES V 365)
1717 James GOODSIR MA	From Strathmartine. Died 1733. Took active part in prosecution of John Glas of Tealing (FES V 365)
1738 George JOHNSTONE MA	Ord. 1738. Pres. by George II 1734. (delay caused by opposition in church courts) (FES V 365)
1774 James HUNTER	From Kirkden. Pres. by George III. Died 1782 (FES V 366)
1783 William MAULE MA DD	From Stracathro. Pres. by George III. DD (St Andrews 1812) Died 1827 (FES V 366)
1827 James MILLER	From Eassie and Nevay. Pres. by George IV. Joined FC 1843; min. of Monikie Free 1843-60. Died 1860 (FES V 366)
1843 Thomas McKIE	Ord. Pres. by Victoria. To Erskine 1852 (FES V 366)
1852 John REID	Ord. Pres. by Victoria. Died 1900 (FES V 366)
1896 Andrew ARMIT	From Pictou Nova Scotia (A&S) Died 1938 (FES V 366, VIII 495)

Monikie Craigton

The minister of Monikie and part of his congregation *came out* at the Disruption of 1843. Lord Panmure prevented the group from obtaining a site for a church and the congregation met in a grain loft of the farm of Affleck, the minister occupying part of the farmhouse. The place of worship was extremely cold and uncomfortable, being just under the slates and without windows. When Fox Maule, Earl of Dalhousie, inherited the estate he granted a site, laying the foundation stone of the church which, along with the manse, was completed in 1853. The earl, who also endowed the stipend, largely met the cost of church and manse. Lord Dalhousie was an elder in the congregation. On his death he left an endowment for it and three other congregations on his estates. Warden described the church as a *very handsome Free Church with a pretty spire, a comfortable manse and a large walled garden.*

The Rev. James Miller, minister of Monikie Free, and his son, the Rev. Samuel Miller, minister of Monifieth Free, appear in the group photograph of Dundee Presbytery Free Church ministers taken at Glasgow on 22 October 1843, reproduced in the catalogue of Hill and Adamson's calotypes. These photographs were used by David Octavius Hill RSA, for likenesses in his large painting entitled, *The First General Assembly of the Free Church of Scotland Signing the Act of Separation and Deed of Demission at Tanfield, Edinburgh, May, 1843.*

*In 1900 **Monikie Free** became **Monikie UF** and in 1929 **Monikie Craigton**.*

Ministers

1843	James MILLER	Min. of Monikie (Died 1860) (Ewing II 163)
1849	Malcolm McINTYRE	Ord. Dem. 1894 (Died 1903) (Ewing II 163, FUF 392)
1894	Robert SCRYMGEOUR MA	Ord. To Jersey (English Presb. Ch.) 1897 (Ewing II 163, PM)
1898	Alexander Reid GORDON MA DLitt	Ord. Res. on appt. as Professor of Old Testament Literature and Exegesis, Presb. College, Montreal, 1907 (Ewing II 163, FUF 392)
1907	John Alexander FLEMING MA	Ord. To Stepps UF 1912 (FUF 392)
1912	Thomas Smith CRICHTON MA	Ord. To Baillieston Rhinsdale UF 1925 (FUF 392)
1925	Quintin Dick WHYTE	From Glasgow Carmyle UF. Dem. 1939 (Died 1944) (FUF 393, FES IX 521)

Monikie

After the union of 1939 both churches continued to be used for worship and the Craigton manse was sold. It became the Craigton Coach Inn.

Ministers

1939	Andrew BURT MA BD	From Insch. Dem. 1960. (Died 1960) (FES IX 521, X 308)
1961	William Douglas CHISHOLM MA	From Crossmichael. Dem. 1983 (FES X 308, YB)

***Monifieth North and Newbigging** was formed by the union on 5 September 1920 of **Monifieth North** and **Newbigging**.*
***Monifieth North and Newbigging** was linked with **Monikie** on 6 September 1967.*

Newbigging

The church is situated in Pitairlie Road in the small village of Newbigging in the parish of Monikie about seven miles north east of Dundee. The building, or meeting house as it was called originally, was erected in 1789. The east gable with a small belfry was added in 1864, and a clock was presented by Mr J P Smith in 1887 to mark the centenary. A cross above the communion table is the work of a craftsman, John Rennie. The Rennies were one of the founding families of the congregation, others included the Fyfes, the Kinnears and the Dicks. Thomas Dick (1774-1857) of Pitkerro House was a distinguished writer on scientific and philosophical matters.

The 150th anniversary of the church was marked in September 1938 when a number of gifts to the congregation were dedicated. An oak communion table in memory of Robert B Galloway, and oak communion chairs in memory of George Galloway, two brass flower vases in memory of the Rev. Alexander Miller, an embroidered communion cloth in memory of Robert Fyfe, and a pulpit hymnary from the Woman's Guild were handed over. A memorial window to the Rev. John Taylor has as its theme, *Suffer the little children.* In 1950 a brass lectern and four offertory plates were gifted by Miss Henderson. In 1953 the Andrew Millar bequest allowed the church to be redecorated and modernised. Stained glass windows were installed in memory of Jeannie Graham, wife of Andrew Millar, Laws Farm, depicting *Christ as the Living Bread*, and in memory of Andrew Millar, Omachie, showing Jesus as *The Sower.* A bequest in 1979 by Mr A Bruce Robertson, organist for twenty-five years, was used to purchase a modern organ.

Newbigging

Newbigging is an old Seceders kirk. During the ministry of the Rev. William Maule some members broke away from the parish church in the period 1786-88. There were other Seceders in the area, most it would seem with Antiburgher leanings. On 8 April 1788 a petition from 171 people in the parishes of Monikie, Monifieth, Barry and Panbride petitioned the Antiburgher Presbytery of Perth for supply of sermon, the first stage in forming a congregation, which was agreed. On 11 July it was reported that ground at Barrymuir had been obtained on which to build their place of worship, and a church was built. Meantime, the minority approached the Rev. James Black of School Wynd Church, the Burgher congregation of Dundee. As a result, application for sermon was made to the Burgher Presbytery of Perth on 5 August 1788. Approval was given, and William Kidston, probationer expressed the wish to form the station into a congregation. The records of Forfar Presbytery show that a group of people purchased an acre of moorland at Newbigging in 1789 for £10, on which they built a church in 1790 and a manse in 1792. They also built two dwellinghouses on the land, which at first were let, then sold to the advantage of congregational funds. The Seceders thus had two churches in the area, the East Muir kirk at Barrymuir for the Antiburghers[1], and the West Muir kirk at Newbigging for the Burghers.

The first managers of Newbigging were elected on 28 March 1789, and their names appear on a stone at the church door. They were David Wilson, Wilsonhall, Monikie; Robert Galloway, Templehall; John Wilson, The Laws; William Horn, Graystone; William Fyfe, Downieken; David Dick, Gagie; David Forbes; and James Dorward. Some of the original members had belonged to School Wynd Church, Dundee. One of the early leaders was Francis Dick, a young man who was ordained to the eldership along with three others. He later joined the Independents, having been involved with the Haldane brothers. In 1790 the people took steps to appoint a minister and the first pastor was ordained and admitted on 26 April 1791.

In 1794 Presbytery considered the inability of the congregation to support their minister. It was reported that the membership was around 44 and 120 seats were let. There was a shortfall of income over expenditure, which did not improve, for in 1796 the first minister demitted with stipend arrears due to him. Thereafter, a vacancy subsisted for almost twenty years, several calls not being sustained, with the pulpit being supplied by eighty-six probationers, and an occasional visit of an ordained minister to dispense the sacrament. During the second ministry the congregation fell in numbers while the debt increased, the pastoral link being broken in difficult circumstances. The next ministry saw a substantial increase in membership. Damage to the roof resulted in a costly repair, but fund-raising on the part of the minister and members in 1830 allowed the church to be renovated and the debt was cleared.

An elder, David Fyfe, began one of the earliest Sabbath Schools in Angus in 1797. Newbigging School was also founded by the congregation. The congregation possesses two communion cups marked, *Newbigging Associate Congregation 1789* and a wine flagon.

In 1854 the congregation was transferred from Arbroath to Dundee Presbytery of the UP Church. On Sunday, 4 June 1989, a service of rededication was held to mark the bi-centenary of Newbigging Church.

Newbigging Burgher *became* ***Newbigging UAS*** *in 1820,* ***Newbigging UP*** *in 1847, and* ***Newbigging UF*** *in 1900.*

Ministers

1791	James HARVEY	Ord. Dem. 1796. To Chair of Oriental Languages, Glasgow. (Died 1826) (Small I 334)
1815	William GRAHAM	Adm. Previously min. of Darlington Burgher. Dem. 1821 (Died 1828) (Small I 335-6)
1828	John ECKFORD	Ord. Dep. 1851 by Presb. of Arbroath following case of *fama. (*Died 1881) His grandson, Col. John McCrae in 1915 wrote the famous poem, *In Flanders fields,* quoted below[2]. (Small I 336)

1852 Alexander MILLER	Ord. In 1895 enrolled min. emeritus (Died 1906) (Small I 336, FUF 393)
1896 George Wyllie HOWIE MA	Ord. To Galashiels South UF 1906 (Small I 336-7, FUF 393)
1906 John Urquhart OGILVY MA	Ord. To Hamilton Saffronhall UF 1914 (FUF 393)
1915 David CONOCHIE	Introd. Formerly min. at Fetterangus. To Bridge of Cally UF 1920 (FUF 393)

Monifieth North

At the Disruption of 1843 the minister of Monifieth, two elders, and many of the congregation left the Established Church. For some time worship was conducted in a tent, as no site for a church could be obtained, the first service being held on 18 June 1843. In 1846 a site was gifted by Mr Arklay of Ethiebeaton and the Free Church of Monifieth was completed in 1847, the opening service being held on 20 June 1847. The rectangular building was constructed in coursed rubble masonry with polished dressings. On the west gable a sculpted circular panel has the date *1846*.

The church was located three miles from the village of Monifieth and, in consequence of a request from Free Church adherents, another charge, called **Monifieth South** (qv), was sanctioned in the village in 1870.

A manse was provided. The membership, which in 1854 had been 254, had fallen to 136 in 1900. The church building is B-listed.

Monifieth Free became Monifieth North in 1900. It was also known as the Hillock Church.

Ministers

1843 Samuel MILLER DD	Min. of Monifieth. To Glasgow St Matthew's Free 1844 (Ewing II 163, PM)
1845 Edward CROSS MA	Ord. Ret. 1890. Died 1892 (Ewing II 163, PM)
1890 Alexander WISEMAN MA	Ord. C&S. Dem. 1920 (Died 1933) (Ewing II 163, FUF 391, FES IX 520, PM)

Monifieth North and Newbigging

After the union of 1920 the Monifieth North manse was sold in 1921. One service was held in each church every Sunday. The North church was closed on 29 June 1982. The building was sold for conversion to houses in the early 1980s.

Monifieth North and Newbigging UF became Monifieth North and Newbigging in 1929.

Ministers

1921 David Chalmers WISEMAN MA	From Kirkurd UF as C&S. To Arbroath Inverbrothock UF 1925 (FUF 391)
1925 Cecil James DAVIDSON	From Oldmeldrum UF. Died 1932 (FUF 391, FES IX 520)
1933 John TAYLOR MA	From Carntyne Old. Died 1944 (FES IX 520)
1945 William FLEMING	From Denbeath. To Dallas 1953 (FES IX 520)
1954 Alexander Duncan MACRAE MA	From Alvie and Insh. To Duror 1956 (FES IX 520 X 307)
1957 Alfred Saunders BARRON MA BD	From Auchtertool. Dem. 1967 (Died 1973) (FES X 307)
1967 William Douglas CHISHOLM MA	Recognised as min. on linking with Monikie on 6 Sept. 1967. Dem. 1983 (FES X 307)

Monikie and Monifieth North and Newbigging

After the union of 1984 both churches continued to be used for worship. The name was later shortened to **Monikie and Newbigging.** In 1999 it was agreed that Newbigging church would be closed and that Monikie church would be the sole place of worship.

Minister

1985 Gordon R MACKENZIE BSc BD	From Kirkmichael and Tomintoul (PM, YB)

Notes

(1) The Antiburgher congregation, originally at Barrymuir, was formed on 3 March 1789. For twelve years, until 1809, the Barrymuir ministers preached occasionally at the *Feus of Taymouth,* which became Carnoustie. They were offered half an acre of ground and built a church at Carnoustie, the congregation transferring in 1810.

(2)
In Flanders fields, the poppies grow
Between the crosses, row on row,
That mark our places: and in the sky
The larks still bravely singing, fly.

We are the Dead. Short days ago
We lived, felt dawn, saw sunset glow
Loved and were loved, and now we lie
In Flanders fields.

Take up your quarrel with the foe;
To you from failing hands we throw
The torch; be yours to hold it high.
If ye break faith with us who die
We shall not sleep, though poppies grow
In Flanders fields.

John McCrae

T Brown, *Annals of the Disruption,* Edinburgh, 1893

W D Chisholm, *The Monikie Story,* Dundee, 1982

    "   " *Precious Stones, the 200 years of an Angus Church, Newbigging,* Dundee, 1979

    "   " *The Hillock Church 1843-1979,* Dundee, 1979

Sara Stevenson (ed.), *David Octavius Hill and Robert Adamson,* Catalogue of their Calotypes taken between 1843 and 1847 in the collection of the Scottish National Portrait Gallery, Edinburgh, 1981

A Warden, *Angus or Forfarshire,* Vol. IV, Dundee, 1885

DCA CH2/499, CH3/612, CH3/612/4

DCC Combined Statutory and Descriptive List

DPL Sp.20/67

Monikie, The Parish Newsletter, No 36, June 1982

MURROES and TEALING

Murroes and Tealing church is situated in the *quoad omnia* parish of Murroes, about three miles north of Broughty Ferry. A stone panel on its south wall is inscribed, *AD 1848, Christo, Luci mundi, et humanae salutis Auctoria haec aedes consecrata est: J.I.C.* (This church was consecrated to Christ, the Light of the World, and the author of human salvation, in the year of Our Lord, 1848)

William Scott, architect, Dundee, rebuilt the church in 1848. The T-plan Gothic building is constructed in stugged snecked rubble sandstone with ashlar dressings. It has pointed windows and there is a porch on the west gable. A heraldic panel above the tower door is dated 1642. There is a fine panelled pulpit. The carved screen in the north aisle has stained glass depicting the McGavin of Ballumbie family arms. There is a moulded stone panel with eight family arms and names on the east wall. The description over the east door reads, *Ora et labora* (pray and labour) and over the west door, *Laus et honor Deo* (praise and honour be to God). The initials *TF* and *MG* on the north gable refer to Thomas Fothringham and Margaret Gibson, his wife. The burial vault of the Fothringhams of Powrie is on the north side of the church.

The church, hall, and Murroes Den with its doo'cot, form a conservation area. The church is B-listed and the hall C(s)-listed.

The church hall was a former single storey stable and coach house built in 1811 in rubble sandstone with ashlar dressings. In March 1998 work began on the complete restoration and extension of the church hall at a cost of £100,000. The single storey building, built in 1811 in rubble sandstone with ashlar dressings, had originally been the manse stables and coach house. One wing had been developed as a hall in the 1960s, as a memorial to the Rev. J O Westwater, formerly minister of Murroes. The restored building incorporates a hall, chapel and kitchen. The opportunity was taken to remove a small number of stone slates, replacing the whole roof with Scotch slate. A courtyard was created using the old table flags found in the excavation. A service of thanksgiving was held on Sunday, 20 December 1998, with the kirk hall being officially opened thereafter by the Earl of Dundee.

*Murroes was linked with **Tealing** on 10 December 1963, under the ministry of the Reverend James Kidd, minister of Tealing. The linked charges were united as **Murroes and Tealing** on 14 December 1982. **Murroes and Tealing** was linked with **Auchterhouse** on 27 February 1983. The manse for the linked charge is situated at Balgray, Tealing.*

Murroes

The church of Murroes, also referred to as Muirhouse or Muraus, belonged to the Abbey of Arbroath in medieval times, having been granted to the Abbey by Gilchrist, Earl of Angus in the period 1201-7.

Ministers

1561	Ninian COOK	Vicar and reader in 1561 (FES V 367)
1563	Andrew AUCHINLECK	Min. in 1563 (FES VIII 495)
1567	William OLIVER	Reader (FES V 367)
1570	Ninian COOK	Reader in May 1570 (FES V 367)
1574	Andrew AUCHINLECK	Min. of Barry, Monifieth and of this par. in 1574 (FES V 367)
1574	William OLIVER	Reader 1574. Pres. to vicarage 1579 on death of Ninian Cook. Died *ante* 18 June 1599 (FES V367)
1585	Henry DUNCAN	Min. of this par. and of Ballumbie. One of forty two ministers who signed Protest to Parliament, 1 July 1606, against introduction of Episcopacy. Died 1618 (FES V 367)
1618	Robert ROLLOCK MA	Pres. by James VI. Dep. by Commission of Assembly, 1639 (FES V 367)
1641	James GARDINER MA	Pres. by Charles I. Died 1647 (FES V 367)
1648	Michael GILBERT	From Garvock. Died *ante* 3 Jan.1652 (FES V 367)
1648	Robert EDWARD MA	From Kirkmichael, Ayrshire. Pres. by Earl of Panmure and adm. *ante* Aug. 1648. Deprived at the Revolution. Died 1696. Published *Description of the County of Angus* in Latin, 1678, along with map of Angus, engraved in Amsterdam (FES V 367)

1684	Charles EDWARD MA	Son of preceding. Recommended for ordination as colleague to his father. Last mentioned 27 Aug. 1692. Par. vacant for over six years. (FES V 368)
1698	James MARR or MAIR MA	Ord. Died 1740 (FES V 368)
1715	James DUNDAS	Episcopal min. intruded Nov. 1715 to Jan. 1716 (FES VIII 495)
1741	George MARR or MAIR MA	Son of preceding. Ord. Pres. by George II. Died 1760 (FES V 368)
1761	Alexander IMLACH	Ord. Pres. by George II. Died 1808 (FES V 368)
1809	David CANNAN	From Kirriemuir. Pres. by George III. To Mains and Strathmartine 1820 (DD 1822) (Died 1854) (FES V 359, 368)
1821	John Irving CURRIE	Ord. Pres. by George IV. Died 1863 (FES V 368)
1864	John BOYD	Ord. Pres. by Victoria. To Kirriemuir 1873 (FES V 368)
1873	James NICOLL	From Rosebank Dundee. Pres. by Victoria. Dem.1919 (Died 1935) (FES V 368, VIII 495)
1919	William Augustus FORBES MA BD	From North Ronaldsay. Died 1942 (FES V 369, VIII 495)
1943	James Pryde BATCHELOR MA	From Alexandria North. Died 1947 (FES IX 521)
1947	John Oswald WESTWATER MA	From Glasgow Woodlands. Dem. 1963 (Died 1963) (FES IX 521, X 308)

Ballumbie

Ballumbie was a pre-Reformation parish that in the 1560s was associated with Monifieth, and linked with Dundee in the 1570s. Thereafter it seems to have been linked with Murroes. The following are shown in the *Fasti* as ministers of the charge.

	Ministers	
1585	Henry DUNCAN	Min. in 1585 with Murroes also in his charge. To Murroes about 1590 (FES V 369)
1604	James FOTHERINGHAM	Min. in 1604 (FES V 369)

Tealing

Tealing church was situated at the Kirkton of Tealing in the *quoad omnia* parish of that name about five miles north of Dundee. It is claimed to have been founded by St Boniface early in the eighth century, or in 690 according to the writer of the OSA, John Gellatly, minister of the parish. The medieval church was dedicated to St Peter the Apostle, and belonged to the Priory of St Andrews before 1199. Before 1275 the church of *Telyn* was disjoined from the Diocese of St Andrews and annexed to the Diocese of Dunkeld. Tealing was a prebend of Dunkeld and the incumbent was an archdeacon of Dunkeld.

The disused building stands on the site of its medieval predecessors. It is a plain rectangular plan, aisleless church, rubble-built with ashlar dressings. A porch and vestry were added in 1806 and other alterations were carried out in 1895 by Alexander Johnston, architect, Dundee. There is a large polished granite memorial to the Scrymgeour Fothringham family, above an earlier sculpted sandstone memorial, at the centre of the south wall. The pulpit is on the south wall and a panelled semi-octagonal gallery is supported on timber Doric columns. The church has a notable collection of sculpted and inscribed stones, including the tombstone of Ingram of Ketheyns, priest of Tealing and archdeacon of Dunkeld who died in 1380. It is now located on the north wall, having been removed from under the floor in 1895. There is part of an early sixteenth century sacrament house depicting Christ and two angels. There is a memorial to John Ramsay, priest at Tealing and archdeacon of Dunkeld, who died in 1618. He was minister of Tealing from 1590 to 1618.

The former Tealing church is A-listed.

Tealing , as it was in 1982, had been formed by the union of **Tealing** *and* **Tealing UF** *on 8 October 1929.*

Tealing

	Ministers
1561 Adam FOWLIE	Vicar 1561, parson 1563, min. 1568 (FES VIII 496)
1567 Andrew GIBB	Reader from 1567 to 1590. Pres. to vicarage 1573 on death of Adam Fowlie (FES V 369, VIII 496)
1567 David ROBERTSON	Min. in 1567, probably holding Rossie in conjunction (FES V 369)
1590 John RAMSAY	Min. in 1590; Inverarity also in his charge. Pres. to parsonage 1591. The charge *has much pepull and requiring an able person to travel in the function of thir ministrie.* Died 1618 (FES V 370, VIII 496)
1623 Alexander BRUCE MA	From Kinfauns. Probably dep. 1649 by Committee of Assembly appointed for Visitation (FES V 370)
1650 John CAMPBELL MA	Adm. Deprived by Act of Parliament and Decreet of Privy Council 1 Oct. 1662, but continued to 30 Oct. 1663 (FES V 370)
1665 Patrick MAKGILL MA	Ord. Died 1684 (FES V 370)
1684 John LYON MA	From Glamis. Archdeacon of Dunkeld in 1687. Dem. 1701 (Died 1702) (FES V 370)
1703 Hugh MAXWELL MA	Ord. To Forfar 1717 (FES V 370)
1719 John GLAS MA	Ord. Dep. 1728 (Died 1773) (FES V 370-2) [1]
1731 John STEWART MA	From Dunkeld. Died 1763 (FES V 372)
1764 John GELLATLY MA	Ord. Pres. by George III. Died 1796 (FES V 372)
1797 Walter TAIT	From Lundie. Pres. by George III. To Trinity Edinburgh 1813. He adopted the teachings of Campbell of Row and Edward Irving and was dep. in 1833. Became pastor of Catholic Apostolic congregation in Carrubber's Close and then in Broughton Street, Edinburgh (Died 1841) (FES V 372, KofE 365) [2]
1814 Charles ADIE	Ord. Pres. by Prince Regent. To Second Charge, Dundee 1826. He was offered, but declined, the moderatorship of GA. DD (St Andrews 1833) (Died 1861) (FES V 317, 372)
1827 George TOD	From Inveresk (Asst.) Pres. by George IV. To Dundee, St David's 1829. He edited the *Montrose Chronicle* 1819-22 and was subsequently editor of *Dundee Courier* (Died 1838) (FES V 326, 372)
1830 Peter BALFOUR	From Evie and Rendall. Pres. by George IV. To Clackmannan 1835 (FES V 372)
1835 David Barclay MELLIS	Previously min. in Douglas I. of Man. Pres. by William IV. Joined FC 1843 and became min. of Tealing Free 1843-61 (Died 1861) (FES V 372)
1843 William ELDER	Ord. as min. of OS Church, Cupar 1836. Joined CofS and became min. of Cupar St Mary's 1839. Although he subscribed the Solemn Engagement he did not join FC but was translated to Tealing 26 Aug. 1843. Died 1890 (FES V 373)
1889 Samuel MACAULAY BA	Ord. Died 1925 (FES V 373, VIII 496)
1925 Ian Forbes McCULLOCH MA	Ord. To Greenock East 1928 (FES VIII 496)

Tealing Free and UF

At the Disruption of 1843 the minister of the Established Church and almost the entire congregation *came out*. A church was built immediately and a manse soon afterwards. The congregation numbers suffered through the extinction of handloom weaving and the absorption of crofts into larger farms.

The former Free Church building now stands roofless. It is rectangular in plan, constructed in rubble sandstone with ashlar dressings. The south elevation has four symmetrically placed windows with the datestone, 1843, at the centre.

The building is B-listed

Tealing Free became *Tealing UF* in 1900. A provisional union of the two Tealing congregations was arranged shortly before the union of the Church of Scotland and United Free Church in 1929.

Ministers

1843	David Barclay MELLIS	Min. of Tealing. Died 1861 (Ewing II 163)
1861	Duncan TURNER	Ord. Dem. 1882 (Ewing II 163, PM)
1883	Neil Stewart ELDER MA	Ord. Dem. 1920 (Died 1928) (Ewing II 163, FUF 393)
1920	James NICOL MA	Ord. To Perth York Place UF 1925 (FUF 393)
1926	James Miller GRAHAM	From Dundee Park UF. To North Queensferry 1929 (FUF 393)

Tealing

After the local union of 1929 the UF buildings were sold and the proceeds of £845 invested for a fabric fund.

Ministers

1929	James Alexander Sutherland WILSON	From Bridge of Allan. Dem. 1941 (Died 1944) (FES VIII 496)
1941	Emmanuel WOOD MA	Adm. from UF Church. To Glasgow Linthouse 1948 (FES IX 523)
1949	Charles Hugh Brew HARKNESS	From Dalton. To Loanhead East 1957 (FES IX 523, X 309, YB 1960)
1958	William Charles SMITH	Intro. on term. appt. Appt. ended 1960 (FES X 309)
1962	James KIDD	From Whiting Bay. Min. of united charge 14 Dec. 1982 (FES X 309, PM)

Murroes and Tealing

After the union of Tealing and Murroes on 14 December 1982, Tealing church ceased to be used for worship. It was intended that the building would be converted to a Church Heritage Centre, but due to lack of monies this has not happened and the building is in a state of disrepair. However, in late 1999 there were moves to conserve the property. Murroes Church became the place of worship of the united congregation.

Ministers

1982	James KIDD	Min. of Tealing. Dem. 1983 (PM, YB)
1983	Helen JOHNSTONE MA BD HdipRE	Ord. To Kitwe Zambia 1989. Died 1999 (PM, YB)
1989	William M MACMILLAN LTh	From Whithorn St Ninian's Priory. To Kilmory with Lamlash 1993 (PM, YB)
1995	Sydney GRAHAM DipYL MPhil	Ind. (PM)

Notes

1. The Rev. John Glas was a very popular preacher. His views on the National Covenants, the relationship of Church and State, and the right of the state to interfere in matters of religion, brought him into conflict with the courts of the Church. He was suspended by the Synod on 18 April 1728, the sentence being confirmed by the GA in the following month. He was deposed on 15 October 1728. Following confirmation of that decision by the Commission of Assembly in 1730 he removed to Dundee where he set up a church whose members became known as Glasites. In 1733 he went to Perth and established a church there with the help of his son-in-law, Robert Sandeman. The sect in England and in America became known as Sandemanians. His tombstone is in the Howff, Dundee. Many items connected to John Glas and Robert Sandeman and the Glasite Church in Dundee are preserved in the Glasite Hall of St Andrew's Church, Dundee. This octagonal building was built by the Glasite congregation and opened in 1777. John Glas had died four years earlier and the meetinghouse in which he preached was in the Seagate.

2. There was a Catholic Apostolic congregation in Dundee, originally in Whitehall Close, then in a chapel in Bell Street. In 1867 they built a church in Constitution Road which is now St Mary Magdalene's Episcopal Church.

C McKean and D Walker, *Dundee, an Illustrated Introduction*, Edinburgh, 1984

A Warden, *Angus or Forfarshire*, Vol. V, Dundee, 1885

DCC Combined Statutory and Descriptive List

DCA CH2/274, 252, CH3/1424

Author's collection of notes on John Glas and the Glasite Church

BONNETHILL
[Dissolved 1978]

*Bonnethill Free became **Bonnethill UF** in 1900 and **Bonnethill** in 1929.*

Bonnethill began as a mission of the Free Church conducted by Hilltown congregation in a hall erected on Bonnethill, also known as Hilltown. In April 1865, Presbytery's Home Mission Committee reported that the mission was in a prosperous state with three services on a Sunday. Communion was first dispensed in the mission hall on 25 February 1866, and in the following year a site was secured in front of the hall for a church with its frontage onto Hilltown. A church was erected at a cost of £2,800, and opened on 30 November 1870 by the Very Rev. Sir Henry Wellwood Moncrieff Bart. DD, minister of Free St Cuthbert's, Edinburgh, and former Moderator of the General Assembly.[1] The charge was sanctioned in 1872. Mr James A Simpson, student missionary, acted as pastor from 1868, being ordained and inducted to the charge in 1872. The parent congregation of Hilltown organised a bazaar in the Kinnaird Hall to clear off the debt of £600 on the church. The bazaar raised enough to liquidate the debt and leave a balance of £300 for the new congregation.

Due to the growth of the Young Men's Bible Class the original hall, which came to be known as the Middle Hall, was enlarged in 1887. The West Hall was added in 1889. Still greater accommodation was required for the expanding Bible Class, and a larger hall was built and opened on 2 October 1892, with a gallery being added a year later. The interior of the church was renovated in 1901 when an organ was introduced. In 1907 ladies of the congregation gifted a font. An eighty fifth-anniversary service was held on Sunday, 29 September 1957, when the guest preacher was the Rev. Dr James Stewart, Edinburgh.[2]

In the post World War II period the area was redeveloped and many of the old houses demolished. The population was considerably reduced and the membership declined to such an extent that dissolution was decided upon. After the dissolution of the congregation in 1978, unsuccessful attempts were made to use the church building in a Community Centre Project and it was demolished. Following closure of the church, its communion silver and communion chairs were handed over to St David's North congregation, being rededicated at a service held there on Sunday, 17 June 1979.

Ministers

1872	James Anderson SIMPSON	Ord. Died 1899 (Ewing II 159, PM)
1899	James CAMERON	Ord. To Arbroath Ladyloan UF 1911 (FUF 381)
1911	Adam Stewart MARSHALL	From Drumblade UF. To Glendoick and Pitroddie UF 1929 (FUF 381)
1929	Donald CAMPBELL MA	From Croy. To Edinburgh St Bernard's South 1934 (Died 1951) (FUF 381, FES IX 503, KofE 157)
1934	Harold ROSS	From Troon St Meddan's. To Newmachar 1948 (FES IX 503)
1949	Robert URQUHART	From Ferryden. To Stirling St Mark's 1957 (FES IX 504, X 299)
1960	James Dennis KEILLOR	From Dennyloanhead. Dem. 1978 (Died 1990) (FES X 299, YB)

Notes
1. Sir Henry Wellwood Moncrieff was very involved in the Disruption, becoming one of the leading figures in the Free Church. He became Principal Clerk to the General Assembly in 1855 and Moderator in 1869.
2. Dr James Stewart was a noted theologian and Professor of New Testament Studies in New College, Edinburgh, being appointed Moderator of the General Assembly in 1963.

C C Barnett, *The Seven Churches of Hilltown*, n.d.
Bonnethill Eighty-Fifth Anniversary Record, 1957
DCA CH3/994
DPL DNC Vol. 10

DUDHOPE CRESCENT ROAD

[Dissolved 15 November 1909]

Temple Lane Relief and UP, Dudhope Crescent Road UP and UF

According to *Small* this congregation of the Relief Church drew its initial membership from *the floating wreck* of two previous Relief charges, Seagate and New Inn Entry, with sermon being supplied (the usual expression then for the beginning of a congregation) in May 1821 in the Seagate Chapel. This may have been at 39 Seagate. The previous membership of Seagate had continued to worship under the informal leadership of the Rev. James Jardine, following the dissolution of the pastoral tie with the Rev. William Strang in May 1820. However, Mr Jardine, who was no longer connected to the Relief denomination, had withdrawn his services in April 1821 when the people were recognised as a *forming congregation.* At least two of the elders were from the New Inn Entry congregation.

The roll of UP congregations, engrossed in the Presbytery minutes of the newly formed United Free Church in November 1900, gives 1788 as the date this congregation was *erected.* This suggests that it may have been regarded as a continuation of the Chapelshade Relief congregation which was the first Relief charge in Dundee. Chapelshade dated from around 1788 (1787 according to *McKelvie*) and joined the Established Church in 1791. The small minority who did not go over to the Church of Scotland had petitioned the Relief Presbytery, calling themselves *the vacant congregation in Dundee* and becoming West Port Relief which, as we shall learn, had a short existence.

In 1833 the Relief congregation removed from their Seagate location to the chapel in Temple Lane, built in 1792 for West Port Relief which ceased as a separate congregation in 1798. This building, popularly known as *The Temple,* was later used by the Independents. The church was bought back from the Independents or Congregationalists for £1,000, leaving a debt of £700. In 1838 the Relief Presbytery met in what was referred to as the *Relief Session House, West Port.* Not all members were happy with the locality and in 1837 a number left to form what became James Church, Bell Street. Presbytery minutes in 1842 refer to the older charge as *1st Relief Church Temple Lane.*

There was a crisis in the congregation's affairs around 1842 with the minister, the Rev James Cross, being unwell and requesting a colleague. When Mr Cross died in 1843 a further ministry was allowed. There was a debt due to Mr Cross' estate as he had advanced the congregation the sum of £200. On 21 March 1844 the congregation, when asking for a pastor, referred to *their present destitute condition and the necessity of obtaining a fixed pastor.* Clearly, they expected a good pastor would build up the ailing congregation and the unanimous approval of Presbytery suggests that they were of a like mind. They all seem to have been proved correct for the membership of what was then known as Temple Lane Relief, and, following the union of 1847, Temple Lane UP congregation, rapidly improved. A financial problem had to be resolved, having been remitted by the Relief Synod on the union. A bill for an unstated amount in the hands of a Mr Hunter was unpaid and presumably past due. This matter exercised the Presbytery for some months but in June 1848 it was reported that the bill had been retired, ending the congregation's liability. Mr Wilson advised presbytery on 13 May 1869 that the congregation had resolved to build a new place of worship in a better locality, and that the estimated cost of the new church was £1,500 to £1,600. The congregation had subscribed £300 and expected to raise £900 or £1,000 from the sale of their present church. Mr Wilson had pledged to raise £300 personally.

Presbytery gave its approval, and next year a new church with accommodation for 650 was completed in Dudhope Crescent Road at a cost of £2,000. Disappointingly, the Temple Lane property realised only £700 at public roup, being bought by Mr O G Miller, leaving a substantial debt. Provost Yeaman laid the foundation stone of the new church on 7 June 1870, and Professor John Eadie opened it for public worship on 22 December 1870[1]. On Sunday, 25 December, the services were taken by Dr George Jeffrey, Glasgow, and Dr John Wilson, Moderator of the Free Church General Assembly.[2] Presumably the name of the congregation was changed at this stage to Dudhope Crescent Road. Sometimes it is referred to as Dudhope Road. Four years later a manse was built at a cost of £800. By November 1887, at the centenary of the Relief Church in Dundee, the debt had been cleared.

***Dudhope Crescent Road UP** became **Dudhope Crescent Road UF** in 1900.*

In 1898 the incumbent became minister *emeritus* with an ordained licentiate being engaged for five years. The congregation was dissolved on 15 November 1909 and the church given to Willison congregation for use as halls. The manse was sold for £510.

Ministers

1823	John CROSS	Ord. Died 1843 (Small I 300-1)
1843	John SYMINGTON	Ord. To Bread Street Edinburgh Relief 1845 (Small I 301)
1846	Robert GEMMELL	From Provost Wynd Cupar Relief. To Arthur Street, Edinburgh UP 1855 (Died 1886) (Small I 301-2)
1856	James WILSON	Ord. Min. *emeritus* 1898. Died 1906 (Small I 302, FUF III 838)
1900	James BAYNE	Ordained licentiate app. for 5 years (Small I 302-3)
1907	John ALEXANDER MA	From Almondbank UF. To Canterbury St Andrew's 1909 (FUF 383)

Notes

1. Dr John Eadie was a leading figure in the UP Church, being Moderator of Synod in 1857. He had a remarkable memory, his biographer claiming that at one time he knew Milton's *Paradise Lost* by heart. A distinguished biblical scholar, he edited *Cruden's Concordance*. Dr Eadie had been minister of Cambridge Street Church in the centre of Glasgow, but by 1863 the area had declined and he and the more affluent members of the congregation removed to the fine new Lansdowne Church, built in the wealthiest part of Great Western Road. On its opening a notice was found pinned to the door:

   > *This church is not for the poor and needy*
   > *But for the rich and Dr Eadie,*
   > *The rich step in and take their seat,*
   > *But the poor walk down to Cambridge Street.*

2. Moves to bring about the union of the United Presbyterian Church and the Free Church began in the early 1860s which may explain Dr Wilson's presence. Although a majority of Free Church presbyteries approved union, the position of the entrenched minority threatened a second Disruption. Both churches reported the ending of the conversations in 1873. Ultimately, the two bodies united in 1900.

W McKelvie, *Annals and Statistics of the United Presbyterian Church,* Edinburgh, 1873
R Small, *History of the United Presbyterian Congregations,* Vol. I, Edinburgh, 1904
DCA CH3/91/1, CH3/91/7

EUCLID CRESCENT

[Dissolved 5 May 1968]

Euclid Crescent congregation was a charge of the United Original Secession Church which acceded to the Church of Scotland on 24 May 1956. The church was in Euclid Crescent.

The Original Secession congregation in Dundee had its origins in Overgate Church (later Bell Street Antiburgher). A dispute resulted in a minority of the congregation withdrawing in 1802, although it was not until 1819 that they had a minister ordained over them. The Constitutional Associate Presbytery (the Auld Licht Antiburghers) was petitioned for *supply of sermon* on 10 May 1808, and moderation was granted on 15 May 1810, meaning they could call a minister. The Rev. Thomas McCrie[1] of Whitfield Chapel, Carrubbers Close, Edinburgh, was appointed to preach and preside on 19 July. A call to a probationer was set aside by Presbytery, despite a petition from the congregation expressing their dissatisfaction. In November 1816, the Rev. James Aitken of Kirriemuir preached and ordained four elders. He moderated in 1818 when a call to Alexander Duncan, probationer, was sustained. Mr Duncan was ordained and inducted as the first minister on 25 March 1819 in New Inn Entry Meeting House.

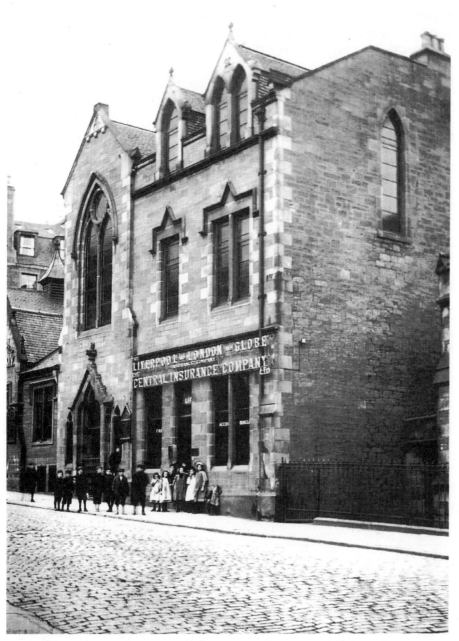

The Original Secession Church Euclid Crescent, early 20th century

The congregation worshipped in this church which they had bought from the New Inn Entry congregation of the Relief Church for £650. The Relief seem to have given up their building around 1817-18 and it is not clear where the Constitutionalists worshipped before acquiring it. When Reform Street was opened this church was sold and taken down. A new church was built in Reform Street, but the debt on the building was beyond the capacity of the congregation and it was sold for £825 to Mariners' Free Church, who afterwards sold it to the Evangelical Union. They in turn sold it and it was converted into offices.

After the sale of the church the congregation met for some time in the High School, but later removed to the Watt Institution. They are shown at the Watt Institution in the Post Office Directory of 1845. Their membership in 1838 was 260. In November 1850 the congregation leased the old Reformed Presbyterian Church in Meadowside. On 1 June 1852 the majority of the Auld Licht Antiburghers or Original Secession Church united with the Free Church. There was division in the congregation over the proposed union, and one Sunday in May there was an unseemly incident. When the minister, the Rev. Edward Thomson, ascended to the pulpit he found it occupied by the Rev. John Blakely, Kirkintilloch, who had been appointed to preach by the Protesting Synod representing the Original Secession minority. After much discussion, agreement was reached that Mr Thomson and his supporters would retain possession of the church for a time. This group, designated *Meadowside congregation* by the Free Presbytery, remained in the building until Mr Thomson was called to and inducted into Dudhope Free in February 1853, when the two congregations of Dudhope and Meadowside were united. The Protesting party, who had agreed to withdraw from the church, met from May 1852 in Lamb's Hall, Reform Street, the Rev. Mr Manson, Perth, officiating. They continued as a congregation of the Original Secession Church, or United Original Seceders, probably worshipping again in the Watt Institution until they obtained the use of premises in Euclid Crescent in 1855 or 1856. What this building was is uncertain but presumably they purchased it, for in 1891 they built a new church on the same site. According to *Lamb,* they erected a church, *a neat and substantial building,* in 1855, but it seems unlikely they would rebuild it only thirty-six years later. It may have been that they fitted out an existing building as a church. The place of worship built in 1891, accommodating 400, cost around £2,000 and was designed by James Langlands, architect, Dundee. The property is on three storeys, Gothic in style, and built of snecked rubble with cream ashlar dressings.

The congregation was dissolved on 5 May 1968. The old Meadow Street hall, belonging to Meadowside Church, was demolished as part of the Wellgate redevelopment. In exchange, this congregation acquired the former Euclid Crescent church property, which they reconstructed to provide hall accommodation for Sunday school and other purposes. The building was purchased by Dundee High School in 1987 and converted, along with the adjacent former Panmure Street Trinity Congregational Church, into the school's Trinity Hall.

There was a manse at 3 Adelaide Terrace.

Ministers

1819	Alexander DUNCAN	Ord. Dem. 1843 (Died 1845) (Scott 313)
1844	Edward Anderson THOMSON	Ord. Dem. 1852 and became min. of Dudhope Free. (Died 1890) (Ewing II 160, Small I 290, Scott 313)
1855	William ROBERTSON	Ord. Dem. 1878 (Lamb)
1879	Peter McVICAR	From Coupar Angus. Died 1920 (DOB)
1921	W S Waters REID	From Arbroath. Mod. of Synod 1922. To Carluke 1926 (Died 1938) (DOB)
1926	John HOWE MA	From Coroneary N. Ireland (UOS Presb. of Ayr) Dem. 1967 (Died 1974) (FES X 301)

Note

1. The Rev. Thomas McCrie, church historian and minister of Potterrow Antiburgher Church, Edinburgh, was the first leader of the Auld Licht Antiburghers. His congregation met in Whitfield Chapel, Carrubber's Close, until in 1813 they built a church in Davie Street. The Original Secession Synod met there. He was a biographer of Knox and Melville.

David Scott, *Annals and Statistics of the Original Secession Church,* Edinburgh, 1886
DPL   Lamb 189(17)
DPL   Dundee Obituary Book (DOB)

HILLTOWN
[Dissolved 22 March 1970]

Hilltown began as a Church Extension charge of the Established Church, Presbytery having approved the erection of a church *within the poor and populous district of Maxwellton* on 5 November 1835. Ground for a church was feued in 1835 at the request of the Kirk Session of St Andrew's. A chapel of ease was constituted on 30 May 1836. Some funds towards the cost of the church were raised by subscription and a grant was obtained from the Church Extension Committee, but a considerable deficit remained. Nevertheless, the building work was put in hand, and in due course, following failure to meet the outstanding debt, the contractor started recovery proceedings. Several individuals met the shortfall against the security of the property. The church was opened on 22 July 1838.

At the Disruption of 1843 the minister, Dr John Baxter, and almost the entire congregation *came out,* but continued to worship in the church. There was a large debt remaining on the church building, which in 1846 was called up by the mortgagees. The church was sold in 1850, being purchased for the upset price of £1,200 for the Free Church congregation assembling in it. A manse was acquired subsequently. Extensive alterations were completed in 1877, the church being entirely refitted with new galleries, seats, and pulpit, at a cost of £3,200, providing seating for over 1,100. Alexander McCulloch, of McCulloch and Fairley, Dundee, was the architect for this work.

A visitor in 1888 recorded that *the kirk is large, and with its great gallery can accommodate a very large congregation.* A mission hall in Hillbank Road was sold in 1924.

Marble plaques were placed on the walls to remember the dead of the wars of 1914-18 and 1939-45, with the baptismal font being dedicated to the memory of those of the Great War.

Under Dr Baxter the congregation had ten Sunday schools, and missions were established at Bonnethill, Hospital Wynd (The High Kirk), Forebank and Coldside. Despite their own debt the Deacons' Court *with great satisfaction* undertook to raise funds to provide helpers for a proposed new church in Dudhope Street (See **Wellgate**).

In 1900 Hilltown Free became Hilltown UF and in 1929 Hilltown.

In the 1960s the area served by the congregation was redeveloped and many of the old houses were demolished. The charge was dissolved on 22 March 1970. The church was sold and became a warehouse.

Ministers

1838	John BAXTER DD	Ord. Previously missionary at Pearsie. Joined FC and became min. of Hilltown Free. To Blairgowrie James St. Free 1858. DD (St Andrew's 1881) (Died 1893) (Ewing II 160, FES V 334, VIII 488, DOB)
1859	John MACPHERSON	Ord. Because of his preaching style was known by sobriquet of *Hellfire Jock.* Dem. 1904 (Died 1915) (Ewing II 160, PM)
1905	William Cumming SKINNER MA	From Kinloss UF. Died 1933 (FUF 384, FES IX 509)
1934	Henry Taylor FERGUSON MA (FES IX 509, KofE 273)	From Musselburgh Millhill. To Inchture and Kinnaird 1941
1942	John PERRY BD	Ord. Dem. on appt. to Jamaica 1946 (FES X 509)
1947	Christopher Charles BARNETT BD	From Bellie. Died 1963 (FES IX 509, X 302)
1964	Joseph Baldwin PERRY	Term appt. To Glasgow Dennistoun 1969 (FES X 302)

CC Barnett, *The Seven Churches of the Hilltown,* Dundee, n.d.
W C Skinner, *The Baronnie of Hilltown Dundee,* Dundee 1927
The Piper O'Dundee, 21 Nov. 1888
DCA CH3/1218
DPL 5/159
DPL Lamb 170(12)

NEW INN ENTRY
[Ceased 1819]

New Inn Entry

Following the demise in 1798 of the West Port Relief congregation, a few former members asked Perth Presbytery on 18 February 1799 for supply of sermon. It was recommended that ministerial members of Presbytery should give them a day each in order to test the strength of support. The outcome was given in the *Missionary Magazine* for October 1799, *A number of people adhering to the Relief connection have recently purchased a house, formerly occupied as a place of public amusement, and have fitted it up as a meeting house.* Presumably, this was the property in New Inn Entry, although the street that connected the Little Meadows to the High Street did not acquire that name until 1808. The building at the north west corner of New Inn Entry, according to *Lamb*, was originally a place of worship, but was used as a theatre for several years before the erection of the Theatre Royal in Castle Street. It then became the chapel of the Original Seceders.

The first minister, called unanimously, *lent dignity for nine and a half years to the Relief cause at Dundee.* The second minister, John Lawson, was censured by Synod for a breach of Church order in Dundee, before his call to the charge. Following his settlement, a number of members who had not opposed him were granted permission to form a new congregation. This was **Seagate**, which dated from about 1811. In 1817 Mr Lawson complained that the doors of his meetinghouse had been closed against him. In 1818 his supporters asked leave to remove to the Tabernacle in Tay Street as the minister had again been locked out of his church. The Tabernacle was the church originally built by the Haldanes and later bought by the Town Council for the Burgh charge of St David's. The New Inn Entry property was then sold for £650 to the Constitutionalists, who had left Overgate Church in 1802, becoming the Auld Licht Antiburghers, later Original Seceders. (See **Euclid Crescent**)

The congregation disintegrated and in 1819 Mr Lawson, ill in mind and body, removed to Manchester. His name was not removed from the roll of Presbytery until 1823.

Ministers

1800 Alexander PATERSON MA	Ord. From Aberdeen Shiprow. Lord Byron referred to him in his Journal, *Afterwards I had a very serious, saturnine, but kind, young man for a tutor...With him I began Ruddiman's Grammar, and continued till I went to the* [Aberdeen] *Grammar School.* Died 1809 (Small I 297-8)
1811 John LAWSON	Formerly Dumfries. In 1819 he removed to Manchester (Died 1836) (Small I 298-9)

A C Lamb, *Dundee Its Quaint and Historic Buildings,* Dundee, 1895

ST COLUMBA'S
[Dissolved 24 November 1991]

*St Columba's became the name of **Dudhope-Lochee Road** in 1958. **Dudhope-Lochee Road** had been formed on 30 November 1955 by the union of **Dudhope** and **Lochee Road**.*

Dudhope, Dudhope Free and UF

*Dudhope Free became **Dudhope UF** in 1900 and **Dudhope** in 1929*

This church was opened on I November 1840 as part of Dr Thomas Chalmers Church Extension[1]. The site had been chosen by the Rev. Murray McCheyne who, along with the Rev. John Roxburgh, minister of St John's, had been a prime mover in the efforts in 1838 to open a church at Dudhope. The local Laird, Mr Rankin of Dudhope, granted a site at a nominal feu, and arranged for the architect, George Angus, to furnish plans and specifications gratis. Presbytery recommended that the building should meet with the *utmost economy that may be consistent with the neatness and respectability of a house devoted to the worship of God*. By the end of 1838 the sum of £750 had been raised for a church and school. In the event the church described as a *large* building *of a mixed Norman style of architecture* cost around £2,200.

A note in a memorandum book of Andrew Cameron, Lower Pleasance, records - *1840 Nov. 1 The Dudhope Church was opened by the Rev. Mr Reid.* [William Reid, minister of Chapelshade Church] *The first psalm that was sung was 102d 13th verse; the chapter read and lectured on was 1st Kings, 8th to 31st verse, Isaiah 60th chapter, 13th verse, Psalm 132d 13th verse.*

The Rev. William C Burns occupied the pulpit for about five months until the first minister was called. At the Disruption the minister adhered to the Free Church, along with most of the congregation. However, he resigned at the meeting of the Free Presbytery in July 1843 on the grounds that the church was burdened with debt, the attendance thin, and the congregation were unable to meet the challenges before them. While his resignation was accepted, the congregation was maintained and the Rev. William Stewart, minister of Lochee, who had been left without a church building, demitted, and was settled at Dudhope bringing many members from his former charge. Because of the debt on the Dudhope property the Established Church allowed the Free Church to retain it.

On 9 June 1852 the Rev. Edward A Thomson and a portion of his Original Secession congregation joined the Free Church, bringing their building. They were designated Meadowside Free congregation. On 17 February 1853 Mr Thomson was called to Dudhope Free with which Meadowside congregation was united.

The congregation had a connection with a school in Scouringburn, described as *that building with a round end at Larch Street*. It had been built by the Rev. George Lewis of St David's and was originally called *The New School*. A day school was operated until it was merged in Dudhope Public School under the School Board. An Industrial School was endowed by Mrs Gardner of Dudhope and placed under the care of the Deacons' Court.

Various improvements were carried out to the properties, largely through the generosity of Mr and Mrs George Johnston. Mr Johnston was Lord Provost of Dundee. Stained glass windows were gifted in 1911. A manse was purchased for £1,550 in 1919. This was probably at 4 Adelaide Place. A clock and bells were installed in the church tower in 1925. Jubilee services were held on Sunday, 9 November 1890.

Following the union of 1900 the congregation left their buildings on 2 April 1905, worshipping in a disused factory in Brewery Lane, until the buildings were restored to them in December 1906 by the Commission set up to allocate disputed properties. The minority who adhered to the remnant Free Church, estimated at one in eight of the congregation, continued to use the church for this period.

Ministers

1841	Alexander MACPHERSON BA	Ord. Joined FC in 1843. Dem. July 1843; thereafter min. of Meigle Free (Died 1892) (FES V 313, Ewing II 160)
1843	William STEWART	From Lochee. Died 1852 (Ewing II 160, PM)
1853	Edward Anderson THOMSON	From Meadowside OS. Dem. 1859 (Ewing II 160, PM)
1860	William STEWART	From Kettle and Cults Free. Died 1867 (Ewing II 160, PM)
1867	Andrew INGLIS	From Ecclefechan Free. Died 1892 (Ewing II 160, PM)
1893	Arthur Clark ABEL	Ord. War service with YMCA in France 1917. Died 1922 (Ewing II 160, FUF 383)

1923 James BAILLIE MA	From Sanquhar South UF. To Strathaven East 1929 (FUF 383, FES IX 507)
1930 Edward BEAL	From Strathmiglo West. To Chapelhall 1942 (FES IX 507)
1942 David Nairn McLEISH MA	From Biggar Gillespie. To Lybster 1947 (FES IX 508)
1947 David Pace PATTERSON	From Newmill. To Ardrishaig 1952 (FES IX 508)
1953 Robert Ernest SLOAN BA	From Tobermore Co. Londonderry. Res. 1955 when appt. terminated (FES IX 508, X 301)

Lochee Road UP and UF

On Sunday, 11 January 1891 the UP Presbytery opened a preaching station to serve the Logie area between Dundee and Lochee. A site was purchased for £700, and a house on the property converted into a hall at a cost of £450 to accommodate over 200 people. A petition by 39 members for *sealing ordinances* was agreed to by Presbytery and the group was placed under the supervision of School Wynd kirk session. On 8 June 1892 the station of 86 members was granted the status of a congregation, and by the end of the year the numbers had grown to 122. The work of the charge had been under a probationer, but towards the end of 1893 the congregation was able to provide for a full time pastor.   The Rev. Dr John Young, Secretary of the Home Mission of the UP Synod, opened the church built in Logie Street, with seating for 700, on 30 September 1897. The buildings, including hall and site, cost £4,200 of which £2,400 was available.

Lochee Road UP became Lochee Road UF in 1900 and Lochee Road in 1929.

Ministers

1894 John BISSETT	From Buckhaven Muiredge UP. To Glasgow Phoenix Park UF 1902 (Small I 314, FUF 385)
1903 James BURNET	From Chapel of Garioch UF. To Garvald UF 1913 (FUF 385)
1913 Robert MITCHELL BD	From Hamilton Low Waters UF. Dem. 1916 (Died 1928) (FUF 385)
1916 Duncan Ross MACKENZIE	Introd. Missionary at Livingstonia. To Peterhead West Associate 1917 (FUF 385)
1917 George HIGGS MA	From Cardenden UF. To Lintrathen 1930 (FUF 385, FES IX 510)
1930 George Robert ROBERTSON MA	From Stonehouse Hamilton Memorial. Dem. 1955 (Died 1967) (FES IX 510, X 302)

Dudhope-Lochee Road - later St Columba's

After union of 1955 a dispute over which church should be used was decided by the General Assembly. The united congregation retained the Lochee Road church, in Logie Street, for worship. The Dudhope church was used initially as a hall but was sold later and adapted for use by Dundee Repertory Theatre. After they removed to their new theatre in Tay Square the building was demolished. The name of the congregation was changed to St Columba's in 1958.

In 1989 the church building was declared structurally unsafe and the congregation worshipped for a time in St David's North Church. The numbers had fallen over the years, and the congregation was unable to meet the substantial cost of repairs. On the retiral of the minister the charge was dissolved and the buildings sold to a developer who demolished the church and erected St Columba's Nursing Home.

For some years the church housed a stone which was claimed to be the original Stone of Scone removed from Westminster Abbey in 1950, it being averred that a substitute had been returned to the authorities. On the closure of the church this stone was removed to a place of safekeeping in Perthshire.

The manse at 7 Inverary Terrace was upgraded for the life occupancy of the retiring minister and his wife. The cost was met from the sale proceeds of the church property with a manse fund of £7,452 being established for its maintenance.

Minister

1956 John MacKay NIMMO MA BD	From Glasgow Elder Park. Dem. 1991 (PhD) (Died 1996) (FES X 301, PM)

Note

1. In 1834 the General Assembly appointed Dr Thomas Chalmers, the leader of the Evangelical Party in the Church, Convener of the Committee on Church Accommodation, to address the problem of church extension. Great activity followed with appeals for financial support to individuals and congregations. In four years over £200,000 was raised and 200 churches erected.

Dudhope Church Dundee from 1840 until 1953, n.d. att. to John Gordon
DYB 1890, 1905

ST CUTHBERT'S
[Dissolved 12 October 1940]

*Willison-Bell Street UF was formed by the union of **Willison** and **Bell Street** congregations in 1928. The name was changed to **St Cuthbert's** in 1934.*

Original Burgher or Barrack Street later Willison.

In 1808 eleven elders and about two thirds of the membership of School Wynd Burgher congregation petitioned the Original Burgher Presbytery of Perth and Dunfermline, asking supply of sermon. This was the start of the process of them becoming a separate congregation in another sect. The reason was given as *a difference that existed between them and the courts of their former connection, in consequence of complaints preferred by them against their minister.* The Presbytery granted their request, and on 6 December 1808 a paper of accession to the Original Burghers was presented to the presbytery, signed by 174 members and 38 adherents. It was not until 1816 that the first minister was inducted. The congregation was known as the Original Burgher Church, Dundee. Along with the minister the congregation acceded to the Church of Scotland in 1839, shortly after the Original Burgher Synod (The Auld Licht Burghers) had done so, but left again in 1843 to join the Free Church. It took the name, Willison Free Church, after John Willison, the distinguished minister of the Second Charge of Dundee from 1716 until 1750.

For several years worship was held in an old factory off Bell Street. Their church in Barrack Street was erected in 1814, the site having formed part of the garden of the Rev. John Willison. The church was extended and renovated in 1869 at a cost of around £1,800, due to the membership exceeding the accommodation and people being turned away at every seat letting. The congregation took over Dudhope Crescent Road Church for use as halls in 1909. An American organ was introduced in 1902 and a pipe organ in 1904.

*Willison Free became **Willison UF** in 1900.*

Ministers

1816	Robert AITKEN	Ord. Original Secession min. at Kirkintilloch, 1811. Ind. to Barrack Street Church, Dundee. Joined Cof S with his cong. 1839. Joined FC 1843 Died 1845 (FES V 342)
1846	Thomas HILL	Ord. Dem. 1889 (Died 1891) (Scott 311, Ewing II 162, PM)
1889	Alexander S INCH MA	Ord. C&S . To Dumbarton Free High 1898 (Ewing II 162, PM)
1898	James HASTINGS DD	From Kinneff Free. To St Cyrus UF 1901 (FUF 390)
1902	William NELSON DD	From Shettleston Sandyhills UF. Min. of united cong. 1928 (FUF 390)

Bell Street

An Antiburgher congregation was formed by a group which broke away from School Wynd Church in 1747. It did not have a minister until 1761. Worship was held in a hall until a church was built off Overgate in 1763-4. A split in the congregation, on the issue of the renewal of covenants, during the ministry of Andrew Scott, resulted in legal action to determine the ownership of the property. On 13 December 1771, the Court of Session decided in favour of the majority. Consequently, Mr Scott and his minority had to vacate the church, worshipping until the close of his ministry in 1791 in a building in Barrack Street. Mr Scott's followers continued as a congregation known as *Scottites* as late as 1803.

In 1802 a division in the mainstream congregation resulted in a minority withdrawing and forming the beginnings of the Original Secession Church in Dundee. They bought a church from the Relief Church but did not have their own minister until 1819. In 1852 about half of their number followed their minister, Edward Thomson, into the Free Church, the other half adhering to the Synod of the Original Seceders. (see Euclid Crescent)

In June 1804 there was a difficulty with services, due to the poor health of the minister, the Rev. James McEwan, and eventually in 1807 the provision of a colleague was approved, despite the lack of funds to meet an adequate additional stipend. There were continuing problems during the course of the joint ministry, which ended in 1813 with the death of Mr McEwan. Thereafter, the sole minister's stipend was augmented and a manse was built for him on open ground beside the church.

Following the union of 1820, when the New Licht Burghers (Associate Synod) and the New Licht Antiburghers (General Associate Synod) became the United Secession Church, the charge is referred to in Presbytery minutes as the *Second Congregation, Dundee.*

In 1840 a new church was built at the corner of West Bell Street and Constitution Road, the architect being James Black. The site was first of all cleared of a group of thatched cottages, popularly known as *Culloden.* A classical building in sandstone ashlar was erected. It has a raised rusticated ground floor, the upper floor being pilastered with blind panels, there being balustrades on the roof. A basement, entered down a flight of stairs from Constitution Road, provided a church hall and offices. The interior of the church, which has a fine plaster ceiling, was described in 1888 as being spacious and lofty but *the gallery is too high, and the pulpit far away from the congregation.* The church, which was opened on Sunday, 31 May 1840, had sittings for 1,300, with the hall accommodating 700. The building cost £5,000.

Following the building of the new church financial problems were experienced. There was dissension arising out of the collegiate ministry, which was resolved with the demission of the senior minister in 1845. There were further problems within the congregation. In 1871 an incident occurred when, following the benediction, the precentor announced that a meeting was to be held to discuss the congregation's finances. The minister declared the announcement to be illegal under church law. The matter seems to have been a sign of factional disputes at the time. The next brief ministry was ended with the minister being suspended, due to charges admitted against his moral character.

A tragic accident occurred on the premises on Monday, 2 January 1865, the day observed as the New Year holiday. The hall beneath the church was used regularly for entertainment and had been let to Springthorpe's Promenade Concerts. A large crowd had gathered outside, awaiting the opening of the hall. Some people slipped on the icy steps leading down to the basement, resulting in twenty deaths.

Bell Street UP became Bell Street UF in 1900. Moves to unite Bell Street with School Wynd congregation fell through in January 1914.

Ministers

1761	Andrew SCOTT	Ord. Dep. 1768 (Small I 287)
1772	William BARLAS	Ord. Died 1779 aged 27 (Small I 288)
1785	James McEWAN	From Buchlyvie. In 1804 he *could not perform his usual ministerial work.* A colleague was agreed on in 1807. Died 1813 (Small I 290-1)
1809	Matthew FRASER	Ord. C&S. Sole min. 1813. Dem. 1845 (Died 1857) (Small I 290-3)
1835	William Broadfoot BORWICK	Ord. C&S. Sole min. 1845. Dem. 1866 (Died 1870) (Small I 292-3)
1867	John BRAND	Ord. To John Street Glasgow UP 1876 (Died 1900) (Small I 293)
1877	James CONWAY	From Linlithgow East UP. Dem. 1879 (Small I 293-4)
1880	Thomas Storey DICKSON MA	From Auchterarder North UP. To Argyle Place Edinburgh UP 1890 (Died 1909) (Small I 294, KofE 265)
1890	James G WALTON BD	From St Paul's South Shields. To Aberdeen St Nicholas UP 1899 (Small I 294)
1900	John W BEVERIDGE BD	From Wolverhampton. To Fossoway UF 1913. In 1938 he was honoured with a knighthood of St Olav from the King of Norway for his services to Norway through his writings (Small I 294, FUF 381)
1914	William Graham BROWN MA	From Lesmahagow Cordiner UF. Dem. 1917 (Died 1928) (FUF 381)
1917	Thomas Cunningham FRASER MA	From Kirkconnel UF. To Everton Valley Liverpool 1924 (FUF 381)
1925	William Lamb FORDYCE MA	From Sunderland St Peter's. To Govan Copland UF 1927 (FUF 381)

St Cuthbert's

The united congregation met temporarily in Willison Church while Bell Street was renovated. After the union of 1928 the Willison church building was sold. It was demolished and John L Robertson, housefurnishers, erected their warehouse on the site, retaining the name in Willison House. On 12 October 1940 the congregation was dissolved at its own request and the buildings sold. The two manual organ by Lawton was overhauled by R L Smith and installed in Lochend Church, Edinburgh.

From the proceeds of the sale of the property, the St Cuthbert's Manse Fund was established under the control of Presbytery. The church building is now the Regional Music Centre and is B-listed.

Ministers

1928	William NELSON DD	Min. of Willison. Died 1933 (FUF 390, FES IX 514)
1933	William POTTINGER MA	From Glasgow Sydney Place and East Campbell Street. Dem. 1940 (FES IX 514)

McKean and Walker, *Dundee An Illustrated Introduction,* Dundee, 1984
The Scots Magazine, May 1990
The Piper O' Dundee, 11 D ec. 1889
A I Dunlop, *The Kirks of Edinburgh 1560-1984*, Edinburgh, 1989
DPL   Lamb Collection 171(12), 171(14)
DA   22 May 1840
DYB   1914
DCC Combined Statutory and Descriptive List

ST JAMES'
[Dissolved 30 September 1988]

St James'

This congregation began as a breakaway from what became known as Dudhope Crescent Road Church. At the time of the split the Relief congregation in Temple Lane was connected to Perth Presbytery, but the disjoining group approached Dysart Presbytery for supply of sermon. Their petition being granted, the Rev. Daniel Kerr of Ceres opened what was called the *Second Relief Congregation* on Sunday, 5 February 1837, reporting an exceedingly good attendance to the next meeting of Presbytery. While clearly the new charge would adversely affect Temple Lane congregation, such matters were allowed to take their course in the Relief Church, unlike the Secession Church where the rights of existing congregations were carefully guarded. The first minister was inducted on 17 January 1838 in Ward Chapel.

The want of a regular place of worship was a serious drawback to the young congregation, five places being used within three years. They met for a time in the Mason Lodge Hall, Murraygate, then in the Sailors' Hall, Union Street, their meeting place when sanctioned as a congregation. In March 1838 they moved to the Caledonian Hall, Castle Street, but transferred in 1839 to the Watt Institution. In June 1840 they obtained the lease of the Old English Chapel in Nethergate (afterwards called Union Hall). Four years later this place of worship was put up for sale and they resolved to build a church. In the interim, they obtained the use of the large hall below Bell Street United Secession Church. On Sunday, 27 April 1845 their new church at the corner of Bell Street and Euclid Crescent with 680 sittings was opened by the Rev. Dr William Anderson of John Street Church, Glasgow. There was a debt of £900 on the building and financial difficulties dogged the congregation for many years. The charge became popularly known as James' Church, probably after the first pastor, James Reston.

Following the union of 1900 there were four UF churches in Bell Street, three next door to one another. In 1904 the building was sold to William Smith, boot manufacturer, for around £2,300. A new church and halls were built in Arklay Street, at the corner of Tannadice Street, and opened on 13 June 1906 by Professor A R MacEwan. The church building, designed by T M Cappon, architect, was cruciform with side and end galleries, being seated for 800. A hall, seating 350, was provided along with a vestry and classroom. The congregation was then named Clepington UF.

This was the first Presbyterian congregation in Dundee to use hymns, worshipping with the Relief Church Hymnbook. A mission school was established in 1868. The jubilee of the removal to Arklay Street was celebrated in 1956 when the Rev. Professor John M Graham, Aberdeen University and Lord Provost of Aberdeen, preached.

James' UP became James' UF in 1900, Clepington UF in 1906 and St James' in 1929. It was also at one time known unofficially as *Robbie's Kirk* out of affection for its long serving minister, the Rev. James Robbie.

Following an unsuccessful attempt to negotiate a union with the nearby Clepington congregation, the charge was dissolved on 30 September 1988. The buildings were sold, with the proceeds setting up the St James' Arklay Street Fund for the upkeep and maintenance of manses within the bounds of Presbytery. The church site was cleared and a block of flats erected with an attempt made to reflect the design of the church in the new building.

Ministers

1838 James RESTON	From Newton Stewart. Mod. of Relief Synod at union with United Secession Church 1847. Died 1865 (Small I 305-6)
1866 Robert LAWRIE	From West Linton UP. Died 1893 (Small I 306)
1894 James ROBBIE MA BD	Ord. From Aberdeen Charlotte Street UP. War Service with YMCA in France in 1917. Dem. 1935 (Died 1935) (Small I 306, FUF 382, FES IX 514)
1935 James Eric McAndrew BAIKIE BD MLitt	Ord. War Service in HM Forces 1939-46. To Edinburgh Burdiehouse 1963 (FES IX 514, X 305)
1964 Robert Duncan SAWERS	Formerly with Overseas Council Nyasaland. To Irvine Muir 1969 (FES X 305)
1969 Andrew Denis WILLIAMS MA	From Grangemouth Kerse (Asst.). Dem. 1977 to take up appt. as Scottish representative of Evangelistic Society (FES X 305, PM)

| 1978 | George S AYRE | From Tayport Queen Street. Intro. on term. appt.Dem. 1983 (YB, PM) |
| 1986 | Robert F DUNCAN MTheol | Ord. and assigned as Auxiliary Min. Appt. terminated 1988 (YB) |

DCA CH3/1384
DYB 1904
DPL Sp. 5/205
DPL Lamb 170(13)

THISTLE HALL, UNION STREET, DUNDEE.

The Thistle Hall and the Caledonian Hall, Castle Street, were used frequently by new congregations as temporary places of worship in the mid nineteenth century

ST STEPHEN'S
[Dissolved 1 December 1906]

St Stephen's

This congregation took its origin from a mission begun by the officebearers of Free St Andrew's in 1850, under the name of Wellgate Territorial Mission or Wellgate Free Church. Meetings were held for a time in a small brick hall. A church was erected in Dudhope Street at a cost of £1,200, and opened on Wednesday, 28 April 1858 by Dr R S Candlish.[1] The charge was sanctioned in 1862. The building was described as *plain but substantial*. Built in stone, its main entrance was by a porch in the east end, the gable of which had a circular window. The building was lit by twelve tall windows with arched tops. Underneath the church were a schoolroom and a vestry. In 1866 the membership was put at 266. Three neighbouring congregations gave financial aid for a few years.

Bailie Gilruth presented a communion service to the congregation. A manse was built in 1872. This was probably at 6 Albany Terrace.

Wellgate Free became St Stephen's UF in 1900.

Following the Union of 1900, the buildings were allocated to the remnant Free Church, and the UF congregation was dissolved. The dissolution was effective from 1 December 1906, by resolution of the Commission of Assembly meeting of 21 November 1906.

Ministers

1863	John DUKE	Ord. To Campsie Free 1879 (Ewing II 162, PM)
1880	Donald COOK BSc	Ord. Dem. 1906 (Died 1928) (Ewing II 162, FUF 389)

Note

1. Dr Robert S Candlish was one of the foremost figures in the Free Church, being its acknowledged leader from the death of Dr Thomas Chalmers in 1847 until his own death in 1873. He was Moderator of the General Assembly in 1861, and Principal of New College, Edinburgh. (See fuller note under **Meadowside St Paul's**)

DPL Lamb 190(12)
UF Presbytery minutes of 12 December 1906

SCHOOL WYND
[Dissolved 1926]

School Wynd

A group of seceders in Dundee was taken under the care of the Associate Presbytery on 18 July 1738. Others joined this congregation, including three elders, and on 9 February 1741 a kirk session was constituted. Supply of sermon by probationers started in September 1740, but was only available about every five or six weeks. This led the Rev. John Willison of the Established Church to complain of the seceders taking people away from their pastors. *People,* he said, *if they obey them, must sit at home on the Lord's Day, and live without the gospel, except when they get a transient sermon now and then from a seceder.* The recommendation of the Associate Presbytery to people under their supervision was to form societies and meet for prayer and conference on the Lord's Day, if no preacher could be had and there was no Secession church within reach. However, it was not uncommon for people to walk twenty miles to attend a Secession church. Three leaders of the Secession Church, Messrs Wilson, Moncrieff and Mair had visited Montrose in 1740, with supply of preachers beginning in December. In 1744 the seceders in Montrose and Dundee were regarded as forming one congregation, although the towns were thirty miles apart, and on 20 December a meeting for the purpose of calling a minister was held in Dundee. The Montrose members nominated John Swanston and the Dundee people James Johnstone. Both were elected, the intention being to make the charge collegiate, but the Synod disapproved and Dundee and Montrose became separate charges.[1]

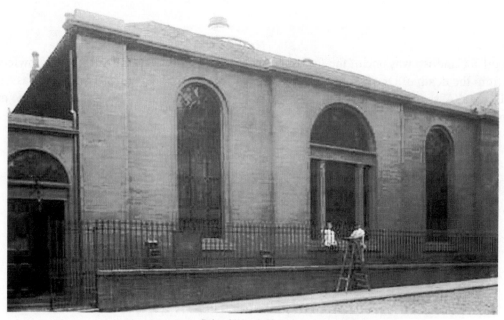

School Wynd Church
The church closed in 1926, the building becoming Kidd's Rooms

The first minister, James Johnstone, was called by 75 members in May 1745, and ordained on 16 April 1746, the church in School Wynd being built in that year. Mr Johnstone preached at Coupar Angus every third Sunday until that congregation became Antiburgher in the division of 1747. Some of the School Wynd people left to form the Antiburgher congregation of Overgate, later Bell Street. In 1773 the minister, William Ballantyne, asked Presbytery to release him from his charge but they did not accede. There were difficulties in the congregation and in 1776 Synod accepted his resignation.

After Mr Ballantyne's demission, John Blackhall was called but never inducted, there being two versions of events. According to *Small,* Mr Blackhall was supply preacher at Rathillet and wrote to Presbytery stating that he would not be coming to Dundee to be ordained. Eventually Presbytery referred the case to Synod who dismissed the call. In the second account[2] we are told that Mr Blackhall disappeared while Presbytery was proceeding to School Wynd Church to ordain him, later confessing that he had been terrified by the short incumbencies of the previous ministers. As a consequence he was publicly rebuked by Synod but allowed a call to Berwick where he remained for 32 years.

There was dissension in the congregation in 1807, and efforts were made to induce the minister, James Black, to demit his charge. The complaints against the minister were not upheld by Synod, and a majority of the congregation left for the Original Burgher Presbytery. This group met for a time in an old factory, but in 1814 a church was erected in Barrack Brae. Their place of worship was extensively altered in 1869, becoming Willison Free Church. (See **St Cuthbert's**) [3]

The residual congregation continued to decline, in part due to the ill health of the minister who died in office in 1814. In the next ministry the church *became full to overflowing* and a new church was built in 1825 at a cost of over £2,000 to seat more than 1,000. This building was erected slightly to the south of the old church, on the site which had been used as the green for the tent communion services.

Following the union of 1820, when the New Licht Burghers (Associate Synod) and New Licht Antiburghers (General Associate Synod) became the United Secession Church, School Wynd is referred to in the Presbytery minutes as the *First Congregation, Dundee.*

A further schism occurred in 1832, due to a dispute over a call, with 235 members leaving to form what became Tay Square congregation. (See **Meadowside St Paul's**) However, the minister who was the subject of the disputed call had a successful, though short, ministry in School Wynd, it being reported in 1835 that *the church was filled anew to overflowing.*

After the death of their ninth minister, the distinguished George Gilfillan, the congregation called the Rev. David McRae of Greenock. However, Paisley and Greenock Presbytery had raised a case against Mr McRae, and, before the call could be dealt with, the Synod declared Mr McRae no longer a minister of the UP Church. Mr McRae accepted the call to Dundee with 870 names and, at a ceremony on 31 October 1879 in the Kinnaird Hall conducted by the Rev. Baldwin Brown of London[4], he was inducted to his new charge, outwith the UP Church. The breakaway group built Gilfillan Memorial Church. At the end of 1879 the membership of School Wynd was reported to have fallen from 900 to 270, but the property remained with the UP Church. An organ was installed in 1876 and in 1882 the interior of the church was renovated. The congregation marked what they termed their 150th anniversary on 20 February 1893.

In 1909 the General Assembly of the United Free Church instructed Presbytery to unite School Wynd with St David's, the intention being that the united congregation would worship initially in School Wynd Church but look for a site in the west of the City. The two ministers were to be colleagues. School Wynd refused to hand over their property to the new Board of Management. Then the St David's people attempted to set up for themselves in a temporary building in the west end. The Commission of Assembly stopped this move and in 1910 the union was dissolved. A proposed union of School Wynd and Bell Street fell through in 1914. Despite the uncertainty of their future the congregation celebrated what they regarded as their 175th anniversary on 22 September 1916. In 1926 the congregation was dissolved. The property was sold and the church building was known for many years as Kidd's Rooms.

School Wynd Burgher became United Secession in 1820, School Wynd UP in 1847, and School Wynd UF in 1900. The street name from which the congregation took its name was changed in the mid nineteenth century to Lindsay Street.

There was a manse at 22 Springfield.

Ministers

1746	James JOHNSTONE	Ord. Died 1750 (Small I 279)
1754	William McEWAN	Ord. Died 1762 (Small I 280)
1762	Thomas LISTER	Ord. Died 1766 (Small I 280)
1767	James CLUNIE	Ord. Died 1768 (Small I 280)
1770	William BALLANTYNE	Ord. Dem. 1776 (Small I 281)
1782	James BLACK	Ord. Died 1814 (Small I 282-3)
1815	George DONALDSON	Ord. Died 1831 (Small I 283-4)
1833	Alexander DAVIDSON	Ord. To Edinburgh Lothian Road UAS 1835 (Died 1836) (Small I 284-5)
1836	George GILFILLAN	Ord. Poet, essayist and leading public figure in Dundee. Died 1878. His funeral procession to Balgay Cemetery was *the largest concourse of mourners that ever honoured the remains of a townsman.* (Small I 285)
1880	Josephus Leishman SKERRET	From Walsall. To Glasgow Cathedral Square UP 1886 (Small I 285)
1887	George SMART	From Denny UP. Dem. 1913 (Died 1929) (Small I 286, FUF 389)

1915   William ADAM   From Glasgow St Rollox UF. Dem. 1926. Introd. Ardclach
                                       UF 1927 (FUF 389)

Notes

1. The probationer who officiated at Montrose in December 1740 was the redoubtable Adam Gib who for many years was minister of the only Antiburgher congregation in Edinburgh. The Montrose congregation became Antiburgher, later taking the name of St Luke's UP.
2. This incident is referred to in *McKelvie.*
3. The Rev. John Willison was the distinguished minister of the Second Charge of Dundee from 1716 to 1750. The site of Willison Church in Barrack Street had been part of his garden.
4. The Rev. James Baldwin Brown was a Congregational minister in London, well known for his liberal theological view. (DNB Vol. VII)

Piper O' Dundee, 11 December *1889*
Small Vol. I pp 68-9 and 279-86
DYB   1893, 1916

SEAGATE
[Ceased 1821]

Seagate

The attempt by a group of members of New Inn Entry Relief congregation in 1811 to form a second Relief charge in Dundee was strongly resisted by its minister, Mr Lawson, and his elder, with the petition being refused three times by Presbytery. However, on appeal, Synod allowed the petitioners to be congregated. Seagate Chapel, which belonged originally to the Episcopalians,[1] was purchased for £400. The Rev. James Jardine supplied the pulpit for some months but withdrew from a call to the charge. The first minister was inducted in 1813 but only remained for a year. There were difficulties in 1819 between the congregation and the bondholder and in 1820 the minister resigned. In 1821 the people were recognised as *a forming congregation,* which suggests that *Seagate* had ceased to exist. The origin of Dudhope Road Relief or **Dudhope Crescent Road (q.v.)** congregation may be dated from this time.

Ministers

1813 Robert HALL	Ord. From Jedburgh High Street. To Berwick Chapel Street 1814 (Died 1834) (Small I 299-300)
1815 William STRANG	From Ford. Dem. 1820. Afterwards at Carrubber's Close Relief Edinburgh (Died 1834) (Small I 300)

Note

1. There were two Episcopal meeting houses in the Seagate. This building may have been the chapel shown on *Crawford's* map of 1777 as *Bp Rait's Meeting House*. It was used by the Scottish Episcopalians from 1763 until 1812 when they built St Paul's Chapel in Castle Street. It was seated below with a gallery.

The Cathedral Church of Saint Paul Dundee, n.d.

WEST PORT
[Ceased 1798]

West Port

Following the admission to the Established Church in 1791 of the minister and most of the congregation of Chapelshade Relief, a petition for sermon was presented to Perth Relief Presbytery on 7 February 1792. The parties styled themselves *the vacant congregation in Dundee* and Mr Grimmond, the Relief minister of Coupar Angus, was appointed to preach to them on the first Sunday of March. In May they applied successfully to the Synod for aid in building a place of worship. Temple Lane Church was built with an inscription on its front, *1792, To the Cause of Religious Liberty. Hear instruction and be wise.*[1] It was popularly known as *The Temple.*

Not long after the induction of the first minister there was dissension, and a complaint against the incumbent was brought to the Synod. The congregation declined in numbers, and on 19 November 1798 the demission of the Rev. Neil Douglas, the congregation's one and only minister as it turned out, was accepted. The Relief congregation can be regarded as having ceased in 1798.

The bulk of the members joined the Independents, taking the building with them, it being burdened with a debt of £1,200. They applied to an English Congregational Academy for preachers. In 1804 the Rev. John Campbell, Dunkeld, later of Nicholson Street Secession Church, Glasgow, became their minister. When Mr Campbell left for Glasgow in 1810 this congregation of Independents joined with the Tabernacle Independent congregation. Thereafter, the united congregation worshipped in Temple Lane church, with the Tabernacle being sold to the Town Council for the use of the new Burgh church of St David's. (See **The Steeple**) The Congregationalists used Temple Lane church until in 1833 Ward Chapel was built. The church was then sold for £1,000 to another Relief congregation. (See **Dudhope Crescent Road**) Temple Lane church was used temporarily by the South Church congregation following the fire in the Burgh Churches in 1841.

Minister

1793 Neil DOUGLAS MA [1]   From Cupar. Dem. 1798. (Died 1823) (Small I 296-7)

Note

1. This inscription has, perhaps, a familiar ring about it. In 1792 the Dundee Friends of Liberty was formed and in November a crowd planted a *Tree of Liberty* in the High Street and there was a week of rioting. The representative sent later by the Friends of Liberty to the General Convention of the Scottish Radical Societies in Edinburgh was the Rev. Neil Douglas. Following the Government's action against Radical leaders, Douglas hurriedly left Dundee for the Highlands. He was the author of *Narrative of a Mission to the West Highlands in 1797,* and an anti-war pamphlet entitled, *Britain's Guilt, Danger and Duty.* He was tried before the Justiciary Court in 1817 for preaching sedition and for attacking George III and the Prince Regent in Sunday evening lectures on the Book of Daniel, but the case was dismissed.

C M Falconer & J C Low, *The Story of Ward Chapel,* Dundee, 1934

WILSON
[Ceased 14 May 1879]

Wilson Territorial Church

The Free Church Presbytery minutes of April 1874 refer to *Wilson Territorial Mission*. The mission was conducted at 145 Overgate, having been opened by St Paul's Free on 25 November 1866 in a densely populated area of the Town. For the previous ten years this work had been conducted in the former Gaelic Church, Long Wynd, relatively nearby. The sum of £2,659 had been subscribed to buy the Overgate site and erect the hall. This was a time of church extension and Dr William Wilson of St Paul's was Convener of the Presbytery's Church Extension Committee, presumably the source of the name.

It was reported on 14 June 1876 that the General Assembly had sanctioned Wilson Territorial Church as a charge and that a site for a church had been obtained. The intention was to purchase an iron church. A minister was ordained on 3 October 1876, and on the following day plans for a church in Annfield Road were submitted to Presbytery.

Evidently this proposal was not proceeded with for, in October 1878, the Deacons' Court of Wilson complained to Presbytery that plans to carry out alterations to the present building were being frustrated, as the Deacons' Court of St Paul's in their capacity as trustees had objected. Dr Wilson had recently retired from active ministry at St Paul's. In a petition the Wilson Deacons' Court claimed that the congregation was losing heart, and that it would like to move to another district. Why they should wish to alter the present building when it was their aim to move is not clear. The Wilson Deacons' Court considered that the charge should not have been sanctioned if it was not to receive assistance. At the next meeting of Presbytery it was intimated that the petition had been withdrawn. Nevertheless, it is evident that the grievances remained.

However, events were to lead to a resolution for, in the following February, the minister received a call which was sustained. A committee was appointed by Presbytery to confer with the congregation. The mission hall used as a church seated no more than 250 and it was unlikely that it would be enlarged. In the circumstances, the officebearers decided that they did not wish to call another minister. Presbytery agreed that, from 14 May 1879, Wilson Territorial Church should cease to exist as a sanctioned charge, but would continue as a mission under St Paul's.

Minister

1876 George MILNE   Ord. To Free Alloa East 1879 (PM)

DCA CH3 Free Church Presbytery minutes 1874-79
D E Stimpson, letter of 9 May 1998

BALFOUR
[Ceased 1845]

Balfour Burgher

On 18 June 1819 a petition for supply of sermon from thirty seven people in the Carse of Gowrie parishes of Abernyte, Inchture, and Longforgan, was received by the Burgher Presbytery of Perth. Their request was granted, and nine months later the group applied to be recognised as a congregation. A congregation was formed on 30 May 1820, with three of their number being ordained to the eldership in the following April. At the end of the year the congregation of Balfour purchased the meetinghouse at Abernyte belonging to Robert Haldane[1] of Airthrey (now Stirling University). This church stood a little to the north west of the old inn known as *The Cauple Stowp*.[2] This chapel, known as *Haldane's Tabernacle,* had been built for Mr Haldane who sometimes preached there himself.

In February 1822 the congregation, which now had a roll of over fifty, called Mr David Smith, promising a stipend of £75, with a two acre glebe and a house and garden. However, Presbytery did not sustain the call and Mr Smith was ordained to Biggar. In 1828 a second and last attempt was made to secure a minister, the membership now being down to forty, but it proved unsuccessful. In 1835 the Rev. James Blyth was located at Balfour for three months and his work was reported to have been highly acceptable. For a time there was an arrangement that preachers would preach at Balfour during the day and conduct a service at Longforgan in the evening. Following the Disruption of 1843 membership declined, there now being Free Churches at Abernyte and Longforgan, and by 1845 the roll was down to thirty-three with a resultant fall in income. The Presbytery minutes for 30 December 1845 record, *The Clerk reported that since last meeting the Balfour people, finding themselves unable to support the station any longer, had requested the preachers to be withdrawn, which he had done accordingly.* This was approved of, and the name of Balfour appears no more in the records of the denomination. The missionary, the Rev. William Ross, whose father was grieve at Pitkindie, was brought up in the Secession Church. He met Dr Moffat of the London Missionary Society and offered his services to the Society. He was sent to Africa along with David Livingstone.

Notes

1. Robert Haldane and his brother, James, are regarded as the founders of the Congregationalist and Baptist denominations in Scotland. They built several large preaching houses, including the building in Tay Street, Dundee, later acquired for the new Burgh charge of Dundee, St David's. Robert Haldane who owned estates in the parish of Abernyte built a chapel for the seceders, which came to be known as *Haldane's Tabernacle.*
2. At one time there were four public houses in the parish of Abernyte, one being known as *The Cauple Stowp.* It stood at the hamlet of Balfour, now known as Abernyte.

R Small, *History of the UP Congregations,* Edinburgh, 1904
L Melville, The *Fair Land of Gowrie,* Coupar Angus, 1939

LIFF
[Dissolved 1801]

Liff Burgher

Messrs Thomas Mair and James Fisher, two of the first ministers of the Associate Presbytery formed in 1733, observed a Fast in the parish of Liff in May 1739. It was the earliest service of the kind held in the neighbourhood under the auspices of the Associate Presbytery There was a small group of seceders in the parish from about this time, members of School Wynd Church, Dundee, which dates from about 1738. It was not until 1785 that an attempt was made to form a congregation at Liff, when there was a dispute about the patron's right of presentation to the parish church. On 8 February 1785 some of the parishioners applied for sermon to the Burgher Presbytery of Perth. The Rev. John Husband of Dunfermline opened the station on the first Sunday of March.

According to the Old Statistical Account, a church and manse were built in what was known as the *Spring Field,* near Denhead of Gray, before the first minister was called by seventy-three members and thirty-eight adherents. This minister, John Auchincloss, was deposed, but a woman snatched the paper containing the decision of Presbytery from the hands of the officiating minister before he could read it. There was division in the congregation over the issue. The minister was allowed to resume his duties, but it came to light that a petition had been presented to the Relief Presbytery of Perth from the *congregation of Springfield in the parish of Liff* asking for their supervision, but the matter with that sect was not concluded. Mr Auchincloss raised an action in the civil courts for defamation but was not successful.

For some years the congregation was supplied with preachers and in 1798 the second minister was inducted. However, numbers declined and the debt on their property was close to £400. By 1801 the congregation was unable to support a minister and the pastoral tie was dissolved by mutual agreement. There was a shortfall from the sale of the property, with the Synod Fund having to accept a partial payment in settlement of the sum which the Fund had lent. Some of the members joined School Wynd Church, Dundee. In 1826 a congregation of the United Secession Church was formed at Lochee in the parish of Liff. The Liff Burgher congregation is remembered in the street name, Myrekirk Road. The former manse, which stood beside the church, is now a private dwellinghouse.

Ministers

1787   John AUCHINCLOSS — Ord. Dep. by Presbytery 1790. Removed to Stockport where he taught in a school (Died 1800) (Small I 331-2)

1798   George WIGTON — Ord. From Penicuik. Dem. 1801 (Died 1849) (Small I 332-3)

R Small, *History of the United Presbyterian Church from 1733 to 1900,* Edinburgh, 1904, Vol. I, pp 278, 330-3
The Courier, 17 December 1999